T.K.Sribhashyam

Emergence of Yoga

Origin and development of the teaching of Yoga

Les Editions Yogakshemam
Les Courtioux,
38680 ST ANDRE EN ROYANS, France.

Original Title: Emergence du Yoga, Origine et développement de l'enseignement du Yoga

Translated by: Geoffrey Finch
Revised by T.K.Sribhashyam
First Edition: 2014

Photography credits (in alphabetical order):

- Luz Studio, Chennai, India
- Pars Media, Berlin, Germany
- Stephane Gerber, Préverenges, Switzerland
- Steve Perrone, Cannes, France
- T.K. Sribhashyam, Nice, France
- V8 Productions, Nice, France.

Cover design by Sumitra Sribhashyam and Anne Levilain, London, United Kingdom.

Page layout by T.K. Sribhashyam and Estelle Lefebvre

Artistic adviser: Claire Sribhashyam, Nice, France

The photographs of the author's father presented in the chapter entitled **'In memory of my father'** were taken in Chennai for his seventy-ninth birthday, and were offered to the author on that occasion. These photographs are published as a sign of recognition.

First published in France in 2011 by Les Editons Yogakshemam, France.

ISBN 978-2-9544855-2-2

To

the revered memory of my father and Guru
Sri T. Krishnamacharya
and to my mother
Srimathi T. Namagiriammal

Table of Contents

TABLE OF FIGURES

Table of figures

TABLE OF FIGURES

TABLE OF FIGURES

Acknowledgement

This book, recounting the emergence of Yoga, is written in testimony to the great gratitude, I owe my parents, Sri T. Krishnamacharya and Srimathi T. Namagiriammal.

I pay deep tribute to my eldest brother, Sri T.K. Srinavasan. The conversations we shared in my youth have always brought fruitful light on my father's teaching.

I have decided to publish this teaching as an acknowledgment to my pupils in India from 1956 to 1970 and in Europe, since 1970. Their sincere interest has encouraged me to transmit the knowledge of Yoga with which my father entrusted me.

I express my sincere gratitude to my wife, Claire, and to my children Sumitra and Satya, who have always supported me in that task.

I especially thank Doctor Nancy Carpentier for her precious support in the preparation of the technical sheets.

I thank the photographers who helped illustrate this book, as well as my students who voluntarily contributed to the photos presented in the practical section with special thanks to Muriel for participating despite her advanced stage of pregnancy at eight and a half months.

I am extremely grateful to Geoffrey Finch who has offered to translate this book, and I thank sincerely all his friends who helped him in this delicate task. I wish to express my thanks to Vivian Thomas for refining the text of the first four chapters.

Coming from a purely oral tradition, this book does not contain published references. However, I will be happy to include, in the next edition, all references to the ancient traditional texts that reach me.

This book is dedicated to all those practising Yoga now, in the past and in the future.

Nice, France, 12 February 2014.

T. K. Sribhashyam.

Preamble

I was often asked to write a book on the Yoga that I taught according to the tradition inherited from my father, persuading me that it would be a proof and an aid to spread and talk about this incomparable discipline.

All the while aware of the difficulties and unavoidable limitations when undertaking to transcribe a purely oral teaching, I was also conscious that after my departure from this physical world, this knowledge, that only my father could transmit, would disappear forever.

I wrote *Emergence of Yoga* to give to the world of tomorrow, a way to continue transmitting this exceptional legacy, in India as well as in the West.

Thanks to the countless philosophical and metaphysical questions asked by my students, and their sincere desire to know the truth, I could appreciate the boundless and invaluable value of the tradition that I received from my father. The method of approach I learnt from him enabled me to teach students from a different culture than mine, without imposing my beliefs. It is precisely because it brought such benefits to their lives and their spiritual development that this priceless aspect of his teaching should not fall into oblivion.

I must confess that encrypting this oral transmission into a written one, all the while remaining faithful to its principles, and to my father was a long and difficult task yet a very rewarding experience.

May this *written transmission* be as valuable as my *oral transmission.* May you enjoy the fruits of the practice of Yoga.

Epigraph

The *Emergence of Yoga* presented in this book was taught to me by my father in circumstances that are worth mentioning here.

In 1954, my father was invited to Madras (Chennai) for professional reasons: his great knowledge of traditional Indian medicine, *Āyurveda*, led him to treat important personalities of post-independent India. He, therefore, left Mysore City to settle in Madras in 1955. I joined him in 1956 and my mother and my younger sister, in 1958. We lived in a small flat near the sea.

From 1956 to 1958, we used to go down to the seashore in the evenings. When the full moon rose over the sea, we used to contemplate on it at the horizon point. It was during these inspirational moments that my father recounted to me the origin of Yoga. Is there a link between the emergence of the moon over the sea and the emergence of Yoga that my father explained to me?

During pilgrimages, my father preferred to walk sometimes fifteen kilometres between two train stations rather than wait for an hour or two for a train and chose these moments to tell me about the origin of the *āsanas* and *mudras.* He seldom gave these exclusive and unexpected teachings in temples, but more often during the walks, during our pilgrimages.

One day, as we were approaching the temple of Kālahasti, we found the doors to the temple closed. It was the first time that he took me on a pilgrimage to a temple dedicated to Shiva. This temple is important for 'Shaivaites', because the five *mahābhūtas* are united there. The five *mahābhūtas* are the five elements which make up the manifested world. They include, *pṛthvi,* the 'earth' element; *ap*, the 'water' element; *tejas,* the 'fire' element; *vāyu,* the 'air' element; and *ākāsha*, the 'ether' element. Out of these five elements, *vāyu* predominates in the temple of Kālāhasti. *Vāyu* is equally important in Yoga.

We sat under a tree, in front of the temple, and there he explained me the origin of *dhyāna.*

During the three-day pilgrimage, he told me a lot about the origin of Yoga. When he enlightened me about *dhyāna,* it was always in temples dedicated to Shiva.

In the temple of Kālahasti, he explained to me the existence and the meaning of the temple's vital points. The sixteen vital points of the temple are sixteen sacred situations, located in precise places and recognisable by Hindu symbols. These are even more noticeable in temples of Shiva. The sixteen vital points of the temple correspond to the sixteen vital points of the body described in the first and the fourth chapters.

The chapter on *dhyāna* described in this book explains the origin of the meditation as my father taught me during our pilgrimage to Kālāhasti.

During my first pilgrimage to Tirupathi, my father showed me the *vimāna*[1], the dome of the temple located on top of a hill. Tirupathi is the most important place of pilgrimage for the devotees of Viṣṇu. Like the temple of Kālahasti, it is located in the state of Andhra Pradesh. The gold covered Dome, represents paradise, meaning the heavenly world. Gold is considered as a divine metal. That is why the *vimāna* is usually in gold on temples of Viṣṇu. It is also the reason a pilgrim must always see and contemplate the *vimāna* of a temple.

Contemplating the dome of the temple of Tirupathi, my father told me that, 'the knowledge of Master Yājñyavalkya is similar to this *vimāna.* The closer you get to it, the more you realize its knowledge is infinite.'

Even if some passages cited in this book come from the Veda, the teaching presented in it, was imparted by my father. I wish to offer to the readers the knowledge, he transmitted to me on the origin of Yoga and on the role the sage Yājñyavalkya played in the transmission of Yoga to humanity.

---

[1] *Vimāna* also means airplane.

1

Emergence of Yoga

The origin of the teaching of Yoga

As a young couple, Brahma Ratha and Sunanda followed the rules of the Veda with great discipline. They had both respected the Veda's[1] principles from a young age. They wished to have a child who would help mankind know Brahman, the Creator. They thus meditated intensely on the Creator in order for them to give birth to a son, who would allow every living being in the world to know Brahman. Brahma Ratha was the name of the young husband. In Sanskrit, *ratha* means 'cart' or 'chariot.' *Brahma Ratha* represents one who continuously tends towards the Creator (Brahman).

By dint of meditation, the Creator's blessing began to bear fruit. One night, the young partners both had the same dream. The dream revealed the life of one of the Veda's greatest *ṛśis*. The *ṛśis* are the seven Sages who transmitted knowledge of the Veda to humanity.

Sunanda became pregnant after that dream. However, when she went into labour, the child refused to leave its mother's womb. In Vedic times, human beings could communicate with other created beings like animals and even uterine forms of life. Sunanda addressed her child. She asked him to have the will to be born. The child answered that it did not wish to leave the real world of its mother's womb to live in a world that was not reality! Brahma Ratha promised his future son that he would prevent him from being trapped in the created world. The two engaged in a grand philosophical discussion. Brahma Ratha eventually convinced his son to be born. The couple decided to name him Brahma Rathi, meaning 'originated from Brahma Ratha.' The name also means 'one who wants to follow the Creator's chariot.'

Sunanda had a brother called Vaiśampāyana. He was one of the few great Masters, who had mastered the four Vedas. When Brahma Rathi reached the age of studying, his parents asked Vaiśampāyana to take him as a disciple. He was initiated and very soon the young boy mastered all the sciences that Vaiśampāyana taught. Brahma Rathi became the Master's favourite disciple. He was unbeatable in philosophical debates, even on subjects dealing with rites and rituals. Although still very young, he had a perfect knowledge of the details of rites, the material and the *mantras* and sacred formulas of the Vedas used in each phase of a ritual. However, as time passed, Vaiśampāyana came to despise his young nephew.

In those far-off days, a large convention of *ṛśis* was organized once a year in India. Brahma Rathi was invited to take part with his uncle. Vaiśampāyana had not been invited when he was Brahma Rathi's age. He started to feel hatred towards his nephew,

[1] The Veda makes up the entirety of the revealed texts, which are divided into four books: the *Ṛg Veda*, the *Sāma Veda*, the *Yajur Veda* and the *Atharvaṇa Veda*.

but did not prevent him from taking part in the debates. He decided to bring Brahma Rathi to the meeting and to withdraw himself, in order to test whether the young boy could defend himself without his Master. According to Indian tradition, a Master evaluates the spiritual progress of his disciples through tests he gives when the opportunity presents itself.

However, on noticing the absence of Vaiśampāyana, the great assembly of *ṛśis* decided to exclude him from the assembly. His absence was considered as a lack of respect for the *ṛśis*. Vaiśampāyana lost all his spiritual power; he lost his conscious vision of the Creator. There are some purification rituals to stop the consequences of errors committed, and Vaiśampāyana's disciples performed these rituals to help their Master recover his lost power. However, their efforts were in vain. Vaiśampāyana fell deeper and deeper into the darkness of ignorance to the point of being unable to recite the *mantras*. His disciples were incapable of purifying their Master. Brahma Rathi was the only resort for Vaiśampāyana. He promised to perform the necessary rites for his uncle's purification and Vaiśampāyana was freed of his impurities thanks to his nephew. He recovered all his abilities and was readmitted to the assembly of *ṛśis*. However, instead of thanking his disciple, Vaiśampāyana asked for a debt of gratitude from him. According to the tradition of the Veda, it is incumbent on everyone to four debts of gratitude: towards the Creator, towards one's Master, towards one's ancestors and towards other human beings[2]. Vaiśampāyana made his request in this context. While a master usually asks his disciple to pursue the teaching he has received, Vaiśampāyana asked Brahma Rathi to forget all the knowledge of the Veda that he had taught him. Brahma Rathi, in turn, renounced his knowledge as a debt of gratitude. He performed a rite to forget all he had learned, and sacrificed his knowledge to satisfy his Master[3].

In pursuit of knowledge

Needless to say, the young boy did not want to remain in this ignorance. He begged his mother to guide him towards knowledge of the Veda. Sunanda told him that he would obtain this through contemplation on the Sun[4]. She taught him a *mantra* for the contemplation[5]. Following diligent contemplation, Brahma Rathi had a vision of *Sūrya,* the Sun. Sūrya answered Brahma Rathi's prayer on these terms, "I can teach you what you are asking, but I cannot stop my evolution because many planets depend on me." He explained that in order to benefit from his teaching, the young boy would have to follow him at the speed of his trajectory. Again, Brahma Rathi asked his mother for advice on how to follow the Sun's (*Sūrya*) trajectory. Sunanda advised him to ask the Sun's wife for help. However, the Sun's wife could no longer accompany her husband herself. She, therefore, reproduced her own image, and it is this image that follows *Sūrya* on his trajectory[6].

Brahma Rathi performed a very intense contemplation on the Sun to obtain the blessings of Sūrya's wife. Sūrya indicated where he could meet his wife who lived under the guise of a golden horse (*aśva*). This is why the horse is a very sacred animal in the Veda. It always represents the Sun's wife and therefore, the Sun himself[7].

Sūrya's wife gave Brahma Rathi a horse to enable him to become a disciple of the Sun. The horse allowed him to follow *Sūrya* and receive his teaching. *Sūrya*, the Sun, taught Brahma Rathi that the Vedas which are known and transmitted by man are incomplete. The *Yajur Veda*[8] was not fully transmitted to man as his dishonesty could have led him to exploit the part of the *Yajur Veda* missing from the *ṛśis'* rendition.

Due to its incomplete nature, the *Yajur Veda* does not contain instructions necessary to acquire knowledge of Reality. This is why it is called *Kṛṣṇa Yajur Veda,* meaning 'Black' *Yajur Veda*. From birth, Brahma Rathi's role was to teach man to know Reality. The *Kṛṣṇa Yajur Veda* does not detail all indications to achieve knowledge of the Creator. Rather, this collection of *mantras* is more focused on the detailed description of the rituals. When Brahma Rathi had completed his studies with the Sun, *Sūrya,* his teaching was referred to as *Śukla Yajur Veda* or the 'White' *Yajur Veda*, as it had come from the Sun.

[2] *Deva ṛna, ṛśi ṛna, pitṛ ṛna* and *manuśya ṛna*.

[3] According to legend, Brahma Rathi 'vomited' knowledge, two parrots (*tittira* in Sanskrit) heard it and later repeated. What came out of parrots (*tittira*) is *Taittirīya*. One *āraṇyaka* (Treaty of the forest) and one *Upaniṣad* are named *Taittirīya*.

[4] *Sūrya,* one of the most important Vedic deities.

[5] Note that Sunanda, Brahma Rathi's mother, had also perfectly mastered the Veda.

[6] *Chāya*, the shadow.

[7] One of the most important *mantras* is an invocation to the horse.

[8] The second *Veda*, composed of *mantras* for rituals.

Brahma Rathi's life in the forest

Following his studies, Brahma Rathi met with great Masters and took part in debates, allowing him to defend his knowledge. He lived in the forest and therefore, dressed differently from people in towns or villages. In the forest, he wore leaves and tree bark, the part of a tree called *valka*, which is used in rites and rituals. He would wear animal skins whenever he went to town to take part in important rituals or take part in philosophical debates held by the king, but in the forest, he only ever wore clothes made from trees. As a result, the assembly of ṛśis named him Yajña Valkya or 'he who is dressed in rites and rituals.' *Valkya* means clothes made from the leaves and tree bark used in Vedic rituals. *Yajña* corresponds to short rites.

Yājñyavalkya wedding

Because of his ability to answer all questions, Yājñyavalkya was considered a very great Master within the assembly of *ṛśis*. The assembly was not reserved to men. Women also took part in philosophical debates. Gārgi, who had met Yājñyavalkya during rituals, was one such woman. Gārgi had a daughter called Maitreyī, who accompanied her mother to the assembly as well as the rituals. Maitreyī's sole preoccupation was to obtain knowledge of the Creator.

Yājñyavalkya had reached the age of marriage. The *ṛśis* proposed that the grand Master marry Kātyāyana, another female philosopher, and so they were married. Kātyāyana also attended the assembly of *ṛśis*. As a philosopher, she appears in two main *Upaniṣads*[9], *Chāndogya Upaniṣad* and *Bṛhadāraṇyaka Upaniṣad*. She questioned her husband on the relation between the mind, senses and the object during an experience. She is present in every chapter dealing with epistemology of perception.

Yājñyavalkya's teaching to his wife

In the days of *Śukla Yajur Veda*, after the time of *Kṛṣṇa Yajur Veda*, Yājñyavalkya highlighted the errors in these philosophical debates about accepted knowledge. He introduced this part of the Veda that the others did not know. Yājñyavalkya had become *ṛśi* Yājñyavalkya, given that he mastered every field of knowledge: philosophy, science, *Āyurveda* (Indian medicine), grammar, language, etc.

One evening, Kātyāyana asked her husband the following questions: While the Veda always adapts itself to a given situation, why do the Veda's injunctions change? Why are human beings no longer capable of applying these injunctions? Despite rites and rituals, why do they seem more attracted by material gains than by the real purpose of the Veda?

Yājñyavalkya described all the influences on man of objects of perception. He reminded Kātyāyana, Gārgi and Maitreyī that in the past, man contemplated with ease because he knew how to master his sense perception. The sense perception of his contemporaries is scattered. Instead of using his body to gain knowledge of the Creator, he uses it as an object.

Yājñyavalkya explained that this situation led to the modification of the rites. Secondary rites were introduced to recover the potency of contemplation that man could no longer preserve. Man had fallen into a trap preventing him from fulfilling contemplations leading him to know the Creator because he had become more dependent on his sense perceptions than on his mind.

However, Kātyāyana, Gārgi and Maitreyī, unsatisfied by Yājñyavalkya's response, asked if there was a way for man to re-establish his former self.

---

[9] The *Upaniṣads* are philosophical texts which make up part of the Veda and mainly deal with the relation between the soul and the Creator.

2
Yoga Sādhana

The method

Yājñyavalkya's answer to the question was clear and precise. Indeed, there is a way for man to regain his power of contemplation. This method is called *Yoga Sādhana.*

Yājñyavalkya began by explaining that man was no longer able to maintain constantly a given position. This is not simply a physical position but also a mental one. Man must first practice remaining in a fixed position for a given period to prevent excitation of sensory and mental activities. Staying in a precise position reduces such excitations and offers the mind the potential to stay without any activity linked to the outside world. Yājñyavalkya calls the position an *āsana.* It allows the mind to be entirely absorbed by the Creator and prevents man from being distracted by sensory activity. The body can only become a tool under these conditions. In all other situations, man is a slave to his body.

Maitreyī asked if there was any other means necessary for the body to become detached from the sense perceptions and the mind. A simple position did not seem sufficient to her to bring the body back to its original purpose of leading man to the Creator.

It is not surprising that Yājñyavalkya's presentation of *Yoga Sādhana* came in response to questions from Kātyāyana, Gārgi and Maitreyī. In Indian philosophical texts, women always ask practical questions. For example, in *Bṛhadāraṇyaka Upaniṣad*, men ask Yājñyavalkya intellectual questions while women ask questions about applicable issues.

During the questioning, Maitreyī confesses to Yājñyavalkya that despite being seated for a long time, her physical position is not uniting her with the Creator. She asks whether there is another way to force her body to become a tool, allowing for contemplation on the Creator.

Yājñyavalkya explains that doubt is preventing her union with the creator, not the *āsana.* He reminds her that doubt comes from breathing. As long as breathing is irregular, it creates doubt. In turn, doubt causes fear and when man is subject to fear, he wilfully looks for situations where death is present. *Prāṇāyāma* is the only means of erasing doubt.

The way in which man breathes allows him either to remove doubt or to sink further into it. The accumulation of doubt automatically leads to the destruction of the individual. Yājñyavalkya continued to give some instructions on *prāṇa,* which make up the first part of the word *prāṇāyāma. Prāṇa* is the name of the ray of Sunshine that is in all of us and which we lose first. It is imperative to recover this ray as it is our chariot's path towards *Āditya,* the Sun. To follow *prāṇa,* it is necessary to perform a ritual, which begins just before sunrise and continues while the sun is rising.

In the *Bṛhadāraṇyaka Upaniṣad,* Yājñyavalkya teaches King Janaka of Videha the importance to man of the Sun's ray. During the presentation in question, Gārgi asked Yājñyavalkya why man lost his values and therefore his capacity. Gārgi belonged to another Veda through family lineage, but she was aware of the consequences of a failure in the path of rituals. Yājñyavalkya spoke of birth and rebirth to explain how man lost his values. He did not expose the theory of rebirth, but he used this theory to explain how man lost his capacity to contemplate.

From rebirth to liberation

Yājñyavalkya taught his female interlocutors that there are sixteen 'exit doors' available to a soul when it is leaving the body. These doors correspond to the sixteen vital points linking the soul to the physical body. The soul does not use these doors on entering a body; however, it knows which world it will be reborn into according to the door from which it exits. Some doors lead the soul to the animal kingdom. The soul can also be reborn among human beings or live in the divine world.

Therefore, rebirth is already programmed by our behaviour in this life. To allow the soul to choose the door from which it will be liberated, *prāṇāyāma* is practiced by concentrating on one of the sixteen vital points. Together, the sixteen 'exit doors' form the *marma sthāna,* literally meaning 'the secret places.' *Prāṇāyāmas* accompanied by concentration on the vital points is called *dhāraṇa.* These sixteen doors explain why *prāṇāyāma* is always practised with sixteen breaths in *Yoga Sādhana.* It is also the reason why there are sixteen rites between birth and liberation.

The sixteen vital points include, the big toes, ankles, knees, top of the thighs, the perineum, the centre of the pelvis, the navel, the centre of the heart, the back of the throat, the throat, the base of the uvula, the back of the palate, the tip of the nose, the point between the eyebrows, the centre of the forehead and the fontanel.

Sagarbha Prāṇāyāma is when a *prāṇāyāma* is carried out along with *dhāraṇa,* concentration on one of the sixteen vital points. In Sanskrit, *garbha* means 'the womb.' Without *dhāraṇa, prāṇāyāma* is considered *nigarbha,* meaning 'sterile.' *Sagarbha Prāṇāyāma* translates as 'fertile *prāṇāyāma*,' as it is the only one capable of liberating the soul. When evoking God, a divine representation or when mentally reciting a *mantra* during *Nāḍī Śodhana,* the *prāṇāyāma* is also *Sagarbha Prāṇāyāma.* By using the sixteen vital points in *prāṇāyāma,* the soul is progressively enlightened to choose the door to liberation. The practice of *Sagarbha Prāṇāyāma* is recommended for the soul to exit through the path of the fontanel, *śīrṣa*[1], and to be freed from the cycle of rebirths.

This path, *Nivṛtti Mārga,* used by *dhāraṇa* in *prāṇāyāma* is the 'path of no return'. In his teaching, Yājñyavalkya calls it *Nivṛtti dharma.*

Pravṛtti Mārga is the path that leads the soul to be reborn as a human being as it always leads to rebirth.

After explaining the concept of *dhāraṇa,* Yājñyavalkya explained the notion of contemplation, *dhyāna. Dhyāna* is contemplation on the Sun, *Āditya,* or the Creator. Thus, there are only two *dhyānas.* Needless to say, all these practices require the support of the individual. This support refers to principles applied in daily life to avoid situations, which could potentially affect contemplation[2].

In other words, Yājñyavalkya indicated the necessary tools for concentration and contemplation. These are the essential elements required to keep the mind on an object of

---

[1] The vital point *śīrṣa* is just above the fontanel

[2] This set of disciplines was later classified as *Yama* and *Niyama. Yama* and *Niyama* are ethical and moral principles with regards to oneself and others.

The 10 yamas are: *ahimsa, satya, asteya, brahmacarya, dayā, ārjava, kṣama, dhṛti, mitha āhāra* and *śauca. Ahimsa* corresponds to not creating suffering in others. *Satya* means to do good to all living beings in this world. *Asteya* is the transmission of the principles taught by the ṛsis. *Brahmacarya* is the interruption of the interaction between the sense perceptions and the world of experience, or sensory objects. *Dayā* is the protection of all that surrounds us. *Ārjava* is the consideration of every path to the Creator as equal: none is considered superior to another. *Kṣama* is the acceptance of pleasure and unhappiness with an equal state of mind. It is most important to equally consider those bringing pleasure and disappointment. *Dhṛti* is stability of mind, free from any influence of activities bringing material goods. *Mitha āhāra* means to feed the body and mind without excess. *Śauca* is the purity of body and mind.

The 10 *niyamas* are *tapas, saṃtoṣa, āstikya, dāna, īśvara pūjana, siddhānta śravaṇa, hrīmatī, japa* and *vrata. Tapas* is the maintenance of a perfectly clean body, internally as well as externally. *Saṃtoṣa* is constant happiness. *Āstikya* is respect for the principles of *dharma* and *adharma*, always in accordance with social and family status. *Dharma* for a *brahmacāri* (bachelor) could be *adharma* for a married man. *Dāna* is the act of respectfully giving what was earned with one's own efforts. *Ishvara pūjana* is the offering of prayers in total sincerity to the supreme God, according to one's capacity. The sincerity of prayer has to grow. *Siddhānta śravaṇa* is the study that confirms conviction. It consists of the study of the Holy Scriptures. *Hrīmatī* is the attitude one must have towards women. A woman cannot be put in a situation of shame. She cannot become an object. *Hrīmatī* corresponds to two *niyamas*, *hri* and *mati. Mati* is the will to know the spiritual entity. *Japa* is the repetition of a mantra. *Vrata* is the strict application of dharmas, which are specific to the individual in searching for the soul.

There are ten *yamas* and ten *niyamas*, even though the authors of Yoga treaties only mention five of them. The other five, having become morals, are not cited anymore.

contemplation[3]. Yājñyavalkya considered the last of these elements as the union with the Creator.

According to Yājñyavalkya, one birth always leads to another. Therefore, to interrupt the cycle of rebirth, birth must end or 'not to be reborn.' During meditation, the soul may unite with the Creator. Yājñyavalkya calls that union *samādhi*. The word *samādhi* also means 'identical to the origin.[4]' That notion was later called *mokṣa* or 'liberation,' but it is a recent term dating back to the time of *darśanas*[5].

The purpose of this approach is to avoid dying again, *punar mṛtyu. Punar* means 'again' and *mṛtyu,* 'death.' The expression *punar janma* meaning 'reborn again' also exists. *Yoga Sādhana* is the name Yājñyavalkya gave to the set of practices whose aim is to stop *punar mṛtyu* or *punar janma.*

Precisions on the *Śukla Yajur Veda*

The *Śukla Yajur Veda* came after the *Kṛṣṇa Yajur Veda.* Like Brahma Rathi, Yājñyavalkya belonged by family tradition to the *Yajur Veda.* The *Śukla Yajur Veda* does not constitute a fifth Veda. Rather, the *Yajur Veda* is made up of two branches, the *Śukla Yajur Veda* and the *Kṛṣṇa Yajur Veda.*

The *Śukla Yajur Veda* is often dated between 3500BC and 3000BC. As with all Vedas, one *Brāhmaṇa*[6] is linked to *Śukla Yajur Veda.* This *Brāhmaṇa's* name, *Śata Patha Brāhmaṇa*, means 'the *Brāhmaṇa* of a hundred and four chapters.' An *upaniṣad* called *Bṛhadāraṇyaka Upaniṣad* also belongs to *Śukla Yajur Veda.* In this *upaniṣad,* we witness a philosophical discourse between Yājñyavalkya, Gārgi, Maitreyī and the great King Janaka. A great philosophical debate with practical elements takes place between King Janaka and Yājñyavalkya. Questions such as, what is the soul's path to rebirth, or what are heaven and hell are posed. Janaka also asks Yājñyavalkya how to put an end to the cycle of rebirth?

Yājñyavalkya then explains *saṃnyāsa* to the king. It is the ninth stage, essential to becoming united with the Creator. *Saṃnyāsa* corresponds to complete renunciation. It is the only way to gain perfect command of the vital points. After *samādhi, saṃnyāsa* is required for the final union of the soul with the Creator.

Yājñyavalkya's teachings

Yājñyavalkya's teachings are always presented through dialogue. For example, it is in response to Kātyāyana, Gārgi and Maitreyī that he explains the importance of the different postures. Maintaining one āsana is insufficient. The sense perceptions cannot be brought under control through one single posture. Yājñyavalkya taught the ladies each āsana's role and function. Similarly, through discussion with King Janaka, Yājñyavalkya highlighted the importance of the rites called *Darśapūrna.* Following the moon's cycle, these rites must be accomplished twice a month. They are part of the sixteen Karmas, the sixteen rites that every human being should carry out in their lifetime. *Darśapūrna* can be broken down as *amāvasya* and *paurṇima*, rites that should be executed on the day of a full moon and a new moon. Yājñyavalkya is the only Master who explains the reasons why these rites should be performed, and the potential consequences of errors committed during their execution. Particular respect should also be shown to guests in our homes during the cyclical movement linked to the two lunar phases.

To replace these rites, which are not accessible to all, my father introduced the practice of *prāṇāyāma* on the day of a new moon and a full moon. These *prāṇāyāma* sessions are described in Chapter 10.

Yājñyavalkya indicates the consequences of errors committed during the performance of rites and the salutary role of *darśapūrna.* The rites of the new moon and full moon days have a direct result on these consequences. The two rites allow redemption from errors committed in other rituals. *Darśapūrna* allows us to make up for neglected seasonal acts, avoiding the potential consequences deriving from these. However, the role of the sixteen *karmas* is to free us from the possessions of this world. We will not achieve

[3] These means later became the 'eight limbs of Yoga' or *aṣṭānga yoga* (*yama, niyama, āsana, prāṇāyāma, pratyāhāra, dhāraṇa, dhyāna* and *samādhi).*

[4] Identical at the origine to the soul in the Creator.

[5] The philosophical interpretations.

[6] The *Brāhmaṇas* represent the philosophical part of the Veda.

liberation, as long as we have the four debts of gratitude[7]. Therefore, living as human beings is an incredible opportunity. It is the only time we can make up for the errors of our previous lives. The cycle of rebirths continues as long as this has not been done. *Darśapūrnas* are the twice-monthly rites that offer man a means of compensating for the loss of other karmas. Our descendants cannot rid us of past errors, but it is our duty to help our children to walk on the path to liberation, in search of the Creator.

The only ritual that allows children 'to be linked to *prāṇa'* is part of *Yoga Sādhana.* It is a *prāṇāyāma* that Yājñyavalkya calls *Prāṇa Agni Hotra.* It carries that name in Yājñyavalkya's teaching because it is considered as an offering of our *prāṇa* to ancestors and descendants.

Yājñyavalkya was the first Master to prescribe a minimum number of *prāṇāyāmas* per day, to enable our mind to be constantly with the Creator. He was also the first to introduce contemplation on *Āditya,* sunlight or the solar disk. Before Yājñyavalkya, the *Ṛg Veda* recommended visual concentration on the rising or setting Sun. These concentrations were done standing either in the morning facing east or in the evening facing west. The contemplations taught by Yājñyavalkya go beyond the solar disk, indicating that contemplation on a point situated in the centre of the Sun leads to the Creator, *Prajāpati.*

This teaching of Yoga did not come from Yājñyavalkya, but he transmitted it from the *Yajur Veda.* In Vedic times, man followed essential discipline to fulfil his duties in this world. Now, however, our body and sense perceptions prevent us from fulfilling our duties. This situation is the *raison d'être* of this teaching allowing man to achieve a disciplined life. Today, we benefit from this teaching, thanks to Yājñyavalkya's answer to Kātyāyana, Gārgi and Maitreyī's questions and also thanks to my father. Our direct ascendant in Yoga is the Sun, *Sūrya.* Yoga is the only science revealed by the Sun. Brahma, the Creator, gave man all other Indian sciences. The Sun transmitted the teaching of Yoga. The word *Sūrya,* referring to the Sun, means 'the one who illuminates.' *Sūrya* is the fire, the one who 'gives light.' This notion is extremely important in Indian thinking because knowledge of the Creator is light. That light can only be found within our hearts, *hṛdaya*[8].

Thus, the Sun is always contemplated in *hṛdaya.* During the practice of *samādhi, hṛdaya,* the centre of our physiological heart, is linked directly to *śīrṣa*[9] through a channel called *hita nāḍī.* The fontanel's importance in the process uniting the soul with the Creator is due to the link that unites *hṛdaya* and *śīrṣa.*

In Yājñyavalkya's period, to achieve *samādhi,* everyone contemplated the Sun in morning, invoking Him in *hṛdaya.* According to Yājñyavalkya's teachings, neither reciting nor study of the Veda is approved before evocation of the Sun.

The tradition of evoking the Masters

Before beginning a study, it is a tradition in India to evoke the *ṛśis* and Masters who transmitted the knowledge from generation to generation. Irrespective of the science being studied, Indian custom advices the evocation of a lineage of teachers who secured the uninterrupted transmission of that science from ancient times. The time or era when the Masters lived is of no significance. Reference to a recognized Master is all that matters. This guarantees authenticity of teaching. He designates his children or at times one of his disciples to continue the transmission.

Yoga is an exception to this rule. The study of Yoga does not begin by paying homage to a lineage of Masters. Yoga is therefore, an exception in a cultural context which shows unlimited respect to tradition. Yet, the science of Yoga dates back to Vedic times and its transmission has been carried out in a traditional manner since then. Certain notional elements we encounter in today's teaching of yoga such as *āsana, prāṇāyāma, dhāraṇa, upāsana*[10], were already present in the Vedas. The Vedas are the reference texts of Indian tradition. They are considered 'non-human'. The word 'Veda' means 'that which comes from God.' They constitute the 'Word of God' or the 'Revelation.' The Vedas represent the absolute reference that cannot be questioned under any circumstances.

[7] Towards the Creator, towards one's Master, towards one's ancestors and towards other human beings.

[8] *Hṛdaya* does not correspond to the physiological heart, but is considered as the location of the soul.

[9] The fontanel.

[10] Postures, respiration accompanying an evocation, concentration, and meditation.

While it is not custom to offer prayers to a lineage of teachers in Yoga, it is a tradition to evoke the Primordial Serpent, *Ananta*[11], which represents infinity. In Indian mythology, Viṣṇu rested on *Ananta*'s body (coiled three times) during Creation. He contemplated his Creation. Viṣṇu lying on *Ananta*'s three coils is called 'The Yogi.' Indians worship him as 'The Great Yogi.' Therefore, it is custom for all those practising meditation to evoke *Ananta,* 'The Great Snake.' In the same way, the traditional invocation before studying a Yoga text, such as Patañjali's *Yoga Sūtra* or Svātmārama's *Haṭha Yoga Pradīpika,* starts with mention of *Ananta.*

In the Veda, the first position for any ritual or meditation is *Ananta āsana.* Irrespective of the ritual or prayer, *Ananta* is invoked before proceeding to the rite or ritual. Viṣṇu lying on the Snake is called *Ananta Āsana.* Homage is paid to the Creator by doing this salutation. This is the origin of the *āsana* in the Veda.

In Indian mythology, all of God's postures are called *yoga āsana.* Since Vedic times, the Fire ritual, prepared with bricks positioned in a precise way has also been called *yoga āsana.* Any divine representation in which the God or Goddess is seated on a bench or represented standing is always *yoga āsana.*

The four foundations of existence, *Puruṣārtha*

The common goal of all Indian sciences is the emancipation of the individual soul (*ātma* or *jīva*), and Yoga is no exception to this rule. This emancipation is called Liberation, or *mokṣa.* Released from the cycle of rebirth (*saṃsāra*), the individual soul (*ātma* or *jīva*) reaches its supreme condition.

This is why, according to Indian thought, man's life is based on four foundations corresponding to the implementation of *puruṣārtha's* values. The word *puruṣārtha* means the pillars of Man (*Puruṣa*). The four *puruṣārthas* are comparable to the four legs of a table. Man's life rests on these foundations, which are four obligations to be fulfilled during his life. Irrespective of age, man must respect the four *puruṣārthas.*

In the *Mahā Bhārata*, one of the two great Indian epics, *puruṣārtha* is referenced in a great philosophical debate. The philosopher Vidura[12] asks what is good in man if he does not comply with the four *puruṣārthas.* Man's degradation comes from the fact that he does not respect the values of *puruṣārtha.*

The four foundations that determine any individual's existence are:

- *Dharma,*
- *Artha,*
- *Kāma,*
- *Mokṣa*

Dharma is the observance of rules keeping the created world from being destroyed. *Artha* corresponds to a balance in material comfort without us being attached to material goods or too many possessions. *Kāma* signifies the desire to respect *Dharma*'s order: the desire to achieve enough comfort in our material lives to sustain our existence and the desire for liberation and union with God. *Mokṣa* is liberation from the cycle of rebirth.

The four *puruṣārthas* outline the path that leads to the Creator. However, they are not enough to reach the supreme destination. They are a means of maintaining physical and emotional balance throughout a lifetime. Man is obliged to respect the four foundations of his existence, irrespective of his age. Man's primary role is to follow the four *puruṣārthas*. According to age and social status, these principles allow man to maintain a balance of material, sentimental, emotional and spiritual needs in his daily life. While the four foundations of existence cannot in themselves lead man to the Creator, they support his progression towards Him.

Study of the Veda shows that there are different ways in which man can fulfil these four foundations. Union with the Creator is the ultimate purpose of their implementation. Their partial or disproportionate implementation prevents man from knowing the Creator and becoming united with Him.

[11] The Primordial Serpent is represented either by seven or ten heads.

[12] Vidura is also adviser and minister to King Dhṛtarāṣṭra.

Union and separation, *Yoga* and *Viyoga*

The non-application of the four *puruṣārtha* values move man away from *Prajāpati*, the name given to the Creator in the Veda. The word used to designate this state is 'separation.' Neglecting them separates the soul from *Prajāpati,* but applying them unites it with the Creator. In the Veda, the concept of *Yoga*, meaning 'be united' and its opposite, the concept of separation, *viyoga,* come from this principle. These two notions are found throughout Indian philosophy under the name of *mokṣa*, liberation, and *bandha*, the stranglehold of matter. In the Veda, the two substantives relating to these notions are *yoga* and *viyoga.*

Vedic rites at different life stages

Vedic rites are a way of practising the *puruṣārthas* at different stages in life. Vedic rites differ according to age, social status and family situation; that is, 'married', 'parent with a daughter', 'parent with a son', etc. For example, if the person conducting the ritual has one deceased parent; the rite will be different if both parents were deceased, or if they were still alive. The choice of *mantras*[13] recited in these rites depends on family and social status. For example, the rituals to salute Sun will be rather simple for a young boy who has not yet been initiated. In addition to the lighting of lamps, he will have to recite short phrases, and the ritual will last no longer than two or three minutes. The rites of a young initiate generally last fifteen minutes and are done three times daily. The rite of Sun adoration lasts longer for a married man and if that married man is over sixty years of age; he will have to do a particularly complicated rite once a month as well as specific rites on the solstices. The set of rites for a man over sixty is a direct means of achieving liberation (*mokṣa*). A child does not have to carry out this type of rite.

By their nature, children are agitated and as they cannot stay still for long, they dedicate only a short period of time to prayer. A married man should carry out longer contemplations and an aged man, free from family worries, should dedicate even more time to rites, prayers, study of holy texts and meditation.

The length of the rites is therefore determined by age and the physical and mental state of the individual doing them. However, the rites imply that the individual is eligible to be initiated and has the knowledge and proficiency necessary to recite the *mantras*. Indeed, a mistake in intonation is considered an error during a rite, and its consequences can be serious.

To perform a rite, one must also know the protocol for this rite. Various means have been offered to those who do not meet the requirements of the rites. Even in the Veda, an alternative is proposed to all those who, by reason of birth or otherwise, cannot carry out the rites leading to liberation[14].

A married man always begins a rite accompanied by his wife. She lights the holy fire at the start of the ritual and finishes the rite by lighting a lamp.

There are more demanding rites which women are not obliged to do as they are responsible for the household during the rite. In addition to the preparation of material necessary for the rite, she has the role of welcoming the priests and providing for their comfort.

A chariot race[15], in which the king participates, is described at the end of the *Mahā Bhārata* epic. The queen escorts the king, and she commands the horse to participate in the race. She gives her consent for the race to take place and orders her horse to win. The race cannot take place without her. The queen is ill in this episode, but nonetheless, she still comes to start the race.

Similarly, in the chapter of the *Mahā Bhārata* describing the war, the Pāṇḍavas's wife Draupadi, gives her consent to start hostilities on the battlefield. With the universal order (*dharma*) under threat, war was inevitable. Yet, without the queen's consent, the war would not have taken place.

Liberation is for all

As union with the Creator is not exclusive to the elite, the Veda gives instructions to those who do

[13] The sacred formulas of the Vedas.
[14] Uninitiated, illness, mourning, etc.
[15] In royal families, a chariot race is a rite.

not have the possibility to conduct the rites. Anyone can be united with the Creator. Irrespective of social status, 'liberation belongs to everyone' as the *Brāhmaṇas* often remind us.

Union with the Creator is not merely for those who have been initiated in rites and rituals.

Thus, the Veda advocates the principles of *puruṣārtha* which can be applied without necessitating rites or rituals.

The principle of *dharma* is linked with the concept of *adharma*, which corresponds to actions to be avoided. However, to be able to avoid these actions, it is essential to reduce or diminish certain physical impulses. In later texts, that notion became 'the perfect discipline over the body.'

Similarly, the evocation of a deity was considered possible through the use of respiration[16]. The deity was evoked through breathing to prevent mental distraction. The use of a concentration point, such as the horizon point or heart, prevented the senses from being distracted during the contemplation and evocation of the deity.

From the Veda to Yoga

Yoga was born from this second non-ritual approach. The approach consisting of various steps has different stages corresponding to our behaviour towards others and us.

Learning equal values, such as facing loss or gain, happiness or unhappiness, was an important step in the teaching. It was the same for the imitation of different species. Imitation of the bodies and attitudes of creatures surrounding us, allows us to acquire the sensorial finesse of these beings. Imitation of the respiratory rhythm of animals or other beings was used as a method of concentration. This progressive learning of concentration allowed for the evocation of divine objects such as a star, the Sun, the Moon…

Man has many preoccupations in addition to the rites and rituals. The Veda thus recommends a morning practice, at dawn, when man has not yet been absorbed by the activities of daily life. According to the Veda, man's mind is clearest at dawn. It is an immutable time. In addition, the practice described in the Veda was more fruitful at dawn. It is worth asking whether the rigour later granted to the morning practice of yoga comes from this practice in the Veda. The fact remains that Yoga is actually a compilation of the non-ritual aspects of the Veda. That is why Yoga is not practised in the strictest tradition of the Veda. Yoga is not practiced in orthodox Vedic *milieu*, as they only carry out the rites and rituals prescribed by the Veda. Sri Rāma, the great hero of *Ramayana*[17], did not practice Yoga, except when he was in the forest with Viśvāmitra, his Master. The prayers or rites that he performed morning, noon and evening were the supreme way towards union with the Creator.

In the *Mahā Bhārata*, Sri Kṛṣṇa brings to light his application of the principles of Yoga. He performed contemplative practices. In the *Bhagavad Gita*[18], Sri Kṛṣṇa gives a detailed description of the different paths which make up Yoga.

However, in India, priests do not practise Yoga. They consider rites and rituals to be of superior value to the practice of Yoga. That is why there is no generally acknowledged genealogy in Yoga. It is important to note that this non-ritual approach is open to everyone.

Yoga is not what we commonly refer to today. The word 'Yoga' has become synonymous with a series of physical exercises or of a certain type of gymnastics. Its primary function has become secondary or even non-existent. Since its origin, Yoga has been a 'way to be united with the creator or God.' Its etymology[19] reminds us of this.

[16] This respiration is called *prāṇāyāma*. Seated (or standing according to the rite) with eyes looking in the direction of the heart ('the spiritual heart'), air is inhaled through the left nostril (the right nostril closed) while mentally reciting a *mantra* and evoking the deity addressed in the *mantra*. The breath is held (closing both nostrils), reciting the same *mantra* mentally and then the air is exhaled through the right nostril (the left nostril closed) reciting the same *mantra* mentally. And so on, either twice or three times according to the rite.

[17] The *Ramayana* and the *Mahā Bhārata* are two epics of great philosophical and ethical value.

[18] 'The Song of the Lord': the philosophical teaching of Sri Kṛṣṇa to Arjuna on the battlefield.

[19] Etymologically, the word Yoga means 'union'.

3

Origin of Prāṇāyāma

Prāṇa

In the Veda, the concept of *prāṇa* as *dhāraṇa* is considered to be the Creator's respiration in this world. The Creator's exhalation is the energy of creation. He created the world through exhalation and reabsorbed it through inhalation. All four Vedas have this theme in common. This is why *prāṇa* is considered the first life. The prefix *Pra* means both 'first' and 'principal.' The Veda mentions creation itself as respiration. This is the origin of the concept of *prāṇa*. From *prāṇa* comes light.

Each of the Creator's respiration cycles is a cycle of creation and absorption.

The Creator can be evoked as Agni, the Creator's Fire; as *Parjanya*, the Water that gives life to earth; as *Vāta*[1], the Wind or the world's breath of life. Fire, Water and Wind are the basic divinities in the Veda, as well as different concepts of *prāṇa*.

As the world was created through exhalation, *prāṇa* is often considered as the original breath. As creation is in a constant state of flux, it goes through a set of transformations. *Prāṇa* is considered to be at the origin of any motion. The notion of motion should be interpreted here as fundamental transformation, not physical motion. *Prāṇa* is time, as the concept of time (*kāla*) comes from motion as well as the duration of non-motion. Non-motion corresponds to when there is no transformation. Motion falls outside non-duration; therefore, *prāṇa* is eternal because non-motion is eternal. Given that non-motion is linked to motion in relation to precedence and subsequence, non-motion is made up of several instants and the period between these instants is imperceptible and eternal. Time is the modification between motion and non-motion, while the modification between two non-durations is eternal, imperceptible, like *prāṇa*, which is also imperceptible. Going into more detail on the concept of *prāṇāyāma*, we will see that *kumbhaka*, the phase between inhalation and exhalation, is also imperceptible. It is the phase corresponding to time.

Note that non-duration is of the same nature as Eternity but is implied by transformation. There is no non-duration without transformation. Without transformation, we perceive eternity. That is *samādhi*.

According to the Veda, there is a time disparity between motion and non-motion in the same way that exhalation is always longer than inhalation in living beings. Lifetime is much longer than the non-lifetime, meaning death. If we can therefore equalise the duration of our inhalation and exhalation, we will understand non-duration. Once we succeed in understanding non-motion, we will understand time, *kāla*, and consequently, the Creator through *prāṇa* since *prāṇa* is time. The Veda deals with *prāṇa* more than ā*yāma.*

There are two different points of view depending on the interpretation of the Veda. Some consider

[1] Not to be confused with the same word used in *Āyurveda* used to indicate certain pathologies.

prāṇa as the force of re-absorption and *apāna* as the force of creation, implying that exhalation corresponds to creation. Others see the Creator's *Prāṇa* as the force of creation. The name of *prāṇa* is therefore, *Ucchiṣṭa Prāṇa*, meaning principal *prāṇa*.

Later in the *Vedānta*[2] and the *Upaniṣads*, *prāṇa* is called *Mukhya Prāṇa*, with *mukhya* meaning important or principal. *Mukhya Prāṇa* is the force of creation as well as the force of re-absorption. These names were given to distinguish the Creator's *prāṇa* from the *prāṇa* within us, which is simply called *prāṇa*.

Invocation of Prāṇa in the Atharvaṇa Veda

The notion of *prāṇa* is much more present in the eleventh *Khaṇḍa*, the eleventh section of the *Atharvaṇa Veda*. A whole chapter, *sarga*, contains mantras to invoke *prāṇa*.

The *Yajur Veda* also includes several invocations of *prāṇa*.

In the eleventh section of *Atharvaṇa Veda*, thirty-two mantras are dedicated to *prāṇa*. *Prāṇa* is evoked as the life of the created world, the Creator's breath. Even though it appears rather late in the *Atharvaṇa Veda*, *prāṇa* represents the most important aspect of any evocation. The following is the translation of the first two mantras of that chapter:

1) Homage and salutation to *prāṇa*:
The whole world is his subject,
He is the King of all creatures,
And the support of all beings.

2) Homage and salutation to *prāṇa*:
He who breathes in this world,
With ferocious strength.
But he breathes with respect.
He converts the wind
Into thunder and lightning.

Prāṇa breathes intensely beyond our atmosphere. Breathing in our universe with 'ferocious strength,' he becomes the Wind. He does not breathe to destroy the world. He generates rain by converting wind into thunder and lightning. Thunder and Lightning form a couple whose child is the rain. They procreate the rain that fertilizes the earth. Rain gives life to Earth, and Earth's produce becomes man's food. All life depends on these four elements: wind, lightning, thunder and rain. It is the Creator's gift.

Five functions of *Prāṇa*

Prāṇa is also invoked as five functions. This invocation introduces the concept of five *prāṇa*s:

Prāṇa is inhalation, meaning 'what enters us'.

Apāna is exhalation, meaning 'what leaves us.' The first two *prāṇa*s called *prāṇa* and *apāna*, not only correspond to thoracic breathing but also to cellular respiration.

The third *prāṇa* is called *vyāna*. It is the 'one that goes askew,' meaning that it moves horizontally and vertically.

Samāna maintains equal distribution in our existence.

Udāna is the *prāṇa* that makes us fly, transcend or go upwards.

Healing Power of *Prāṇa*

Prāṇa is evoked for its healing power. Medicine and magic are largely present in the *Atharvaṇa Veda*. Indian medicine, Āyurveda, finds its origin in the *Atharvaṇa Veda*. In the *Atharvaṇa Veda*, curing a creature is not solely a matter of healing its body but also involves soothing the *duḥkhas*, meaning relieving its suffering.

Prāṇa is evoked as cloth (*dhara*). It dresses creatures like a father dress his son. The cloth represents the body because *prāṇa* gives life to the cells.

[2] One of the six *Darśanas*, philosophical interpretations.

The Lord of what breathes and what does not breathe

Prāṇa is the Lord of what breathes and what does not, meaning that he is present in what lives as well as in death. Death is not re-absorption.

Prāṇa is death and illness. *Prāṇa* is fever. Fever is the beginning of the destruction of cells. It is considered as the sign of death. Death is a change in the state of a creature; therefore, a dysfunction of the body leads to the destruction of cells. In Vedic times, man enjoyed perfect health, but feared modifications because dysfunction leads to death.

Therefore, the *Atharvaṇa Veda* contains a mantra to appease fever, fever being considered as destruction and not just a rise in body temperature.

Prāṇa, the Creator, rice and barley

Prāṇa is the power of creation, *Virāj*. It is also the deity that guides us. Therefore, all creatures worship *prāṇa*. *Prāṇa* is the Sun and the Moon; it is *Prajāpati*, the Creator.

In the *Atharvaṇa Veda*, the Sun and the Moon are the most important divinities for man. In the other Vedas, the most important divinities are *Indra*, *Vāyu*, *Varuṇa* …

In one *mantra*, we learn that rice and barley are considered as the inhalation and exhalation[3] of the Goddess Earth[4].

From conception to death

Prāṇa governs life from the moment of conception. In the womb, the embryo inhales and exhales. Man is dead when he no longer breathes. The cessation of respiration is synonymous with death.

Prāṇa arrives in the body before the soul, *ātma*. The soul penetrates a body only after *prāṇa*. It is the same for death. *Prāṇa* leaves the body before the soul. At the time of death, the soul is still present when *prāṇa* is leaving the body.

Like breathing, *prāṇa* is present in man, whether asleep or awake.

The Honey of creation

The *Atharvaṇa Veda* gives *prāṇa* the same name as *Āditya*, the Sun. *Prāṇa* has a golden, honey-like colour. As honey is the womb of all living creatures, 'the great embryo', *prāṇa* moves among living creatures. *Prāṇa* moves freely in honey. *Prāṇa* is immortality. It is eternal.

Prāṇa is common to all, divinities and human beings. It is the faithful friend of divinities, demons, animals and men.

The Creator's vision and the higher path

In the most important part of the *Atharvaṇa Veda*, we learn that vision is the first thing *prāṇa* gives to creatures in the embryo. This is perception rather than eyesight. *Prāṇa* then gives all living creatures the power of expression, *vāk*.

Thus, sight promoting a vision of the Creator is the first power given by *prāṇa*, meaning that during all uterine life, the embryo has a vision of the Creator.

Vāk or expression allows for transcendence. In the Rāmāyaṇa epic, Sri Anjaneya[5] soared towards the Sun at birth. In the same way, *vāk* is the impulse that all beings have towards the Creator. This is given by *prāṇa*.

Any impulse towards the Creator is *udāna.*

In the same *Veda*, an invocation invites *prāṇa* to 'escape towards the zenith.' The person reciting asks *prāṇa* to follow the transcendental path, *ūrdhva gati*, in order to escape upwards. The more recent concept of *ujjāyi* comes from that evocation. *Ujjāyi* breathing allows for transcendence, the transcendental movement of *prāṇa*.

[3] Rice and barley are offerings in Vedic rituals. In *Āyurveda*, Indian medicine, rice water mixed with barley water is considered to bring a dying person back to life. A sick person drinks a few drops of the mixture to bring him back to health.

[4] This metaphysical concept also governs agriculture. In the Vedas, there are many references to agriculture, for example, cultivating alternately rice and barley in a field, or sesame and mustard. In the same field, rice is not cultivated for two consecutive years, but sow rice and barley alternately to allow the Earth to breathe.

[5] Sri Ānjaneya is the spiritual son of the Wind God who was incarnated to help the Lord Rāma find his wife, Sītā, who had been kidnapped by the king of the Demons.

The entire history of Yoga can be found in the *Atharvaṇa Veda*. At the beginning of the first section, the origin of *prāṇāyāma* can be found in the rite of *Prāṇa Agni Hotra*.

Prāṇa is divided into nine parts in the head. The nine doors of *prāṇa* are the two eyes, two ears, two nostrils, the mouth, *śīrṣa*[6] and *brahma randhra*[7]. *Śīrṣa* and *Brahma Randhra* correspond to the upward movement of *prāṇa*, *ūrdhva gati*, while the other doors signify downward movement, *adho gati*. When we evoke for *prāṇa* to escape through the top, we pray for it to follow the Higher Path that passes through the fontanel and *brahma randhra*.

Prāṇa's cloth

Before eating, we must first give food to the five *prāṇa*s. We must nourish the *prāṇa*s before feeding the body. At death, the last nourishment is water, *Parjanya*. *Parjanya* is *prāṇa*'s cloth. In Indian medicine, Āyurveda, medication must always be taken with water even if a different 'vehicle'[8] is indicated. *Prāṇa* can only be nourished with water. If *prāṇa* is not nourished, an illness can never be healed.

Thus, in death, we offer water to the nine doors because they are the nine paths of *prāṇa*.

The two buffalo and the plough

Prāṇa and *apāna* are like two buffalos yoked (Yoga) to a plough. To be able to pull the plough (the body), the two buffalo must move in the same direction. Death occurs if they separate. *Prāṇa* is invoked in order for *prāṇa* and *apāna* to always go in the same direction. *Prāṇa* and *apāna* are inhalation and exhalation.

The separation of *prāṇa* and *apāna* corresponds to the beginning of old age. This translates into loss of sensory and motor activity.

Blessing of new-born babies

Prāṇa governs all creatures, including animals, plants, etc. It governs what was and will be born (in the past, present and future). *Prāṇa* is present in any invocation recited at the birth of a creature. The priest's blessing is formulated as follows, 'May Heaven, Earth, *prāṇa* and *apāna* protect you for a hundred winters, guided by *prāṇa* and *apāna.'*

In the *mantra* that follows this, a prayer is addressed to *Agni* (the Fire) to unite with *prāṇa* in order for *prāṇa* to free man from any illness and any sensory or motor disability. In the *Atharvaṇa Veda*, the same prayer is said for animals.

The benefactor of the created world

Through *prāṇa*, the divinities awakened the Sun's power to nourish the created world. The Sun, *Sūrya*, is therefore, the benefactor of the created world. He is somehow the intermediary between *prāṇa* and the created world. Creatures breathe thanks to the Wind, and they see thanks to the Sun. Creatures exist in this world thanks to the soul. Existence also means complete function of the body and strength of the mind.Two wise men of the Veda

Prāṇa resembles two alert and vigilant wise men. They are all-knowing of the Veda. The two wise men are alert even during sleep. They are the two guardians of respiration and life. They are awake day and night, whether we are ill or in good health, awake or asleep. Always present, they constantly watch over us. Death occurs when they are not awake.

The Higher Path

The fourth section of the *Atharvaṇa Veda* indicates that the soul, *ātma*, must reside in the body to provide sensory and motor activity. Similarly, at death, the mind function leaves the body first, then sensory activities escape from the body, followed

[6] The vital point *śīrṣa* is just above the fontanel.
[7] *Brahma randhra* is the ninth door situated above the fontanel.

[8] For example, water, milk and honey represent 'vehicles' favouring the effectiveness of a medicine.

by *prāṇa* before the soul finally leaves its bodily envelop.

In a prayer from this section, man evokes *prāṇa* while standing. He asks for his heart to explode, opening brutally to let *prāṇa* escape upwards, *ūrdhva gati*. Incidentally, the standing position is the most important for invocations in the *Atharvaṇa Veda*.

The above-mentioned *ucchiṡṭa prāṇa* is the principal *prāṇa* in the Veda. The designation of *prāṇa* as *ucchiṡṭa* comes from the word *ut* meaning erect. It is called *ucchiṡṭa* because it was born above, without anything higher. It forms the link between the Creator and created beings. The *ūrdhva gati* movement of *prāṇa* is also *ut*. The word *ud* meaning to erect oneself towards the sky also comes from the word *ut*. Any movement towards the Creator is *ut*. This noun recurrently appears in *Bṛhadāraṇyaka Upaniṣad*. *Ut* is also *śīrṣa*, meaning superior to all.

It is worth noting that the Sanskrit word for water is *udaka*. The etymological root of the word *udaka* is *ut*. In fact, water helps us to rise. Water is offered to the superior beings, the Gods, in the rites. In rites addressed to the ancestors, water along with sesame, rice and barley are offered.

The prayer for *prāṇa* to escape upwards is recited daily. *Prāṇa* breathing through *śīrṣa* is the last breath of existence. That breath is also *ut*. This *ut* is the most important movement, the greatest impetus of our existence. Going towards the Creator is considered as the greatest movement. This respiration is called *rohita* because it is the purest movement. Hita means pleasant. *Rohita* is the purest, whitest and the most agreeable. The last exhalation of our existence becomes the inhalation of the Creator. By opening our heart, the forced movement of *prāṇa* leads our soul through *śīrṣa* to the Creator.

The divisions of *Prāṇa*

In one mantra of the *Atharvaṇa Veda*, *Prajāpati* independently supports the soul of all created beings through breathing. *Prajāpati* moves freely, protecting the souls of all creatures. The expression *brahmacārin* means 'one who moves freely in the soul of any being.' Therefore, *Prajāpati* is also called Brahmacārin. As Brahmacārin, it produces inhalation (*prāṇa*), exhalation (*apāna*), transversal breathing (*vyāna*), *samāna*, *udāna*, speech (*vāk*), the mind (*manas*), the heart (*hṛdaya*) and wisdom in creatures. It also provides sight, hearing, glory, food, sperm, blood and the womb (*garbha*).

According to the *Veda*, *prāṇa* is divided into seven and these seven *prāṇa*s are situated in the head. *Prāṇa* is often compared to seven fires. It is also said that in order to gain knowledge of the Creator, the seven *prāṇa*s must be managed or the seven fires must be offered to Him. The verb 'to offer' is interpreted as bringing (in the sense of Yoga) the seven fires, or rather the seven flames, towards the Creator. In reality, the seven *prāṇa*s are the five sense perceptions, the mind (*manas*) and the intellect (*buddhi*). The seven *prāṇa*s are used as twigs in a fire to produce the flame that brings us towards the Creator. The seven fires are considered as seven worlds to which man is attached. Man must defeat these seven worlds to transcend them in order to know the Creator. The rituals, the stages which enable man to go beyond the seven worlds have long been called *agni hotra*. As these seven worlds are the *prāṇas*, these rites or contemplations are called *Prāṇa Agni Hotra*.

Unifying *Prāṇa*

Man only commits sin through the five sense perceptions, the mind or the intellect. *Ananta*, the snake with seven heads in Indian mythology, corresponds to this concept of seven sins. The Sanskrit word for sin is *pāpa*. It does not have any religious connotation. *Pāpa* simply means 'that which takes away from the Creator.' The only way man can put an end to sin is by preventing the seven *prāṇas* from reaching their respective targets. In order to break the relationship between the seven *prāṇa*s and the world, and to bring *prāṇa* towards the Creator, the Veda recommends inhaling through the left nostril[9] and then exhaling through the right nostril. The following inhalation must be done through the right nostril and the last exhalation through the left nostril.

The objective of inhaling through the left nostril is to take the *prāṇas* away from their target, meaning the perceptible world. Exhalation through the right nostril aims to unify the seven *prāṇa*s to lead them towards the Creator. The unified *prāṇa* can then

[9] Let us not forget that we are seated facing east.

direct itself towards the place of meditation, which in Indian thinking is always the heart, *hṛdaya*, by inhaling through the right nostril. Exhaling through the left nostril allows the place of meditation to unite with the Creator[10].

The *Veda* recommends repeating this cycle three times. In the *Veda*, three times represent the past, present and future; in other words, the known, the living and the unknown. The known corresponds to ancestors, the living to our present life, and the unknown to our descendants.

Also, according to the Veda, every human being has three *aṁśas*. The word *aṁśa* means 'residue.' The three residues of a human being are *pitṛ aṁśa, ṛśi aṁśa* and *deva aṁśa*. *Pitṛ* are the ancestors, *ṛśi* the Sages and *deva* the deities. In view of these three 'residues,' we often repeat the same action three times. For example, three convolutions take place in the temple, the same *mantra* is repeated three times, and the Earth is offered three pinches of food before eating. Salutations traditionally occurred in threes and when a Master blessed a disciple, he touched his head three times.

The time-honoured formula for any evocation, *Om, Śānti*, is always repeated three times. *Śānti* means peace. This formula is recited three times to obtain peace. Later, in the times of the *darśanas*, singing *Om Śānti* three times meant eliminating the three kinds of sufferings affecting creatures, called *duḥkhatraya*. These three sufferings include, suffering coming from the celestial, suffering coming from others and our surroundings and suffering coming from oneself[11]. Doing three cycles of this alternated breathing allows for the elimination of the three *Duḥkhas*. Irrespective of the ritual, the number three can always be found. To pay homage to his Master, a disciple does three convolutions presenting his right shoulder.

The breathing recommended by the Veda repeated three times, allows man to bring together his sensory activities, directing them towards an object of meditation of his choice. In the Veda, it was of course the Creator.

All ritual acts always started with these three breathing cycles and to make them even more efficient, more 'fertile', the Veda recommends the repetition of *Gāyatrī*, a *mantra* of twenty-four *pādas*[12], during these three breathings.

Later, this ritual was called *Nāḍī Śodhana*. It is the name given in Yoga to the *prāṇāyāma* that applies the technique of breathing alternately through each nostril.

In the section of the *Atharvaṇa Veda* that interests us, this is the first *prāṇāyāma* described in the *Vedas*. All other *prāṇāyāmas* come after this one.

In a daily ritual, this breathing cycle is executed at least four times, making a total of twelve cycles. Adding the three daily rituals, we obtain a total of three times twelve cycles that correspond to the minimum duration of a *prāṇāyāma* in Yoga. In fact, Yoga recommends 36 *prāṇāyāma*-cycles per day.

These respirations are rituals called *Prāṇa Agni Hotra*. Later, they became known as *prāṇāyāma*.

[10] In the Veda that breathing is named *prāṇāyāma*. Later on it will be called *Nāḍī Śodhana*.

[11] Respectively, *adhi daivika, adhi bhautika* and *adhi ātmika*.

[12] The word *pāda* (foot) indicates a rhythmic unit in a *mantra*.

4

The 'New' Prāṇāyāmas

Body purifiers

The practice of these breathing cycles has remained unchanged over the past 2500 years. Other *prāṇāyāmas* described in Yoga texts, for example, *Ujjāyi* or *Śītalī,* appeared much later. These *prāṇāyāmas* serve as 'body purifiers' to restore a certain physical and physiological balance.

As the Veda evolved, a long period of consistency was observed in the practice of *prāṇāyāma*. Then, either because man did not apply all the disciplines, or because he lost his faculty of mental attention, other types of *prāṇāyāmas* were introduced to restore the minimal physical condition necessary for contemplation or the fulfilment of rituals. The very large range of *prāṇāyāmas*, including *Ujjāyi Anuloma, Ujjāyi Viloma, Ujjāyi Pratiloma, Śītalī, etc.*[1], is to respond to man's need to re-establish conditions lending to contemplation.

The emergence of these *prāṇāyāmas* can be dated back to the time of the first invasions. Man begins to lose his innate faculties, as soon as he loses his environmental basis. The first invasion of a different culture was that of Alexander. The arrival of the Aryans on the Indian peninsula long before Alexander was not considered an invasion. It seems that the Aryans pursued the same quest for the divine as the Dravidians, India's first inhabitants.

The oldest *prāṇāyāma* to appear at that time was *Ujjāyi Viloma,* as man was first affected by mental distraction. *Ujjāyi Viloma* enabled him to re-establish his peaceful state of mind and reduce mental distraction.

Man of this era was attracted by sensory objects. Once man was trapped by sensory distraction, he became emotionally distracted. *Ujjāyi Pratiloma* was introduced after *Ujjāyi Viloma.* This *prāṇāyāma* is concerned with emotional activity. Lessening or removing of emotional distraction is one of the main virtues of *Ujjāyi Pratiloma.*

The loss of all notions of discipline was the consequence of sensory and emotional distraction. Man started to neglect the discipline of his body. Lack of physical discipline was the origin of a third *prāṇāyāma*, *Ujjāyi Anuloma.*

From sensory distraction to the loss of all bodily discipline, a 'certain poison' had affected man. Poisoned by sensory, emotional and physical

[1] The technique of these *Prāṇāyāmas* is described in Chapter 15.

attractions, he seemed to have lost any hope of salvation. The poisoning made him 'hot.' The mind is considered to be 'hot' when it is overcome by emotions such as passion, anger[2], etc. The *Śītalī Prāṇāyāma* was introduced some five hundred years ago to neutralise this mental poison. Derivations of *Śītalī* were elaborated on more recently.

Given the seriousness of this poisoning, it was necessary to find a faster means to detoxify man. This is the purpose of *Kapāla Bhāti*[3], a fast-paced *prāṇāyāma,* which often comes immediately before other *prāṇāyāmas*.

Man's nervous system suffers the direct effects of poisoning. A second fast paced *prāṇāyāma, Bastri* (the 'goldsmith's blower'), was introduced to calm the hyperactivity of nervous impulses. Symbolically, this breathing does not cause the flames to rise. It is supposed to extinguish the fire fuelled by the different stages of man's decadence.

This is the chronological order in which these different *prāṇāyāmas* appeared. The Masters who introduced them did not leave their names to posterity. We will never know the identities of the Great Masters who adapted *prāṇāyāmas* to the needs of their contemporaries.

However, there is one exception. According to Indian tradition, God instructed the *prāṇāyāma* called *Nāḍī Śodhana*.

Ujjāyi

Ujjāyi[4] breathing is specific to Hatha Yoga. This technique of breathing is not found in the Veda. All *prāṇāyāmas* recommended by the Veda belong to the family of *Nāḍī Śodhana* and therefore, do not use *Ujjāyi*. However, the notion of *Ojas* is often found in the Veda, and this is intimately linked to *Ujjāyi.*

Ujjāyi is present in a lion's breathing. The lion refers to all that is spiritual. The lion, swan or royal eagle is frequently mentioned in reference to spirituality.

Mudra

Traditionally, rigorous hand gestures accompanied each *mantra* during recitations of the Vedas. That rule obviously did not apply when reciting *mantras* during rituals, as the ritual itself occupied the hands. But in the traditional technique of reciting the Vedas, the hands played a significant role, consisting of a gesture rather than a movement. The fingers of each hand were placed in a precise way. The exact position of the hands for each *mantra* was specified to unite body and mind. The harmony of gesture, voice and speech captured the mind during the evocation. Each *mantra* evoked one deity. For example, the forefinger was extended and the middle and ring fingers bent or the tip of the thumb touched the root of the middle finger. The thumb on the forefinger always accompanied a quick recitation. Not only did the gesture enable knowledge of the evoked divinity, but it also guided the manner in which the *mantra* was recited.

Hand gestures had great importance in the Veda because of the correlation between the five fingers and the five *prāṇas*. Each finger corresponds to one of the *prāṇas*. Therefore, the position of the fingers is always defined in relation to the five *prāṇas*. Furthermore, looking at the inside of the hand, the middle and ring fingers represent God, the thumb and forefinger represent the ancestors, the space between the little finger and wrist is the place of the *ṛśis*, while the base of the hand corresponds to *Prajāpati*, the Creator.

In a clockwise direction the hand represents, *Prajāpati* (the Creator), the *ṛśis* (the Vedic Seers), *deva* (God) and *pitṛ* (the ancestors). The extremities of the five fingers correspond to the five *prāṇas*.

The synchronization between the *mantras* and the corresponding hand gesture is called *mudra.* As long as the position of the hands remains in harmony with the *mantra*, the mind is embraced by the evocation. Therefore, *mudra* belongs to the recitation of the *mantras* in the same way as speed (tempo) or breathing (*prāṇa*)[5].

The secret of the *mantra* lies in the *mudra.* The concept of *mudra,* using the body to seize the mind, was developed from this. By giving the body a specific position, the mind is prevented from

[2] Sensual desire (*kāma*), anger (*krodha*), greed (*lobha*), mental confusion (*moha*), passion (*mada*) and jealousy (*mātsarya*).

[3] Also known as *Bhastrikā*.

[4] *Ujjāyi* breathing is described in Chapter 6.

[5] This technique has been used for thousands of years but is now disappearing in the recitation of the Vedas. During the processions, however, reciting mantras while walking continues to be generally accompanied by *Mudras*.

distraction and the sense perceptions keep the mind from being attracted to objects of experience. Certain gestures used in prayer, like joining the palms of the hands (*anjāli*), are found in most religions. Meditation gestures (*dhyāna*) are used to prevent mental distraction.

Use of *Mudras* outside the Veda

While recitation of the Veda was reserved solely for the initiated, *hand gestures* independent of the Veda were accessible to all. *Hand gestures* alone were sufficient to obtain and maintain concentration to the point where *Padma Āsana*[6],

Fig. 1 Ananta Āsana
(Satya)

the lotus posture, became a *mudra* even outside Yoga. The posture, which consists of placing the right foot on the left thigh and the left foot on the right thigh, immediately leads to a state of concentration. However, *Padma Āsana* is not used in reciting the Veda.

Instead, a posture called *Ananta Āsana* is advised, with the right foot placed on the left thigh and the left foot resting under the right thigh.

Indeed, the right thigh is used for several reasons. A book of *mantras* should not be touched by the feet. This is why the right foot is placed on the left thigh and *Padma Āsana* is not used. Musicians also adopt this position to sing. They put the right hand on the right thigh to count the timing (*tāla*).

Mudras in Yoga

The principle of *mudras* is to use the body to obtain the same thing that was given by the Veda. In order to make this power of mind available to everybody, Yoga added *mudra*s to its practices. Indeed, Yoga offers both *mudra*s and Āsanas. The great Masters of Yoga in the classical period, Yājñyavalkya and Svātmārāma, dedicated a part of their teaching to *mudra*s. These Masters introduced certain postures like *Mahā Mudra*, meaning 'the great *mudra*', which does not feature in the chapter dedicated to Āsanas. Holding these postures gradually leads to mental control[7]. *Mahā Mudra* enables the mind to concentrate on a *dhāraṇa* or vital point.

The generalisation of *Ujjāyi* breathing in the practice of Yoga has appeared rather recently. The classical treaties, with the exception of *Haṭha Yoga Pradīpika,* say very little about *Ujjāyi* breathing. Yet, *mudras* have always been executed with *Ujjāyi* breathing. The *mudras* involved not only sustained concentration, but also a specific breathing rhythm with the exhalation often longer than the inhalation. By imposing specific breathing, which is always slower than normal in *mudras,* as well as sustained concentration, the individual created a sort of barrier against emotions affecting him in daily life. These emotions are called *kleśas* in Yoga.

For the same reason, in order for the person reciting the Veda to be liberated from all human emotions, a great deal of discipline was required. *Mudras* used by a singer had the identical purpose of purifying the mind. Therefore, a *mudra* is defined by a physical and mental position, preventing the *kleśas* from developing. The definition given to *mudras* in Yoga comes from the

[6] Technique of *Padma Āsana* and *Ananta Āsana* is described in Chapter 13.

[7] A few *Mudras* are described in Chapter 14.

previous definition: a *mudra* enables the deactivation of emotions affecting us.

In the same way as there are rules for the recitation of the Veda. Yoga defines several parameters for the practice of *mudras*:

- A precise *āsana*,
- A defined number of breaths, 6, 8, 12 or 16 according to the *mudra*,
- Long breaths, with exhalation twice as long as inhalation,
- A concentration,
- *Kumbhaka*, retention which traditionally comes after exhalation.

The only concentration in the original *mudras* was *bhrūmadhya*, the vital point situated between the two eyebrows. The eyes were directed towards the *mudra*. Later, other points were introduced, such as *mūla* (the perineum), *nābhi* (the navel), *anāhatā* (the centre of the heart), *hṛdaya* (the heart) and *kaṇṭha* (the throat). However, *bhrūmadhya*, the point situated between the eyebrows, was the only concentration indicated at the beginning. *Bhrūmadhya* is always attributed to the God Shiva. Other concentrations were introduced to allow other religious convictions to benefit from the practice of *mudras*.

As already mentioned, the practice of *mudra* requires the use of *ujjāyi*[8] breathing, which the texts of *Haṭha Yoga* name as *Ujjāyi Kumbhaka*.

The practice of *mudra* can also be independent of the practice of *āsanas*. At the beginning of *Hatha Yoga,* around five centuries ago, the *mudras* were so valued that a prayer (*nyāsa*) always preceded them. The purpose of that prayer was to purify the body, not the mind because the mind would be purified by the *mudra* itself. The same rigours did not apply to the practice of *āsanas*. In the beginning of *Haṭha Yoga*, God was always evoked when practicing a *mudra*. According to Svātmārāma, at the origin of *Haṭha Yoga*, a God was evoked according to the *mudras* practised. Each *mudra* had a different corresponding God. Shiva was much evoked at beginning of *Haṭha Yoga*.

Āsana

In the past, man constantly preserved harmony with the values of *puruṣārtha*[9]. He could maintain a perfect balance between the four foundations of life, *dharma*, *artha*, *kāma* and *mokṣa*, according to his social and family status. This equilibrium was far from being fixed for everybody. For example, a Brahmin by vocation granted more importance to *dharma* and had much less interest in *artha*. On the other hand, a Vaiśya granted more importance to *artha*. The merchant's activity, which opposes the principle of *dharma*, was tolerated for storekeepers without threatening the harmony of *puruṣārtha.*

As time went on, man started to calculate the benefit his actions could bring him. The quest for material gain became more and more important, even in rituals. In Vedic times, man carried out a ritual for the sake of the ritual. Then, man asked himself what it would bring him, whether it was liberation for a Brahmin or an increase in material gain for a Vaiśya. Man ended up searching for material advantages in everything he did. That attraction to these advantages brought him to a state of impurity on both physical and mental levels. Man's permanent search for personal benefit is considered a loss of purity. In fact, four types of errors are encountered at bodily, sensory, mental and spiritual levels. The loss of *ātma śuddhi* explicitly means 'loss of the soul's purity.' Man's way of thinking changed with these impurities. The permanent quest for benefit led him to greed and an increased desire to constantly own more. He lost his sincerity. Lying developed as he looked for personal gains at any cost.

Bodily impurity, a direct consequence of this, translates into a deficient lifestyle. This includes lack of dietary discipline, absence of body hygiene, erratic behaviour, etc.

Now, man only uses his sense perceptions in order to acquire something. This sensory impurity is considered as *adharma.*

Mental impurity is characterized by a change in man's thoughts. He is only interested in the profit he can take from any situation. He looks to benefit himself and not others. From there, he develops a sense of the 'self.' This sense of 'self' is considered an impurity of the soul, and it comes

[8] The technique of the *ujjāyi* breathing is explained in Chapter 6.

[9] The four *puruśārtas* are the four foundations of the existence previously referred to.

from pride. Pride is the impurity that covers the soul, but the soul itself remains pure.

Yājñyavalkya exposed the principles of *yama* and *niyama* to purify the individual and to restore harmony and the balance of the values of *puruṣārtha*. *Yama* and *niyama* are maxims to be applied towards oneself and the world in order to reclaim a certain purity of *dharma*.

The role of the *āsanas* is to purify the body, because the body is the container of all impurity. The function of *prāṇāyāmas* is to purify the mind, while that of *pratyāhāra*[10], known as *indriya śuddhi,* is to purify the sense perceptions or rather to purify sensory activity.

As society is in a state of flux, man applies the principles of *yama* and *niyama* less and less. He is evermore attracted by physical pleasures, neglecting a healthy lifestyle on physical, sensory, mental and spiritual levels. Increasing passion develops, which drives him to blindness and jealousy. The Sanskrit word *kāma* is used to denote the sensual desire which drags man into a vicious circle of anger, greed, confusion, passion and jealousy. Therefore, passion, *mada*, is synonymous with suffering, *duḥkha*.

In reality, the body is the driving force of either good or evil. At the same time, it is the recipient of pleasure and the pivot of action, but it is not responsible for harmony. The status of the *āsanas* has become particularly important as the body represents the driving force of all actions. It is also easier to adjust the senses through the body rather than the mind. By practising different *āsanas*, man purifies his sense perceptions and his mind. The adequate practice of *āsanas* enables the purification of the body, senses and mind in order to restore the harmony of the four fundamental values. *Āsanas* were traditionally practised with retention, *kumbhaka*, and concentration, *ekāgrata*[11].

The body's action is like a set of gears; it is capable of gearing up its action so much that it finishes by short-circuiting the cerebral impulses.

The influence of the body is so important that it has the potential to govern different activities totally by itself, as though entirely independent of sensory and mental impulses. A wide range of *āsanas* was introduced to reduce this effect.

By imitating human and non-human beings like animals, birds, reptiles and insects, the body modifies certain basic behaviours, thus changing the desires it has developed. Man does not become a dog by doing *Śvāna Āsana*[12], but it enables him to regulate the different values of his existence. By holding a specific position, the body modifies its functions. Similarly, by imitating the meditative posture chosen by the *ṛśis* for their *tapas*, the body adjusts its desire for pleasure. Several *āsanas* carry the names of *ṛśis*. These *āsanas* correspond to the postures adopted by the Masters to devote in their austerities, and the positions invented by the spiritual Masters to restructure the demands of the body.

For example, an individual adopts the position of a bird in order for his body to modify its basic demands. By adopting the position of a Yogi, *Bhāradvāja Āsana* or *Bhagīratha Āsana*, the individual reshapes his sense perceptions. Practising *āsanas* introduced by spiritual Masters allows him to reduce his bodily and mental demands.

In the *Rāmāyaṇa* epic, the great King Viśvāmitra held immense power. He wished to buy the *ṛśi* Vasiṣṭha's cow which was capable of feeding his whole army. When the *ṛśi* refused, he decided to take the cow by force. He deployed his troops, but they were unable to defeat the *ṛśi* who only had his ascetic's stick to defend him. Vasiṣṭha's serenity was superior to Viśvāmitra's anger, greed and the power of his army. The stick, called *daṇḍa* in Sanskrit, represents the ascetic's equanimity. The stick stands for emotional steadiness The Sage is so even-tempered that he succeeds in defeating the King and his army.

Viśvāmitra withdrew and abandoned his reign to lead the life of an ascetic. Vālmīki, the author of the *Rāmāyaṇa*, tells us that it took thousands of years for Viśvāmitra to overcome his anger. This is why we have *Viśvāmitra Āsana* in Yoga. The *Vasiṣṭha Āsana* position carries the name of the great *ṛśi* honoured by Vālmīki. *Daṇḍa Āsana*, the position of the stick, is described in Chapter13 of this book. It is easy to guess that one of the fruits yielded by this *āsana* is stability.

In the list of *āsanas* shown in Chapter 13, there are all types of animals, insects and *ṛśis*.

[10] Withdrawal of the senses.

[11] My father, in his books, *Yoga Makaranda* and *Yoga Āsanagalu*, published in Kannada language by the University of Mysore, gives detailed guidance on holding of breath and concentrations for each *asana* presented in the books.

[12] In the same way, a grandfather does not become a child by getting down on his hands and knees beside his grandchild. He does, however, get closer to the spirit of the child.

My father is one of the few Masters who used this large repertoire of *āsanas* in his teaching. He widely contributed to the teaching and disclosure of these *āsanas*. As a Master of *Āyurveda*, Indian medicine, he also explained the *fruit*[13] of each *āsana,* using terminology specific to the pathology of *Āyurveda*. In Chapter 13 of this book, readers will get an insight of some of the *āsanas* along with their corresponding fruits.

Several types of body dysfunction, which are considered impurities in Yoga, appeared along with passion. The practice of *āsanas* enables the reduction of passion and its corresponding dysfunctions. However, one has to be particularly vigilant to avoid producing the opposite effect. For example, lust is often accompanied by typical body dysfunctions. The recommended *āsanas* help the recovery of bodily functions provided they do not seek physical sensation during execution. In order to prevent a practice consisting solely of *āsanas* from deviating from its objectives by awakening passions, a Yoga session always commences and concludes with a *prāṇāyāma*. By practising *āsanas* alone and given the risk of being attracted by bodily sensations, an individual could be feeding impurities. The practice of Yoga, like any Vedic ritual, starts and ends with *prāṇāyāma*[14].

Dhyāna

All the Vedas begin with an evocation. There is always an evocation before reciting *mantras* or performing a Vedic ritual. The *Veda* is considered a Revelation, and its ultimate aim is to know He who revealed it. Therefore, the Author of the Veda must be evoked at the beginning of any study or recitation. Man carries out an evocation during which his mind should be wholly with God. This evocation is the preamble to the *Veda* and is known as *dhyāna*.

Each of the four Vedas has a specific invocation. Therefore, there are four corresponding invocations. Each Veda begins with an oration. The Creator, *Īśa* and *Viṣṇu* are evoked. *Īśa* means happiness and when Viṣṇu is evoked in prayer, reference is being made to the Creator rather than the mythological God. The *dhyāna* at the beginning of each Veda is identical even if the invocation differs.

Dhyāna and *mantra* are specific to the Veda. They represent two aspects of the Veda: evocation and reciting aloud.

Reciting aloud follows the oration. The person reciting the Veda cannot be classified as a reciter or reader because the terms overlook the religious aspect of the reading. 'Cantor' is a preferred designation. The word refers not only to a precise melodic and rhythmic manner, systematically accompanying the reciting of the Veda, but it also refers to a mental posture because the cantor is entirely in the uninterrupted evocation. During this time, the cantor withdraws, implying that he has forgotten the world. He is 'selfless.'

Depending on the Veda, the phase of oration preceding the recitation can last for two to two and half minutes.

As the invocation is carried out aloud, the cantor invites other participants to meditate. He guides them to *dhyāna*.

Irrespective of the Veda being studied, it is invariably recited, as it is known by heart. The first step of the recitation is always *dhyāna*, meditation. In the same way, the recitation ends with an identical meditation. A ritual cannot be left until *dhyāna* is complete. Our life is defined by two cupolas. These are the *dhyānas* at the beginning of the act and the *dhyāna* at the end of the act. This is the reason why the word Veda also means meditation. *Dhyāna* is a more recent term referring to the evocation without which no Vedic rite can take place.

A cantor can recite the Veda alone, but most often he is surrounded by family members, his wife and his children. Other priests also accompany the cantor.

All the participants passively follow *dhyāna*. They remain silent, even if they are busy with other activities. This passive meditation is comparable to devotional music. An audience is transported by the devotion even if it is not singing. This situation represents the origin of the word *Sāma Veda*. Everybody around the cantor takes part in the meditation passively.

There are two types of meditation:

1) Active meditation, executed by the person doing the evocation and reciting the *mantras*.

[13] The word used by my father to indicate the effects of *āsanas* on health is '*phala'* which literally means 'fruit'.

[14] A Vedic ritual also includes *prāṇāyāmas* at regular intervals.

2) Passive meditation, done by those who receive or listen to the invocation.

Originally in the Veda, *dhyāna* was carried out by reciting the *mantras* aloud[15].

Therefore, people who had not been initiated in the Veda could benefit from a passive learning of it. In order for the minds of non-initiates to become capable of meditating, even if they were not used to reciting the Veda, there are two types of *dhyāna* in the Veda:

1) *Dhyāna* with the support of *mantra*.

2) *Dhyāna* without the support of *mantra*.

Two conditions have to be fulfilled for the *dhyāna* of a non-initiate:

1) Eyes shut.

2) Sitting or standing facing east[16].

Later, keeping the eyes shut became the most important condition.

There is a section in the Veda, which consists of an invocation of the Sun. It is *Taittirīya Āraṇyaka* and is part of the *Yajur Veda*. The set of *mantras* making up the *Taittirīya Āraṇyaka* is an invocation to the Sun, lasting about an hour and a half. These *mantras* are not eulogies of the Sun God, but are considered as the ultimate meditation. The text of *Taittirīya Āraṇyaka* itself is even considered as a support to the contemplation of the Sun. In past times, the *Taittirīya Āraṇyaka* had to be recited every Sunday, Sunday being the day of the Sun. The text was recited once a week for an hour and a half while facing east. It is the first *dhyāna* on *Aruṇa*, the rising Sun, to be found in the Veda.

The second *dhyāna* in the Veda is a meditation on *Agni*, Fire, as all Vedic rituals are carried out with *agni*.

This *dhyāna* is slightly more complex as it is entirely dependent on a Vedic ritual. The second great divinity serving the meditation is *Agni*, the ritual Fire, the sacred Fire. It is useful to recall here that *dhyāna* refers to meditation on an object rather than a subject. For example, the ritual Fire is entirely captured by the mind without any intellectual deliberation or thinking.

There are two types of *agni* in a house:

- The household Fire.

- The ritual Fire. This is not the same *agni* even if lit with the household fire.

In the morning, the housewife lights the kitchen Fire and evokes the Fire that she has just lit, in the same way as the master of the household evokes the Fire when lighting the ritual Fire.

Lamps lit in a house always represent *agni*. Long after Vedic times, lamps were considered as the goddess Lakṣmī.

The flame that lights the house, and the flame lit for prayer have become a divinity in themselves and this is a divine object of meditation. It is an aid for meditation.

The Fire or lamp is the second most important object of meditation after the Sun. In the way *agni* corresponds to an initiate's evocation, the lamp represents the non-initiate's meditative object. That does not prevent non-initiates from invoking Fire in their meditation, just as an initiate might meditate on a lamp. Fire and the lamp both have identical values as objects of meditation.

The third object of meditation in the Veda is *Sūrya* and *Candra*, the Sun and the Moon. When alluding to these objects of meditation, we refer to the rising Sun and the full Moon.

It is necessary to differentiate between initiates and non-initiates of the Veda with regards to these *Dhyānas*. However, in *Taittirīya Āraṇyaka*, the Sun is so important that the evocation of the morning Sun is also recommended for non-initiates, irrespective of their family or social status.

All Indians who pray for a moment while lighting their lamps carry out this rite, *Sūrya Upasthāna*. *Sūrya* is the name given to the Sun and '*upastha*' means 'standing upright.' Standing up is a sign of respect. Prayer can take place in any position, but when the first ray of Sunshine appears, the birds start to sing and man must stand up to greet the Sun. It is specified in several *Upaniṣads* that as soon as the Sun rises; birds greet it with their song, and their heads turned up towards the light watching the dawn.

Sūrya Upasthāna later became known as *Sūrya Namaskāra*, simply meaning the 'act of saluting the Sun.' The act of saluting the Sun should not be confused with the set of exercises of the same

[15] In the beginning, the Veda was always recited aloud. A different way of reciting the Veda appeared around the time of the invasions of India by non-Hindu forces. The invasion of the country led cantors to whisper the Veda. In that hostile environment, cantors were obliged to hide and to recite their *mantras* in a quiet voice. But at the beginning, *dhyāna* was always accompanied by a *mantra* recited out loud.

[16] The east facing position became secondary from the time of the invasions. For the invaders, the sight of a native facing east with his eyes shut seemed like suspicious behaviour. Hinduism succeeded in adapting itself to history without losing its core values.

name, *Sūrya Namaskāra*, even if that set of exercises translates as 'salutations to Sun.'

In Vedic times, the standing position adopted for *Sūrya Upasthāna* consisted of placing the sole of the right foot against the upper left thigh, hands joined together above the head, arms slightly bent. This position called *upasthāna* was later renamed *Ardha Candra Āsana*[17] in Yoga, and an alternation of the legs was added.

Sūrya Upasthāna is always done facing east at dawn and west at dusk.

We now come to the third object of meditation, composed of the Sun and the Moon.

In the Veda, there are situations when different deities are evoked according to the rituals. For example, peasants evoke the Clouds or Thunder, *Indra*, while fishermen evoke *Varuṇa*, Water.

A warrior will evoke the Wind, as *Vāyu*[18]. In Vedic times, traders evoked *Hiraṇyagarbha*, the golden form of the Creator.

All these individuals, irrespective of profession, evoke a jug filled with water or cereal. Often that jug is replaced with a coconut. The coconut, with its fibres, has the same shape as the jug. The jug or coconut represents the cosmos, the created world and the Creator. The word *purṇa* comes from here.

This part of meditation specific to the Veda remained unchanged for a very long period, until the times of the *Purāṇas* and the *Itihāsas*.

In the time of the *Purāṇas*, the different manifestations of Gods and Goddesses became supports of *dhyāna*. Indeed, they became *dhyāna* itself.

At the time of the *Purāṇas,* the meditations of *dhyāna* were accompanied by a *mantra* that took the form of a prayer. This specific prayer encouraged the evocation of God. It was a special appeal to support meditation on the manifestation of God. These prayers and appeals have been designated by the term *dhyāna śloka*. *Dhyāna mantra* is therefore, specific to the Veda and *dhyāna śloka* is specific to the evocation of God.

Therefore, there is an evocation and a *mantra* or prayer, according to the evocation. *Dhyāna*, before and after the prayer or *mantra* are comparable to two hemispheres. According to the Veda, *dhyāna* protects our lives. There should be at least two daily moments of *dhyāńa* in our lives. Indeed, it is possible to have more than that. Our day should start and finish with a *dhyāna*.

Three *saṃdhyās*[19] are recommended in the Veda:

- In the morning, or more precisely 'the moment of union between night and day.'
- At midday, 'the moment of union between morning and afternoon.'
- At dusk, 'the time situated between day and night.'

Saṃdhyā vandana signifies the ritual carried out at the moment of these three transitions, and the technical term used in the Veda for the three meditations is *trisaṃdhyā*, to insist upon the importance of *dhyāna* in our lives.

It is because of this *trisaṃdhyā* that meditation is omnipresent in daily life, whatever the evolution of Indian thinking.

Dhyāna has as much importance in the Vedas, *Āraṇyakas*, *Upaniṣads* and *Purāṇas,* as well as in more recent texts on Yoga. An entire chapter of *Hatha Yoga Pradīpika* is dedicated to *dhyāna*.

Note that the word *samādhi* was originally a word used for *dhyāna*. In Yoga, *samādhi* signifies a prolonged *dhyāna*[20]. In the sub-chapter dedicated to *dhyāna,* we see how *ṛśi* Yājñyavalkya introduced *dhāraṇa*, the vital points, as a means for non-initiates to reach *dhyāna*.

Dhāraṇa

The technique of *dhāraṇa* consists of directing the eyes towards a vital point, *marma sthāna*, referenced by an anatomical location. It is important to specify for *dhāraṇa* that **the image of the anatomical reference must not be evoked under any circumstances**. The organ or anatomical place is not evoked, but the eyes are directed towards the vital point.

[17] Technique of *Ardha Candra Āsana* is described in Chapter 13.

[18] In the *Mahā Bhārata,* an effigy of Sri Ānjaneya is surmounted on the chariot of the hero Arjuna who is not considered a monkey, but the incarnation of the Wind God.

[19] The word *saṃdhyās* means the temporal conjuctions.

[20] The noun *samādhi* has several meanings in Sanskrit. A burial is designated by *samādhi,* as well as the relics of a Master considered to have reached enlightenment. *Samādhi* also designates one who hibernates: when one willingly interrupts the biological functions of the body, that interruption is called *samādhi*. In the *Mahā Bhārata,* Bhishma puts himself into *samādhi* before dying. The word *samādhi,* like the word Yoga, can have several meanings.

Dhāraṇa can be performed in *āsanas*, *mudras* or *prāṇāyāmas*. As already mentioned, a *prāṇāyāma* done with *dhāraṇa* is called *Sagarbha Prāṇāyāma*, meaning 'fertile *prāṇāyāma'*. This *Prāṇāyāma* also corresponds to *prāṇāyāmas* accompanied by an evocation of God or a mental recitation of a *mantra*.

By looking at an object attentively, we are carrying out *trāṭaka*. Directing our eyes towards an object with sustained attention is called *trāṭaka*. There are two types of *trāṭaka*:

- *Bahistrāṭaka*: eyes open.
- *Antastrāṭaka*: eyes closed.

By directing our eyes towards a part of God's body, we are carrying out *dhyāna*. God becomes supreme in *dhyāna*. However, looking at the flame in front of God is *trāṭaka*. Evoking God's image corresponds to *dhyāna*, while watching the flame, without evoking it, corresponds to *trāṭaka*. *Trāṭaka* is linked to *ekāgrata*, mental attentiveness. Generally, *trāṭaka* is done before *dhāraṇa*.

The sixteen vital points used in *dhāraṇa* are:

↑ The fontanel, *śīrṣa,*

↑ The middle of the forehead, *mūrdhna,*

↑The point situated in between the eyebrows, *bhrūmadhya,*

↑ The point situated at the extremity of the nose, *nāsāgra,*

↑ The point situated at the back of the palate, *tālu mūla,*

↑ The point at the root of the uvula, *lalāṭa,*

↑ The throat, *kaṇṭha,*

↑ The back of the throat, *kaṇṭha kūpa,*

↑ The middle of the heart, *hṛdaya,*

↑ The navel, *nābhi,*

↑ The centre of the pelvis, *śroṇī,*

↑ The perineum, *mūla,*

↑ The point at top of the thighs, *jangha*

↑ The point at the middle of the knees, *jānu,*

↑ The point at the middle of the ankles, *gulpha,*

↑ The point of the big toes, *pāda aṅguṣṭa,*

Irrespective of the point indicated, *dhāraṇa* is executed without moving the position of the head in an *āsana*, *mudra* or *prāṇāyāma*. Let us specify once more that *dhāraṇa* is practised by directing the eyes towards the vital point and not by imagining that point.

There are two types of *dhāraṇa* in practice:

- *Dhāraṇa* on a single point.
- *Dhāraṇa* on several points.

Depending on the *āsana*, *mudra* or *prāṇāyāma*, it is possible to direct the eyes successively to several vital points during inhalation, but during exhalation, concentration is always maintained on a single point. For example, in *Taṭāka Mudra*, also known as *Tāḍagi Mudra*, the concentration can be directed during inhalation towards the sixteen vital points, from *aṅguṣṭa,* the big toe, to *śīrṣa*, the fontanel. During exhalation, it can be maintained on a single point. In this *mudra,* this point could be *kaṇṭha*, the throat, *nābhi*, the navel, or even *mūla*, the perineum. In *Aśvinī Mudra, dhāraṇa* is found on the points located between *mūla,* the perineum, and *kaṇṭha*, the throat, during inhalation; on *bhrūmadhya*, the vital point located between the eyebrows, during retention after the inhalation; on *nābhi*, the navel, during exhalation; and on *mūla*, the perineum, during retention after exhalation.

In *mudras* practised in sitting positions, concentration is directed towards the vital points located between *mūla* and *śīrṣa*, always in the ascending direction. In *prāṇāyāmas* and *mudras*, concentration can be introduced on a single point between *mūla* and *śīrṣa*.

The vital points located between *mūla,* and *śīrṣa* have a greater spiritual value. According to my father, the points located between the big toe, and the perineum relate to the sensory sphere; the points located between the perineum, and the heart are linked to the emotions; and the points located between the heart, and the fontanel are associated with spirituality. Therefore, according to him, three levels can be distinguished within the sixteen vital points.

In addition to these sixteen vital points, *Ṛśi* Yājñyavalkya mentioned *tāraka*, the horizon point, considered to be one of the vital points of the world. *Tāraka* is one of the points on which *dhāraṇa* can be carried out. Concentration on *tāraka* consists of directing the gaze horizontally in alignment with the eyes, on the most distant point, without evoking any image. Traditionally, *dhāraṇa* on *tāraka* is always practised in the standing position or seated, except if otherwise indicated. For example, in case of illness, *dhāraṇa* on *tāraka* can be done lying on the back. My father recommended this concentration to sick people who were unable to sit.

Tāraka constitutes the central point of the ten cardinal points. These ten cardinal points are the four principal points, east, south, west and north, the four intermediate points, the zenith and the nadir.

Dhāraṇa on *tāraka* is used as a preliminary to *dhyāna*.

By definition, *dhyāna* is a *dhāraṇa* on *tāraka* followed by:

- An evocation of the Creator, or
- An evocation of God, or a representation of God, or
- An evocation of the solar disk.

An oration, a prayer or eulogy emphasizing the qualities of the divine object being evoked, always accompanies *dhyāna*. Therefore, one does not lie down after *dhyāna*. The divine value of the evoked object requires that *dhyāna* conclude with salutation and not rest on the back.

5
In memory of my father

Fig. 2 Utthita Trikoṇa Āsana N° 1

Fig. 3 Utthita Trikoṇa Āsana N° 2

Fig. 4 Utthita Pārśva Utthāna Āsana

Fig. 5 Utthita Pārśva Koṇa Āsana

Fig. 6 Prasārita Pāda Utthāna Āsana

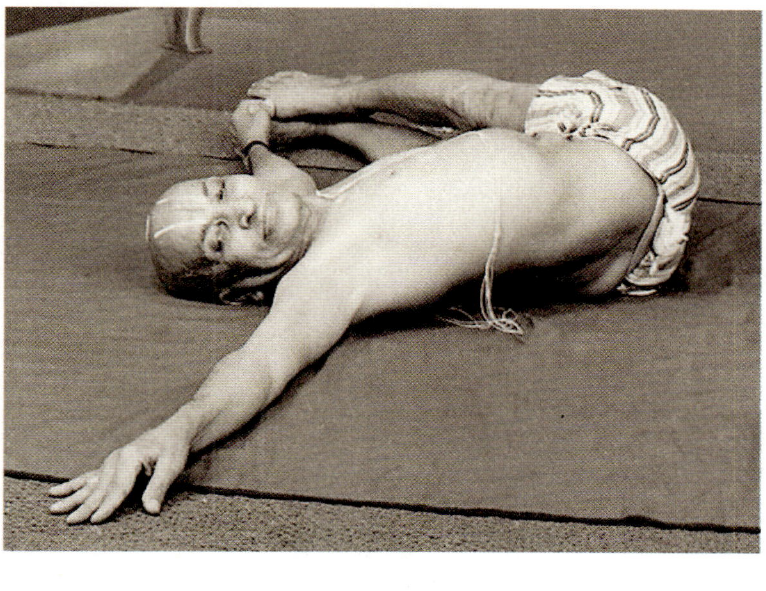

Fig. 7 Jaṭhara Parivṛtti

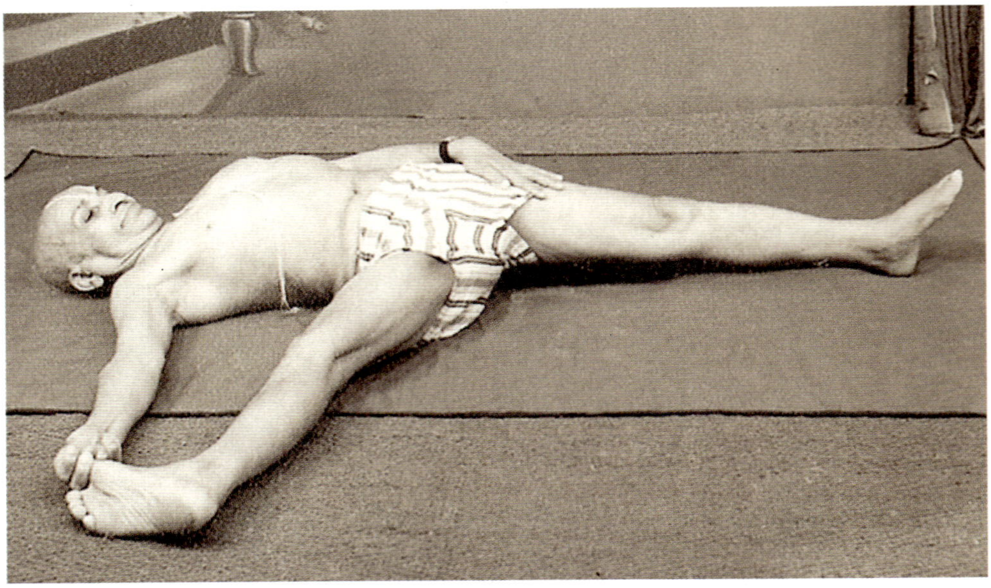

Fig. 8 Supta Pārśva Pāda Anguṣṭa Āsana

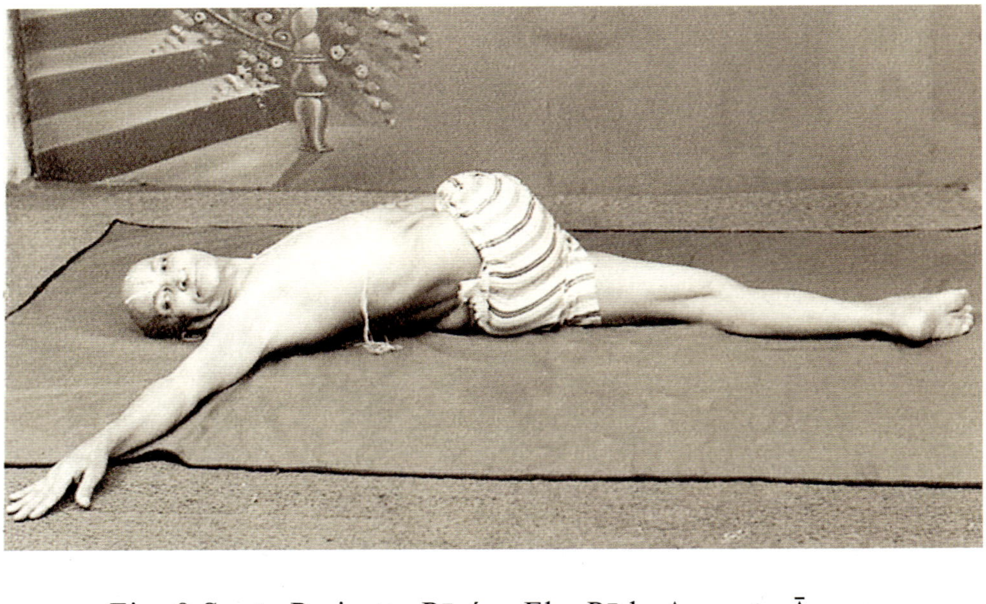

Fig. 9 Supta Parivṛtta Pārśva Eka Pāda Anguṣṭa Āsana

Fig. 10 Ūrdhva Prasuta Pāda Āsana

Fig. 11 Supta Pāda Anguṣṭa Āsana

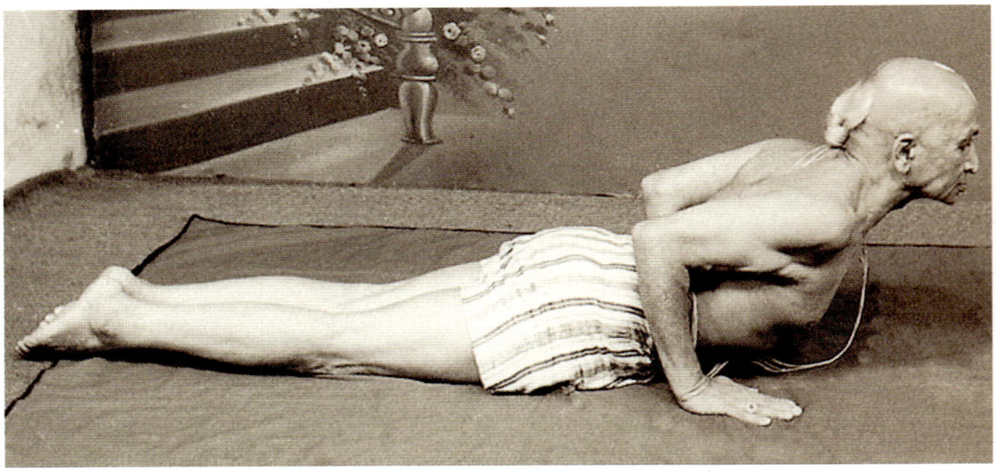

Fig. 12 Bhujaṃga Āsana

Fig. 13 Sarvānga Āsana

Fig. 14 Śīrṣa Āsana

Fig. 15 Pinḍa Āsana

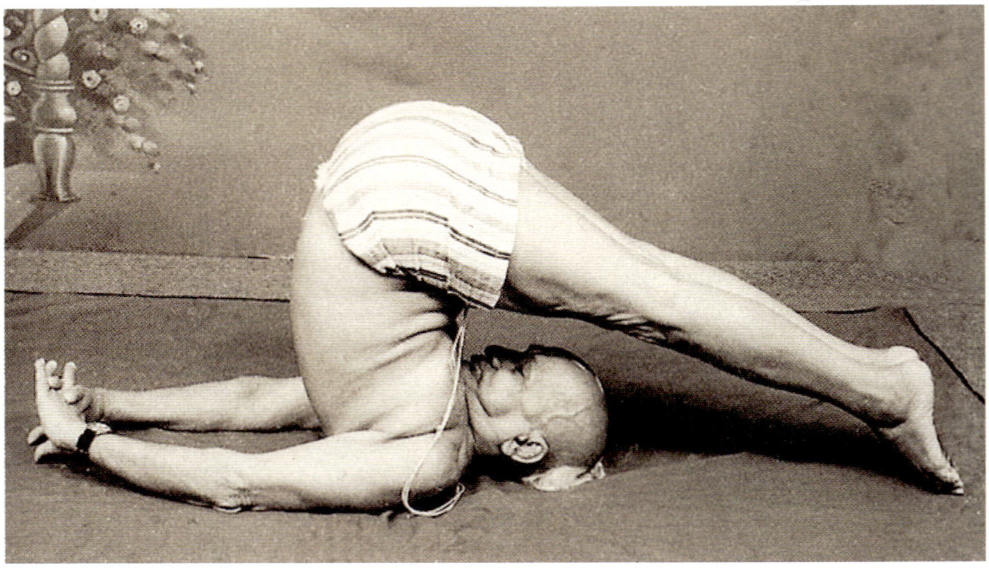

Fig. 16 Hala Āsana

Fig. 17 Simha Āsana

Fig. 18 Daṇḍa Āsana

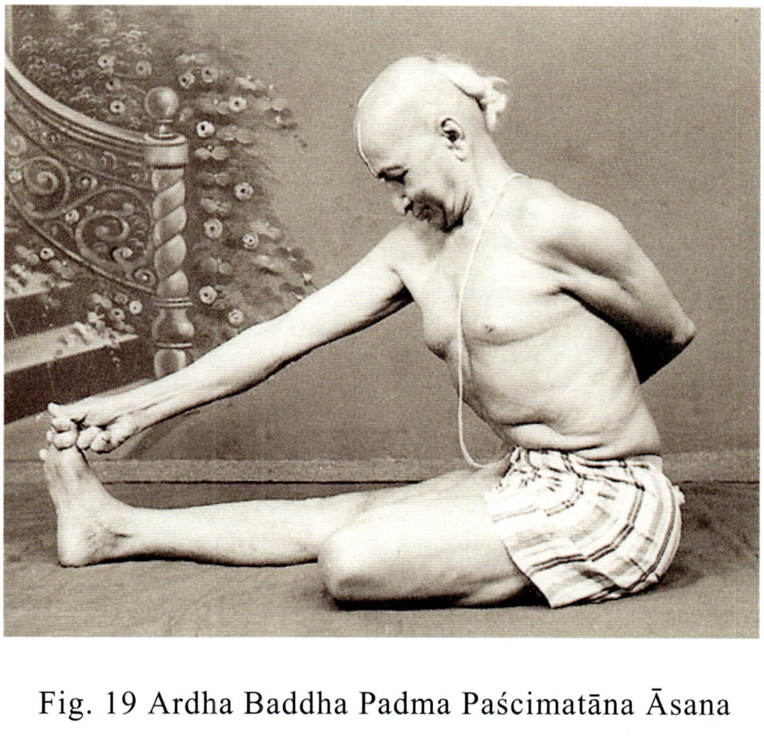

Fig. 19 Ardha Baddha Padma Paścimatāna Āsana

Fig. 20 Ardha Matsyendra Āsana N° 1 (front view)

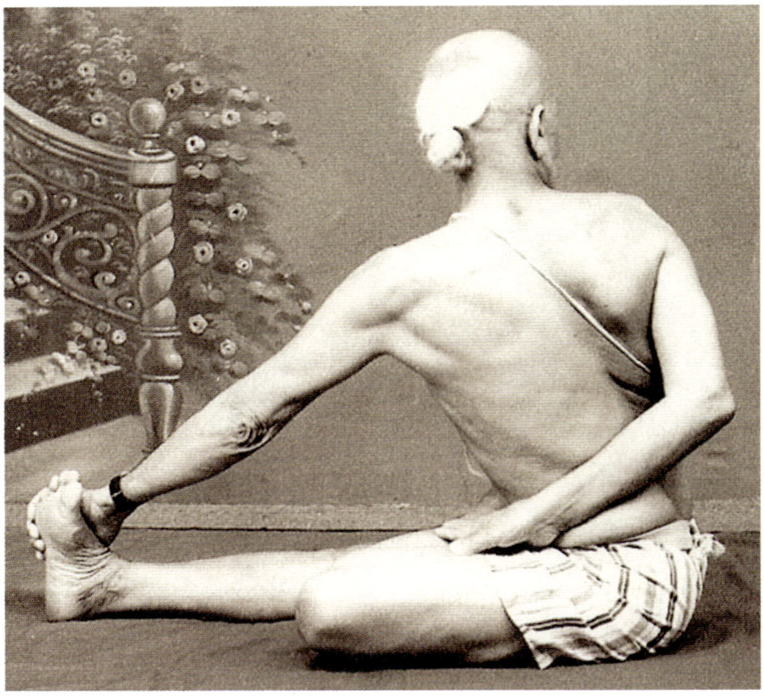

Fig. 21 Ardha Matsyendra Āsana N° 1 (back view)

Fig. 22 Ardha Matsyendra Āsana N° 2
(front view)

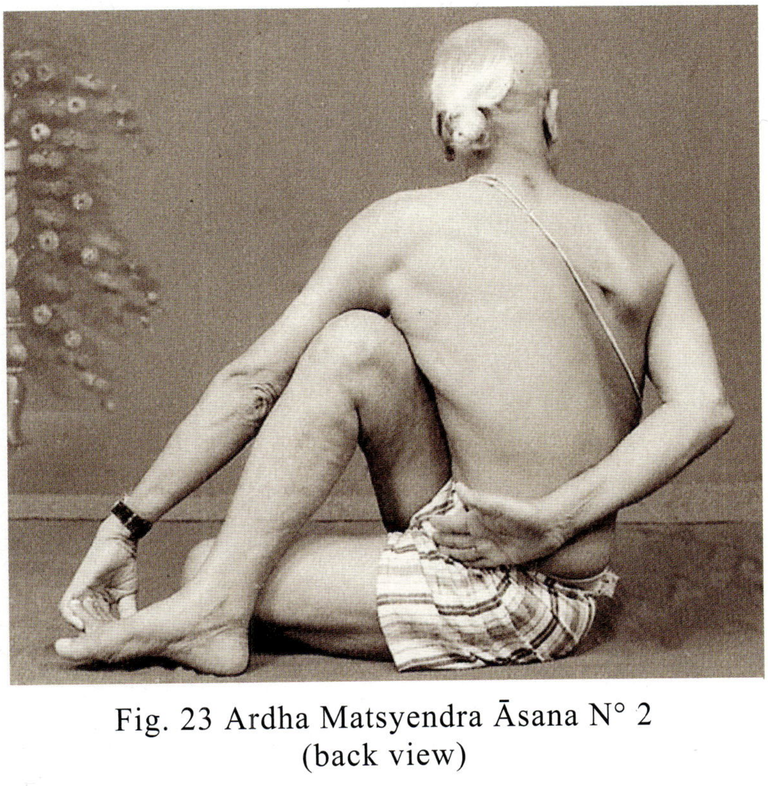

Fig. 23 Ardha Matsyendra Āsana N° 2
(back view)

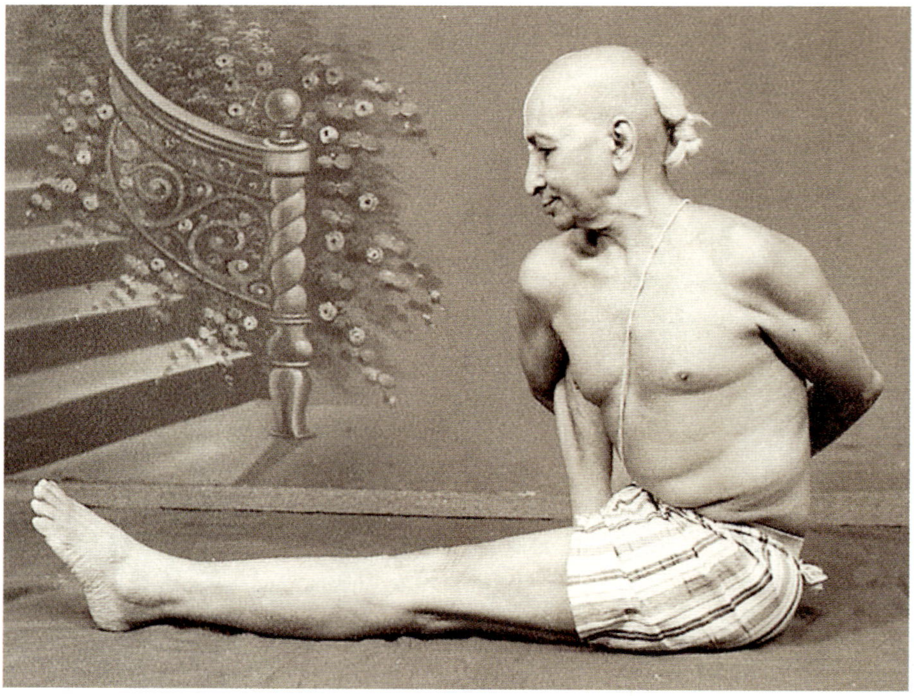

Fig. 24 Marīcya Āsana N° 1

Fig. 25 Upaviśṭa Koṇa Āsana 1

Fig. 26 Upaviśṭa Koṇa Āsana 2

Fig. 27 Upaviśṭa Koṇa Āsana 3

Fig. 28 Pūrvatāna Āsana in Upaviśṭa Koṇa Āsana

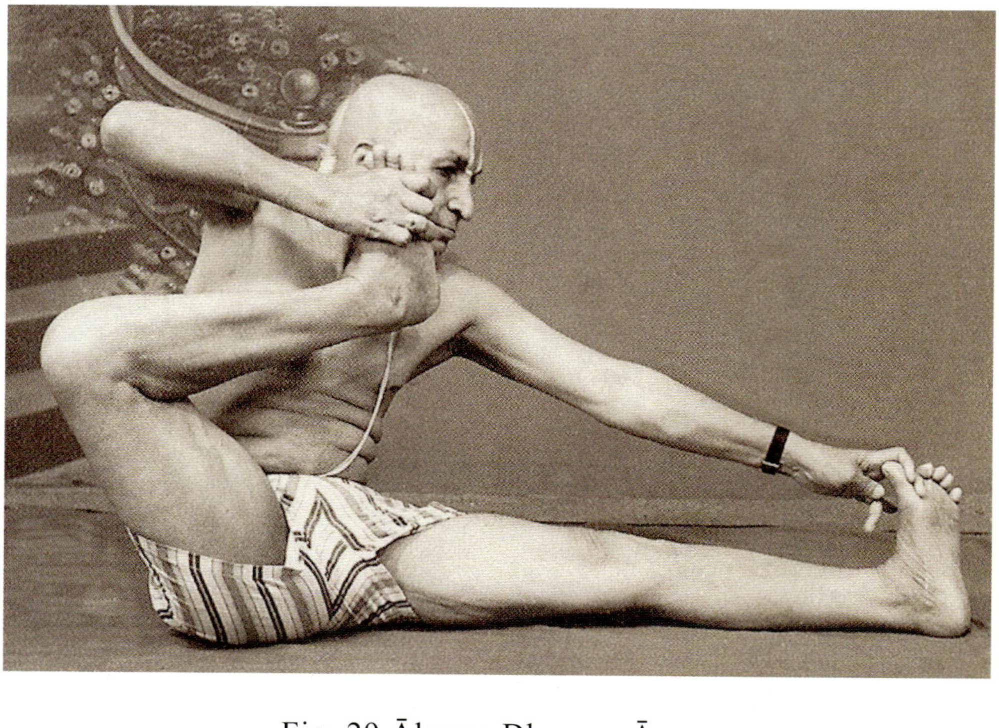

Fig. 29 Ākarṇa Dhanura Āsana

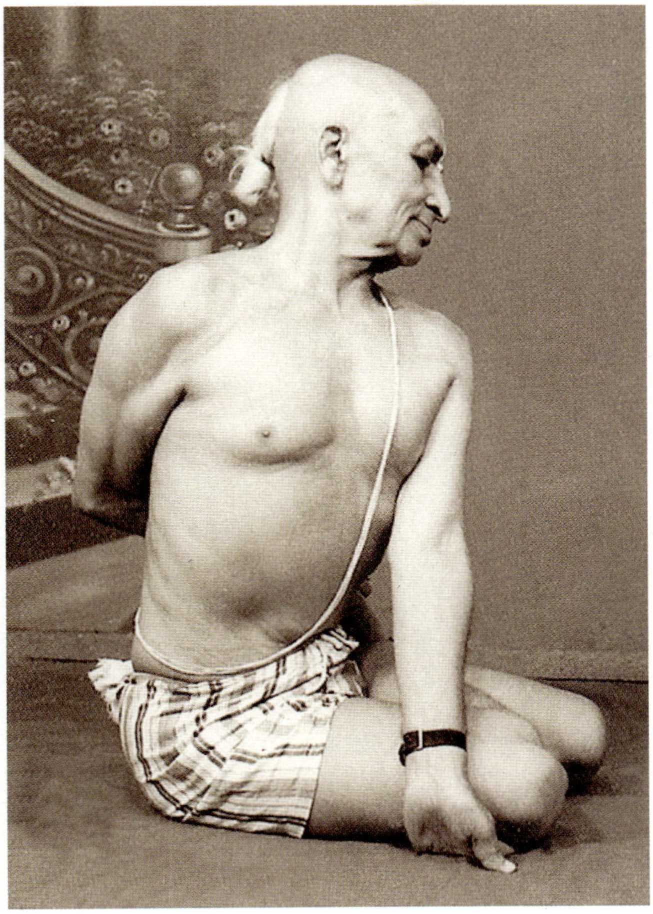

Fig. 30 Bhāradvāja Āsana

Fig. 31 Baddha Koṇa Āsana

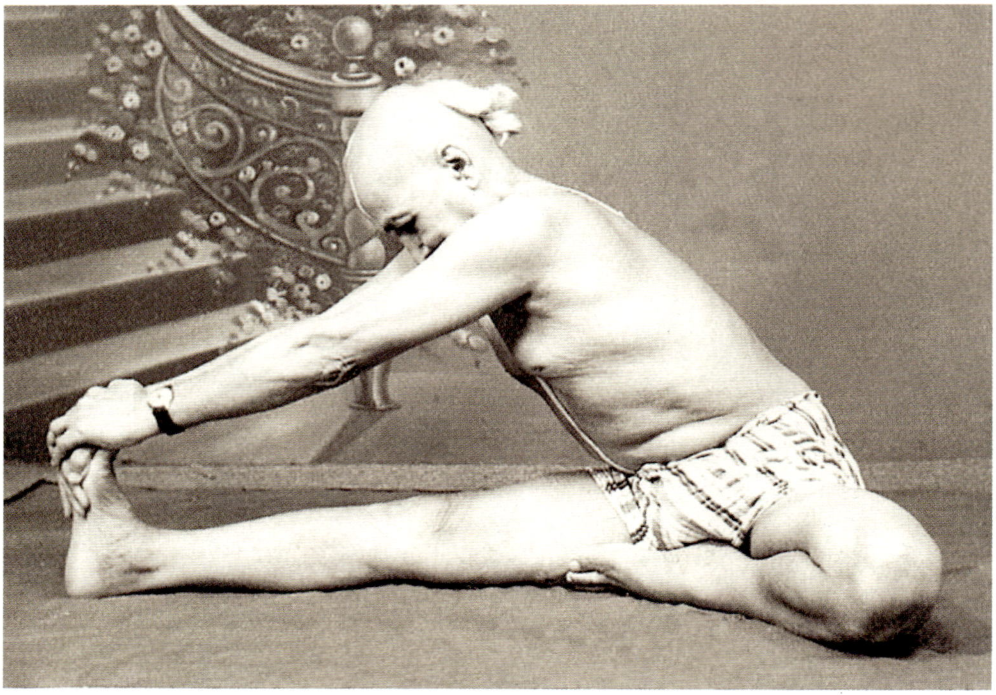

Fig. 32 Mahā Mudra

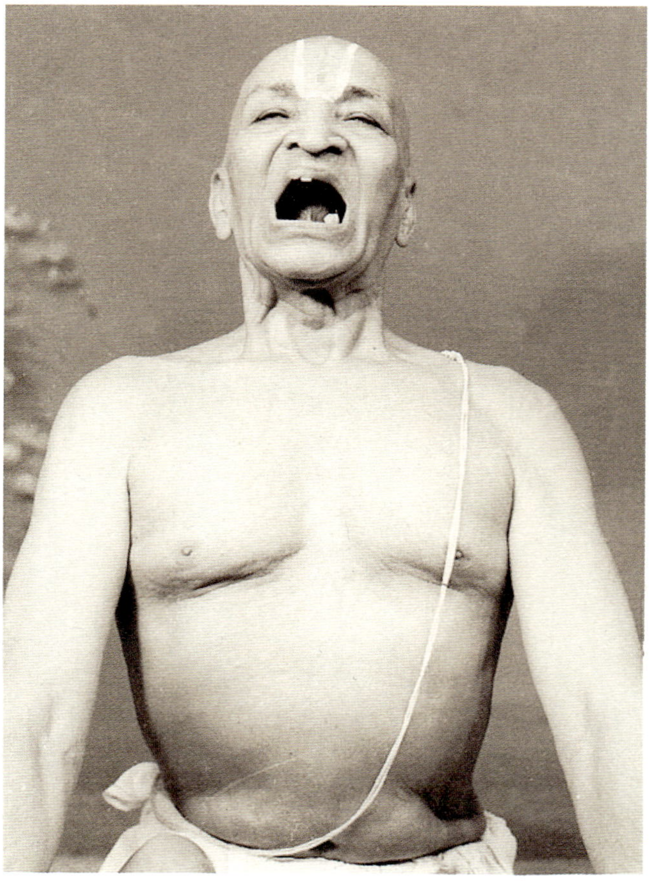

Fig. 33 Khecarī Mudra

Fig. 34 Padma Āsana

6

General instructions for Practice

Unless otherwise indicated, *Ujjāyi* is the breathing technique recommended in the *āsanas* and the *mudras*.

Ujjāyi breathing technique

Ujjāyi is a natural breathing with a specific sound produced by the friction of air at the back of the palate, behind the uvula. *Ujjāyi* is practiced breathing in and out through both nostrils, mouth closed.

Rest Position

Lie flat on the back, legs together, feet together, arms along the body, palms of the hands on the floor, chin lowered, eyes closed. Breathe normally through the nose. Take a rest after each *āsana*, *mudra* and *Prāṇāyāma*.

Duration of rest

Length of rest after each *āsana*, *mudra* or *Prāṇāyāma* from 1 to 2 minutes.

Duration of an *Āsana*

3, 6 or 12 *Ujjāyi* breaths

Note that:

1. Length of an āsana on the stomach must not be more than 3 breaths.

2. In case of laterality: 3 repetitions of 3 breaths on each side are equivalent to the length of 3 breaths.

3. In case of laterality, start the āsana, *mudra* or Prāṇāyāma with the left leg, or the left side, unless otherwise stated.

Duration of a *Mudra*

6 or 8 breaths in Mahā Mudra. 6 or12 breaths in other *mudra*s.

Duration of a *Prāṇāyāma*

12 or 16 breaths.

Note that: A *Prāṇāyāma* can be practiced longer: take a rest on the back after a cycle of 12 or 16 breaths.

Basic structure of a Practice Session.

(Approximate duration: 45 minutes)

- 1 Prāṇāyāma (Ujjāyi Anuloma, Ujjāyi Viloma, Ujjāyi Pratiloma or Śītalī) - 12 breaths

-1 āsana standing up - 6 breaths

-1 āsana on the back– 6 breaths

-1 āsana on the stomach– 3 breaths

- Sarvānga Āsana – 12 breaths

-Śīrṣa Āsana – 12 breaths

-Sarvānga Āsana variations – 12 breaths

- 1 āsana on the stomach– 3 breaths

- 1 āsana sitting - 6 breaths

- 1 Mudra – 12 breaths

- 1 Prāṇāyāma (preferably Nāḍī Śodhana) 12 breaths.

Parameters for a Practice Session

-A session always starts with a *Prāṇāyāma*.

-Total number of breaths during the āsanas on the stomach cannot exceed 6 breaths.

-The number of breaths in śīrṣa āsana and Sarvānga Āsana is equal or inferior to the number of breaths during the Prāṇāyāmas.

-Total number of breaths during the *mudra*s should be equal or inferior to the number of breaths of all the prāṇāyāmas during one session.

-The number of breaths in the āsanas standing up should not exceed 6 breaths.

-The number of breaths in the āsanas on the back can be equal to the number of breaths of the sitting āsanas.

-The number of breaths in the sitting āsana- s should be inferior to the number of breaths during one *mudra*.

-The number of breaths during all the āsanas (without counting the *mudra*s) should be inferior or equal to the number of breaths of all the prāṇāyāmas and *mudra*s. Do not take into account the number of breaths during Kapāla Bhāti or Bastri.

End up a session with a *Prāṇāyāma*.

Frequency of Practice Sessions

General Session: One daily session. See examples of General Sessions.

Mudra session: One session every 5th day of practice. See Examples of Mudras Sessions.

Prāṇāyāma session: One session a day after a Mudra Session. Refer to Examples of *Prāṇāyāma* Sessions.

Advice: Introduce or replace *mudra*s or prāṇāyāmas according to the progression of your practice and according to your capacity.

Caution: In any case, respect the instructions given by your teacher.

Indications for practicing

-Do not practice right after the ingestion of a drink.

-Wait at least 2 hours after a major meal or a minimum of 1 hour after a breakfast.

-Do not practice on an empty stomach. Drink a glass of milk or an herbal tea or eat a fruit at least 10 minutes before practicing.

-Dress comfortably, without a belt.

-Take off contacts, glasses, hearing aids, rings, collars, etc.

-Do the practice with the eyes closed.

-At the beginning of a session, remain seated at least 1 minute, directing your gaze towards the tip of the nose, eyes closed.

-At the end of a session, remain seated at least 1 minute to maintain the mental state.

Advice: Bastri and Śītalī during the spring and the summer; Kapāla Bhāti and Ujjāyi Anuloma or Ujjāyi Viloma during the fall and the winter.

For the technique of concentration, refer to Chapter 4, sub-chapter on *dhyāna* and *dhāraṇa*.

Notes on the abbreviations:

A.K. = *Antah Kumbhaka* (holding of breath after inhalation)

B.K. = *Bāhya Kumbhaka* (holding of breath after exhalation)

s. = second

We decline all responsibility for any damage that might occur due to practicing the instructions contained in these pages.

We strongly advise that you obtain your doctor's consent before you practice yoga.

The examples of the sessions follow a pedagogical progression. It is advisable therefore to practice them in the given order and to refer to the technique indicated in the chapters 13, 14 and 15.

7
Examples of General Practice Sessions

Example 1

Taṭāka Mudra - 12 breaths

Eka Pāda Apāna Āsana - 3 breaths on each side

Eka Pāda Ūrdhva Prasuta Pāda Āsana - 3 times alternating

Jaṭhara Parivṛtti N°1 - 3 breaths

Bhujaṃga Āsana - 3 times

Vajra Āsana - 6 breaths followed by Vajra Āsana (Variations) 6 Breaths

Daṇḍa Āsana (Variations) - each movement 2 times

Ujjāyi Anuloma - 6 Cycles

Example 2

Ujjāyi Anuloma - 6 Cycles

Tāḍa Āsana - 3 breaths

Ardha Candra Āsana - 3 breaths

Ūrdhva Prasuta Pāda Āsana - 4 times

Apāna Āsana - 6 breaths

Śvāna Āsana - 3 times

Sarvāṅga Āsana - 6 breaths

Bhujaṃga Āsana - 3 times

Parvata Āsana – 2 times for each of the 4 movements of the arms, then flex forward 3 times.

Ujjāyi Anuloma - 6 Cycles

Example 3

Ujjāyi Anuloma - 6 Cycles

Utthita Trikoṇa Āsana N°1 - 3 breaths

Supta Pāda Aṅguṣṭa Āsana - 6 breaths

Supta Parvata Āsana - 6 breaths

Śvāna Āsana - 3 times

Sarvāṅga Āsana - 8 breaths

Bhujaṃga Āsana - 3 times

Paścimatāna Āsana - 6 breaths followed by Pūrvatāna Āsana 3 times followed by Catuś Pāda Pīṭam 3 times

Ujjāyi Anuloma - 6 Cycles

Example 4

Ujjāyi Anuloma - 6 Cycles

Baddha Koṇa Āsana - 6 breaths

Ardha Nāva Āsana - 3 breaths

Bhujaṃga Āsana - 3 times

Sarvāṅga Āsana - 12 breaths

Utthita Pāda Aṅguṣṭa Āsana - 6 breaths

Sarvāṅga Āsana - 6 breaths

Bhujaṃga Āsana - 3 times

Upaviśṭa Koṇa Āsana - 6 breaths followed by Pūrvatāna Āsana in Upaviśṭa Koṇa Āsana 3 times

Ujjāyi Viloma - 6 Cycles

Example 5

Kapāla Bhāti - 16 breaths

Ujjāyi Anuloma - 6 Cycles

Supta Pāda Aṅguṣṭa Āsana - 6 breaths

Śvāna Āsana- 3 breaths

Sarvānga Āsana -12 breaths

Utthita Pāda Aṅguṣṭa Āsana - 6 breaths

Sarvānga Āśana - 6 breaths

Bhujaṃga Āsana, variation - 3 times

Parvata Āsana - 6 breaths sitting and then bending six times

Kapāla Bhāti - 24 breaths followed by

Ujjāyi Anuloma - 6 Cycles

Example 6

Kapāla Bhāti - 24 breaths

Ujjāyi Anuloma - 6 Cycles

Ardha Candra Āsana - 3 breaths

Supta Parvata Āsana - 6 breaths, Concentration *kaṇṭha*

Śvāna Āsana - 3 times

Sarvānga Āsana - 12 breaths

Viparīta Karaṇi - 6 breaths

Variations of Sarvānga Āsana:

- Eka Pāda Sarvānga Āsana - 2 times alternating
- Eka Pāda Ākuñcana Āsana - 2 times alternating
- Dvi Pāda Ākuñcana Āsana - 2 times

Bhujaṃga Āsana - 3 times

Paścimatāna Āsana - 6 breaths, Concentration *nāsāgra*

Kapāla Bhāti - 24 breaths followed by

Ujjāyi Anuloma - 6 Cycles

Example 7

Ujjāyi Anuloma - 6 Cycles

Upaviśṭa Koṇa Āsana - 6 breaths, Concentration *nābhi*

Bhujaṃga Āsana - 3 breaths, Concentration *kaṇṭha*

Sarvānga Āsana - 12 breaths

Viparīta Karaṇi - 6 breaths

Variations of Sarvānga Āsana:

- Eka Pāda Sarvānga Āsana – 2 times
- Eka Pāda Ākuñcana Āsana – 2 times
- Dvi Pāda Ākuñcana Āsana – 2 times

Ūrdhva Mukha Śvāna Āsana - 3 breaths

Baddha Koṇa Āsana - 6 breaths, Concentration *nābhi*

Sitting, Concentration *nāsāgra*, followed by Ujjāyi Viloma - 6 Cycles B K 5 s Concentration *kaṇṭha* during Exhalation.

Example 8

Kapāla Bhāti - 24 breaths followed by

Ujjāyi Anuloma - 6 Cycles

Sitting, normal breaths, Concentration *nāsāgra*

Taṭāka Mudra – 8 breaths, Concentration *kaṇṭha*

Bhujaṃga Āsana - 3 breaths

Sarvānga Āsana - 12 breaths

Baddha Koṇa Āsana - 8 breaths, A.K. 5 s Concentration *nāsāgra*

Sarvānga Āsana - 8 breaths

Eka Pāda Śalabha Āsana - 3 times

Paścimatāna Āsana – 8 breaths, Concentration *kaṇṭha*

Ujjāyi Viloma - 6 Cycles, Concentration *kaṇṭha* during Exhalation

Example 9

Kapāla Bhāti - 24 breaths followed by

Ujjāyi Anuloma - 6 Cycles

Ardha Utkaṭa Āsana - 3 times followed by

Utthāna Āsana - 6 breaths

Ardha Nāva Āsana - 3 breaths

Adho Mukha Baddha Koṇa Āsana - 3 breaths

Sarvānga Āsana - 12 breaths

Śīrṣa Āsana - 12 breaths; or Utthita Pāda Aṅguṣṭa Āsana 6 breaths

Variations of Sarvānga Āsana:

- Eka Pāda Ākuñcana Āsana - 2 times
- Dvi Pāda Ākuñcana Āsana - 2 times
- Baddha Koṇa Āsana in Sarvānga Āsana - 2 times

Dhanura Āsana - 3 times

Nāva Āsana - 3 breaths

Baddha Koṇa Āsana - 6 breaths B K 3 s

Nāḍī Śodhana - 6 Cycles

Example 10

Kapāla Bhāti - 24 breaths followed by

Ujjāyi Anuloma - 6 Cycles

Tāḍa Āsana - 3 breaths followed by

Tāḍa Āsana Parivṛtti - 1 time

Ardha Padma Apāna Āsana - 6 breaths

Adho Mukha Padma Āsana - 3 breaths

Sarvānga Āsana - 12 breaths

Śīrṣa Āsana - 12 Breaths; or Utthita Pāda Aṅguṣṭa Āsana 6 breaths

Variations of Sarvānga Āsana:

- Eka Pāda Sarvānga Āsana - 3 times
- Eka Pāda Ākuñcana Āsana - 3 times
- Dvi Pāda Ākuñcana Āsana - 3 times
- Prasārita Sarvānga Āsana - 3 times

Daṇḍa Āsana - 6 breaths, then Paścimatāna Āsana 6 breaths, then Pūrvatāna Āsana 3 times, then Catuś Pāda Pīṭam 3 times

Taṭāka Mudra – 12 breaths, B.K. 3 s

Example 11

Śītalī - 12 breaths

Ūrdhva Prasuta Pāda Aṅguṣṭa Āsana and Ardha Setu Bandha Āsana - 3 times

Parvata Āsana – The 4 arm movements - 2 times

Sarvānga Āsana - 12 breaths

Śīrṣa Āsana – 12 breaths; or Viparīta Karaṇi 12 breaths

Variations of Sarvānga Āsana:

- Prasārita Sarvānga Āsana - 3 times
- Baddha Koṇa Āsana in Sarvānga Āsana - 3 times and 3 breaths
- Ākuñcana Āsana Parivṛtti - 2 times

Adho Mukha Śvāna Āsana - 3 breaths

Baddha Koṇa Āsana - 12 breaths Śītalī

Upaviśṭa Koṇa Āsana - 6 breaths B.K. 5 s

Ujjāyi Anuloma - 6 Cycles A.K. 5 s

Example 12

Vajra Āsana - Concentration *nāsāgra* followed by Śītalī 12 breaths

Utthita Pāda Aṅguṣṭa Āsana – 6 breaths, B.K. 5 s, Concentration *kaṇṭha*

Jaṭhara Parivṛtti N° 2 - 3 breaths

Parvata Āsana or Vajra Āsana – The arms over the head 6 breaths followed by bending forward, 6 breaths

Sarvānga Āsana - 12 breaths

Śīrṣa Āsana – 12 breaths; or Viparīta Karaṇi 8 breaths

Variations of Sarvānga Āsana:

- Ardha Padma Ākuñcana Āsana - 2 times
- Ākuñcana Āsana Parivṛtti - 2 times
- Pārśva Eka Pāda Sarvānga Āsana - 2 times

Dhanura Āsana - 3 breaths

Mahā Mudra - 6 breaths A.K. 5 s and B.K. 5 s, Concentration *kaṇṭha*

Nāḍī Śodhana - 6 Cycles

Example 13

Baddha Koṇa Āsana (back against the wall) - 12 breaths Śītalī

Tāḍa Āsana - 3 breaths followed by Utthāna Āsana 6 breaths

Ardha Setu Bandha Āsana - 4 times, then 4 breaths

Bhujaṃga Āsana, variation - 3 times

Sarvānga Āsana - 12 breaths

Śīrṣa Āsana – 12 breaths; or Taṭāka Mudra 12 breaths B.K. 5s, Concentration *kaṇṭha*

Eka Pāda Śalabha Āsana - 3 times alternating

Daṇḍa Āsana - Arms over the head 3 breaths followed by Paścimatāna Āsana bending forward 4 times, followed by Paścimatāna Āsana 6 breaths, followed by Pūrvatāna Āsana 3 times

Concentration *nāsāgra*, more or less 1 Minute followed by

Nāḍī Śodhana - 6 Cycles Concentration *kaṇṭha*

Example 14

Bastri -30 Cycles or more followed by

Śītalī - 12 breaths A.K. 5 s

Utthita Trikoṇa Āsana N°2 - 3 breaths

Dhanura Āsana, Variation - 3 times

Sarvāṅga Āsana - 12 breaths

Śīrṣa Āsana – 12 breaths;
or Viparīta Karaṇi 8 breaths B.K. 3 s

Variations of Sarvāṅga Āsana:

- Dvi Pāda Ākuñcana Āsana - 2 times
- Prasārita Sarvāṅga Āsana - 3 times
- Ākuñcana Āsana Parivṛtti - 2 times
- Ardha Padma Ākuñcana Āsana - 3 times or 3 breaths

Śalabha Āsana - 3 times

Upaviṣṭa Koṇa Āsana – 6 breaths, then Pūrvatāna Āsana in Upaviṣṭa Koṇa Āsana 3 times

Bastri - 30 Cycles followed by

Nāḍī Śodhana - 6 Cycles, A.K. 5 s, Concentration *hṛdaya*

Stay sitting, concentration *tāraka* during 2 or 3 minutes

Example 15

Kapāla Bhāti - 24 or 32 breaths followed by

Ujjāyi Anuloma - 6 Cycles, A.K. 5 s

Bhagīratha Āsana - 3 breaths

Ūrdhva Prasuta Pāda Āsana and Ardha Setu Bandha Āsana - 6 times

Bhujaṃga Āsana, variation - 3 times

Sarvāṅga Āsana - 12 breaths

Śīrṣa Āsana -12 breaths;
or Viparīta Karaṇi 8 breaths B.K. 3 s

Variations of Sarvāṅga Āsana:

- Eka Pāda Sarvāṅga Āsana - 2 times alternating
- Eka Pāda Ākuñcana Āsana - 2 times alternating
- Dvi Pāda Ākuñcana Āsana - 2 times
- Ākuñcana Āsana Parivṛtti - 2 times

Eka Pāda Dhanura Āsana - 3 times

Upaviṣṭa Koṇa Āsana - 6 breaths followed by Pūrvatāna Āsana in Upaviṣṭa Koṇa Āsana 3 times

Bastri - 30 Cycles followed by

Nāḍī Śodhana - 6 Cycles, A. K. 5 s, Concentration *hṛdaya*

Stay sitting, concentration *nāsāgra* during 2 or 3 minutes

Example 16

Taṭāka Mudra – 12 breaths, A.K. 5 s and B.K. 5 s, Concentration *lalāṭa*

Tāḍa Āsana - 6 breaths followed by Tāḍa Āsana Parivṛtti 3 times

Adho Mukha Śvāna Āsana - 3 breaths

Sarvāṅga Āsana - 12 breaths

Śīrṣa Āsana – 12 breaths; or Viparīta Karaṇi 6 breaths

Variations of Sarvāṅga Āsana:

- Prasārita Sarvāṅga Āsana - 3 times
- Baddha Koṇa Āsana - 3 times and 3 breaths
- Ākuñcana Āsana Parivṛtti - 2 times
- Pārśva Eka Pāda Sarvāṅga Āsana - 2 times

Eka Pāda Śalabha Āsana - 3 times

Parvata Āsana, flexion - 3 times

Kapāla Bhāti - 12 breaths followed by

Ujjāyi Viloma - 6 Cycles, Exhalation longer than Inhalation

Example 17

Taṭāka Mudra – 12 breaths, A.K. 5 s and B.K. 5 s

Utthita Trikoṇa Āsana N°2 - 3 breaths

Ardha Nāva Āsana - 3 breaths

Śvāna Āsana - 3 times

Sarvāṅga Āsana - 12 breaths

Śīrṣa Āsana - 12 breaths

Sarvāṅga Āsana – 12 breaths

Śalabha Āsana - 3 times

Upaviṣṭa Koṇa Āsana complete - 3 breaths

Kapāla Bhāti - 12 breaths followed by

Ujjāyi Viloma - 6 Cycles, Exhalation longer than Inhalation

Example 18

Kapāla Bhāti - 16 or 24 breaths followed by

Ujjāyi Anuloma - 6 Cycles A.K. 5 s

Ardha Utkaṭa Āsana - 4 times followed by Utthāna Āsana 3 breaths

Ardha Padma Apāna Āsana - 3 breaths

Śvāna Āsana - 3 times

Śīrṣa Āsana – 12 breaths; or Utthita Pāda Aṅguṣṭa Āsana 6 breaths B.K. 5 s, Concentration *kaṇṭha*

Variations of Sarvāṅga Āsana:

- Eka Pāda Sarvāṅga Āsana - 2 times alternating
- Eka Pāda Ākuñcana Āsana - 2 times alternating
- Dvi Pāda Ākuñcana Āsana - 2 times

- Prasārita Sarvānga Āsana - 3 times

Parigha Āsana - 3 times

Baddha Koṇa Āsana - 6 breaths

Bastri - 30 Cycles or more followed by

Nāḍī Śodhana - 6 Cycles A.K. 5 s. or 10 s., Concentration *hṛdaya*

Stay sitting, concentration *nāsāgra* during 2 or 3 minutes

Example 19

Kapāla Bhāti - 32 breaths followed by

Ujjāyi Anuloma - 6 Cycles A. K. 3 s

Utthita Pārśva Utthāna Āsana - 3 breaths

Jaṭhara Parivṛtti N° 2 - 3 breaths each side

Eka Pāda Śalabha Āsana - 3 times alternating

Sarvānga Āsana - 12 breaths

Śīrṣa Āsana – 12 breaths; or Supta Pāda Aṅguṣṭa Āsana 12 breaths

Sarvānga Āsana - 12 breaths

Dhanura Āsana - 3 breaths

Upaviṣṭa Koṇa Āsana - 6 breaths

Kapāla Bhāti - 32 breaths followed by

Ujjāyi Anuloma - 6 Cycles

Example 20

Kapāla Bhāti - 24 breaths followed by

Ujjāyi Anuloma - 3 Cycles

- Repeat 2 times

Ūrdhva Mukha Āsana - 4 times

Supta Pārśva Eka Pāda Aṅguṣṭa Āsana - 3 breaths

Śvāna Āsana - 3 times

Sarvānga Āsana - 12 breaths

Śīrṣa Āsana – 12 breaths; or Supta Pāda Aṅguṣṭa Āsana 12 breaths with legs against the wall

Variations of Sarvānga Āsana:

- Eka Pāda Sarvānga Āsana - 2 times alternating
- Prasārita Sarvānga Āsana - 3 times
- Ākuñcana Āsana Parivṛtti - 2 times
- Pārśva Eka Pāda Sarvānga Āsana - 2 times

Śalabha Āsana - 3 times

Vajra Āsana, Variations - 3 times of each followed by Uṣṭra Āsana – 3 breaths

Paścimatāna Āsana - 6 breaths

Nāḍī Śodhana - 6 Cycles

Example 21

Taṭāka Mudra - 12 breaths B.K. 3 s

Vīra Bhadra Āsana - 1 breath followed by Garuḍa Āsana – 1 breath

Bhujaṃga Āsana, variation 3 times

Sarvānga Āsana - 12 breaths

Śīrṣa Āsana - 12 breaths; or Baddha Koṇa Āsana 8 breaths, Concentration *kaṇṭha*

Sarvānga Āsana – 12 breaths

Śvāna Āsana - 3 times

Parvata Āsana or Vajra Āsana – the 4 arm movements, 2 times each

Upaviṣṭa Koṇa Āsana - 6 breaths

Nāḍī Śodhana - 6 Cycles

Example 22

Śītalī - 12 breaths

Bhagīratha Āsana - 3 breaths

Ūrdhva Prasuta Pāda Āsana and Ardha Setu Bandha Āsana - 4 times

Adho Mukha Padma Āsana - 3 breaths

Sarvānga Āsana - 12 breaths

Śīrṣa Āsana - 12 breaths; or, Baddha Koṇa Āsana 8 breaths B.K. 5 s, Concentration *nāsāgra*

Variations of Sarvānga Āsana:

- Eka Pāda Ākuñcana Āsana - 2 times alternating
- Dvi Pāda Ākuñcana Āsana - 2 times
- Prasārita Sarvānga Āsana - 3 times

Eka Pāda Viparīta Śalabha Āsana - 3 times alternating

Daṇḍa Āsana, Variations - 3 times each followed by Paścimatāna Āsana - 3 times bending forward, followed by Paścimatāna Āsana - 6 breaths

Nāḍī Śodhana - 6 Cycles

Example 23

Śītalī - 12 breaths

Prasārita Pāda Utthāna Āsana - 6 breaths

Eka Pāda Ūrdhva Prasuta Pāda Āsana - 2 times alternating then followed by Ūrdhva Prasuta Pāda Āsana 4 times

Śvāna Āsana - 3 times

Sarvānga Āsana - 12 breaths

Śīrṣa Āsana – 12 breaths; or Utthita Pāda Aṅguṣṭa Āsana 6 breaths

Variations of Sarvānga Āsana:

- Ākuñcana Āsana Parivṛtti - 2 times
- Pārśva Eka Pāda Sarvānga Āsana - 2 times
- Ardha Padma Ākuñcana Āsana - 3 times or 3 breaths

Rāja Kapota Āsana - 3 breaths

Upaviṣṭa Koṇa Āsana complete - 3 times each phase

Kapāla Bhāti - 24 breaths followed by

Ujjāyi Anuloma - 6 Cycles

Example 24

Kapāla Bhāti - 32 breaths followed by

Ujjāyi Anuloma - 6 Cycles

Bhagīratha Āsana - 3 breaths

Supta Parvata Āsana - 6 breaths

Śvāna Āsana - 3 times

Sarvānga Āsana - 12 breaths

Śīrṣa Āsana – 12 breaths; or Utthita Pāda Aṅguṣṭa Āsana 6 breaths

Variations of Sarvānga Āsana:

- Eka Pāda Sarvānga Āsana - 2 times alternating.
- Eka Pāda Ākuñcana Āsana - 2 times alternating
- Dvi Pāda Ākuñcana Āsana - 2 times
- Ardha Padma Ākuñcana Āsana - 3 times or 3 breaths

Simha Āsana or Adho Mukha Padma Āsana - 3 times

Baddha Koṇa Āsana - 6 breaths

Śītalī 2nd Technique - 12 breaths

Example 25

Śītalī - 12 breaths

Supta Parivṛtta Pārśva Pāda Aṅguṣṭa Āsana - 3 breaths

Dhanura Āsana - 3 times

Śīrṣa Āsana - 12 breaths; or Viparīta Karaṇi 12 breaths

Sarvānga Āsana - 12 breaths

Variations of Sarvānga Āsana:

- Prasārita Sarvānga Āsana - 3 times
- Pārśva Eka Pāda Sarvānga Āsana - 2 times

Eka Pāda Dhanura Āsana - 3 times alternating

Baddha Koṇa Āsana - 6 breaths

Bhāradvāja Āsana – 3 breaths

Mahā Mudra - 6 breaths Śītalī (without lifting the head during Inhalation)

Ujjāyi Anuloma - 6 Cycles B.K. 5 s

Example 26

Bastri - 30 Cycles followed by

Śītalī - 12 breaths B.K. 5 s

Utthita Pārśva Koṇa Āsana - 3 breaths

Matsya Āsana - 3 breaths

Sarvānga Āsana - 12 breaths

Śīrṣa Āsana - 12 breaths; or Utthita Pāda Aṅguṣṭa Āsana 6 breaths B.K. 5 s

Hala Āsana - 3 breaths followed by Karṇa Pīḍa Āsana – 3 breaths

Dhanura Āsana, Variation - 3 times

Marīcya Āsana N°1 - 3 breaths

Kapāla Bhāti - 24 breaths followed by

Ujjāyi Anuloma - 6 Cycles, Concentration *kaṇṭha* during Inhalation

Example 27

Kapāla Bhāti - 16 breaths followed by

Ujjāyi Pratiloma - 4 Cycles

Vīra Bhadra Āsana - 1 breath followed by Garuḍa Āsana – 1 breath

Utthāna Pāda Āsana - 3 breaths

Sarvānga Āsana - 12 breaths

Śīrṣa Āsana – 12 breaths;
or Viparīta Karaṇi 8 breaths B.K. 3s

Hala Āsana - 3 breaths followed by Karṇa Pīḍa Āsana – 3 breaths

Eka Pāda Viparīta Śalabha Āsana - 3 times alternating

Vajra Āsana, Variation - 3 times each followed by Uṣṭra Āsana – 3 breaths

Bastri - 30 Cycles followed by

Nāḍī Śodhana - 6 Cycles, Inhalation Concentration *mūla to śīrṣa*, Exhalation Concentration *hṛdaya*

Stay sitting, concentration *hṛdaya*

Example 28

Kapāla Bhāti - 16 breaths followed by

Ujjāyi Viloma - 6 Cycles B.K. 5 s

Utthita Pārśva Utthāna Āsana - 3 breaths on each side

Ardha Padma Apāna Āsana - 3 breaths

Sarvānga Āsana - 12 breaths, Concentration *kaṇṭha*

Śīrṣa Āsana - 12 breaths, Concentration *kaṇṭha* or Baddha Koṇa Āsana 8 breaths B.K. 5 s, Concentration *nābhi*

Variations of Sarvānga Āsana:

- Prasārita Sarvānga Āsana - 3 times
- Baddha Koṇa Āsana – 3 times

Śalabha Āsana - 3 times

Ardha Padma Paścimatāna Āsana - 3 breaths

Bastri - 30 Cycles followed by

Nāḍī Śodhana - 6 Cycles Concentration *hṛdaya*

Maintain mental state during more or less 2 minutes.

Example 29

Taṭāka Mudra – 12 breaths, Inhalation Concentration Mūla to *bhrūmadhya*, Exhalation Concentration *kaṇṭha*

Utthita Trikoṇa Āsana N°2 - 2 breaths

Ardha Nāva Āsana – 3 breaths

Eka Pāda Śalabha Āsana - 3 times alternating

Sarvānga Āsana - 12 breaths

Śīrṣa Āsana - 12 breaths; or Utthita Pāda Aṅguṣṭa Āsana 6 breaths B.K. 5 s

Variations of Sarvānga Āsana:

- Eka Pāda Sarvānga Āsana - 1 time alternating
- Dvi Pāda Ākuñcana Āsana - 1 time
- Prasārita Sarvānga Āsana - 1 time
- Pārśva Eka Pāda Sarvānga Āsana - 1 time
- Ardha Padma Ākuñcana Āsana - 3 times

Śvāna Āsana - 3 times

Vajra Āsana, variations - 2 times of each followed by Uṣṭra Āsana - 3 breaths

Paścimatāna Āsana - 6 breaths B.K. 5 s, Concentration *nābhi*

Bastri - 30 Cycles followed by

Nāḍī Śodhana - 6 Cycles B.K. 5 s, Concentration *hṛdaya*

Stay sitting, concentration *tāraka* during more or less 2 minutes.

Example 30

Kapāla Bhāti - 24 breaths (in Vajra Āsana) followed by

Ujjāyi Viloma - 6 Cycles B.K. 5 s (in Vajra Āsana)

Ardha Setu Bandha Āsana - 4 times or 4 breaths

Utthita Pāda Aṅguṣṭa Āsana - 6 breaths

Adho Mukha Baddha Koṇa Āsana - 3 times or 3 breaths

Sarvānga Āsana - 12 breaths

Śīrṣa Āsana - 12 breaths; or Baddha Koṇa Āsana - 8 breaths Concentration *nābhi*, B.K. 5 s

Variations of Sarvānga Āsana:

-Prasārita Sarvānga Āsana - 1 time

-Baddha Koṇa Āsana – 3 times

-Pārśva Eka Pāda Sarvānga Āsana – 2 times

Hala Āsana - 3 breaths

Dhanura Āsana - 3 breaths

Upaviṣṭa Koṇa Āsana complete - 2 times

Sit in Padma Āsana - 6 breaths Ujjāyi, Inhalation Mūla to *bhrūmadhya*, Exhalation Concentration *kaṇṭha* followed by Bastri - 30 Cycles or more followed by

Nāḍī Śodhana (Abhyantara Vṛtti) - 6 Cycles A.K. 5 to10 s, Inhalation Concentration *nāsāgra* to *hṛdaya*, Exhalation Concentration *hṛdaya*

Stay sitting, concentration *hṛdaya* during more or less 2 minutes.

Example 31

Kapāla Bhāti - 24 breaths followed by

Ujjāyi Anuloma - 6 Cycles A.K. 5 s

Parigha Āsana - 3 breaths

Utkaṭa Āsana (back against the wall, arms above the head) - 6 breaths

Ūrdhva Mukha Śvāna Āsana - 3 breaths

Sarvānga Āsana - 12 breaths

Śīrṣa Āsana - 12 breaths; or Utthita Pāda Aṅguṣṭa Āsana 8 breaths

Variations of Sarvānga Āsana:

- Eka Pāda Sarvānga Āsana - 1 time alternating
- Eka Pāda Ākuñcana Āsana - 1 time alternating
- Dvi Pāda Ākuñcana Āsana - 1 time
- Ardha Padma Ākuñcana Āsana - 3 times

Adho Mukha Padma Āsana - 3 times or 3 breaths; or Adho Mukha Baddha Koṇa Āsana - 3 breaths

Baddha Koṇa Āsana - 6 breaths B.K. 5 s, Inhalation Concentration Mūla to *bhrūmadhya*, Exhalation Concentration *nābhi*

Bastri - 30 Cycles

Nāḍī Śodhana - 6 Cycles A.K. 5 s and B.K. 5 s, Inhalation Concentration *nābhi*, Exhalation Concentration *hṛdaya*

Stay sitting, concentration *hṛdaya* during more or less 2 minutes.

Example 32

Kapāla Bhāti - 12 breaths followed by

Ujjāyi Viloma - 6 Cycles, B. K. 5 s

Bhagīratha Āsana - 3 breaths

Supta Parvata Āsana - 6 breaths; or Matsya Āsana 3 breaths

Adho Mukha Padma Āsana - 3 breaths; or Adho Mukha Baddha Koṇa Āsana 3 breaths

Śīrṣa Āsana - 12 breaths; or Taṭāka Mudra 12 breaths B.K. 5s, Concentration *kaṇṭha*

Variations of Sarvānga Āsana:

- Prasārita Sarvānga Āsana - 1 time
- Pārśva Eka Pāda Sarvānga Āsana - 1 time
- Ardha Padma Ākuñcana Āsana - 3 times

Bheka Āsana – 3 breaths

Ardha Baddha Padma Paścimatāna Āsana - 3 breaths

Bastri - 30 Cycles or more followed by

Nāḍī Śodhana - 6 Cycles, A.K. 5 or 8 s and B.K. 5 of 8 s, Concentration *kaṇṭha kūpa*

Stay sitting, Concentration *tāraka* during more or less 2 minutes.

Example 33

Paścimatāna Āsana - Kapāla Bhāti 12 breaths followed by Ujjāyi 4 breaths B.K. 5 s Concentration *nābhi*

- Repeat 3 times

Prasārita Pāda Utthāna Āsana - 6 breaths

Utthāna Pāda Āsana - 3 breaths

Sarvānga Āsana - 12 breaths

Śīrṣa Āsana - 12 breaths; or Supta Pāda Angusṭa Āsana 12 breaths

Variations of Sarvānga Āsana:

- Eka Pāda Sarvānga Āsana - 1 time alternating
- Ardha Padma Ākuñcana Āsana - 3 times
- Ardha Padma Hala Āsana 3 breaths

Dhanura Āsana - 3 times or 3 breaths

Parivṛtta Paścimatāna Āsana - 3 breaths

Ardha Matsyendra Āsana N°1 - 3 breaths

Bastri - 30 Cycles followed by

Nāḍī Śodhana - 8 Cycles, Concentration *hṛdaya*

Stay sitting, Concentration *nāsāgra* during more or less 2 minutes.

Example 34

Kapāla Bhāti, variation 12 breaths followed by Samasthiti, 3 breaths Ujjāyi B.K. 5 s

- Repeat 3 times

Ardha Candra Āsana - 3 breaths

Eka Pāda Viparīta Śalabha Āsana - 3 times alternating

Sarvānga Āsana - 12 breaths, Concentration *kaṇṭha*

Śīrṣa Āsana - 12 breaths B.K. 5 s or, Baddha Koṇa Āsana 12 breaths, Concentration *nābhi*

Hala Āsana - 3 breaths followed by Karṇa Pīḍa Āsana 3 breaths

Rāja Kapota Āsana - 3 breaths

Marīcya Āsana N°1 – 6 breaths

Bastri - 30 Cycles followed by

Nāḍī Śodhana - 6 Cycles, Inhalation Concentration *mūla to śīrṣa*, Exhalation Concentration *hṛdaya*

Stay sitting, Concentration *hṛdaya* during more or less 2 minutes.

Example 35

Vajra Āsana - Concentration *nāsāgra* followed by Ujjāyi Viloma 6 Cycles

Utthita Pāda Angusṭa - 6 breaths, Concentration *kaṇṭha*

Matsya Āsana - 3 breaths; or Supta Parvata Āsana 6 breaths

Sarvānga Āsana - 12 breaths

Śīrṣa Āsana - 12 breaths; or Viparīta Karaṇi 8 breaths

Ūrdhva Mukha Śvāna Āsana - 3 breaths

Pinḍa Āsana – 3 breaths

Uṣṭra Āsana – 3 breaths

Ākarṇa Dhanura Āsana – 2 breaths

Mahā Mudra - 6 breaths A.K. 5 s and B.K. 5 s, Concentration *kaṇṭha*

Bastri - 30 Cycles followed by

Nāḍī Śodhana - 6 Cycles

Example 36

Taṭāka Mudra - 12 breaths B.K. 5 s, Inhalation Concentration Pāda *aṅguṣṭa to śīrṣa*, Exhalation Concentration *kaṇṭha*

Tāḍa Āsana - Concentration *nāsāgra* - 3 breaths

Śvāna Āsana - 3 breaths

Sarvānga Āsana - 12 breaths

Śīrṣa Āsana - 12 breaths; or Baddha Koṇa Āsana - 12 breaths (back against the wall), Concentration *nābhi*

Variations of Sarvānga Āsana:

- Eka Pāda Ākuñcana Āsana - 2 times alternating
- Ākuñcana Āsana Parivṛtti - 2 times
- Ardha Padma Ākuñcana Āsana - 3 times or 3 breaths
- Prasārita Sarvānga Āsana - 3 times
- Baddha Koṇa Āsana - 3 times and 3 breaths

Adho Mukha Padma Āsana - 3 breaths; or Simha Āsana (if you do Padma Āsana) - 3 breaths

Ardha Baddha Padma Paścimatāna Āsana or Ardha Padma Paścimatāna Āsana - 3 breaths

Bastri - 30 Cycles or more followed by

Nāḍī Śodhana - 6 Cycles A.K. 5 s Concentration *kaṇṭha kūpa*

Stay sitting, Concentration *tāraka* during more or less 2 minutes.

Example 37

Kapāla Bhāti - 24 breaths followed by

Ujjāyi Anuloma - 6 Cycles A.K. 5 s

Utthita Pāda Aṅguṣṭa Āsana - 6 breaths B.K. 5 s

Supta Parvata Āsana - 3 breaths B.K. 5 s

Sarvānga Āsana - 12 breaths

Śīrṣa Āsana - 12 breaths B.K. 3 s or Sarvānga Āsana 6 breaths B.K. 3 s

Dhanura Āsana - 3 breaths or 3 times

Upaviśṭa Koṇa Āsana - 12 breaths A.K. 5 s

Baddha Koṇa Āsana - 6 breaths A.K. 5 s

Marīcya Āsana N°2 - 3 breaths

Bastri - 30 Cycles followed by

Nāḍī Śodhana - 6 Cycles A.K. 8 s or 10 s

Example 38

Kapāla Bhāti - 24 breaths followed by

Ujjāyi Viloma - 6 Cycles

Utthita Trikoṇa Āsana N°2 - 2 breaths

Eka Pāda Viparīta Śalabha Āsana - 3 times alternating

Sarvānga Āsana - 12 breaths

Śīrṣa Āsana - 12 breaths; or Supta Pāda Aṅguṣṭa Āsana - 12 breaths B.K. 5 s

Variations of Sarvānga Āsana:

- Eka Pāda Sarvānga Āsana - 2 times alternating
- Prasārita Sarvānga Āsana - 3 times
- Baddha Koṇa Āsana in Sarvānga Āsana - 3 times and 3 breaths
- Pārśva Eka Pāda Sarvānga Āsana - 2 times
- Ardha Padma Ākuñcana Āsana - 3 times or 3 breaths

Śalabha Āsana - 3 times

Parigha Āsana - 3 times

Bastri - 30 Cycles or more followed by

Nāḍī Śodhana - 6 Cycles

Example 39

Kapāla Bhāti - 12 breaths followed by

Ujjāyi - 3 breaths A.K. 5 s and B.K. 5 s

- Repeat 3 times

Vīra Bhadra Āsana - 1 breath followed by Garuḍa Āsana 1 breath

Matsya Āsana - 3 times or Supta Parvata Āsana 3 breaths

Sarvānga Āsana - 12 breaths

Śīrṣa Āsana - 12 breaths; or Viparīta Karaṇi 8 breaths

Ūrdhva Mukha Padma Āsana – 3 breaths

Pinḍa Āsana – 3 breaths

Uṣṭra Āsana - 3 breaths

Ardha Baddha Padma Paścimatāna Āsana - 3 breaths or Ardha Padma Paścimatāna Āsana - 3 breaths

Ardha Matsyendra Āsana N°2 – 3 breaths

Bastri - 30 Cycles followed by

Nāḍī Śodhana - 6 Cycles, Inhalation equal to Exhalation (Inhalation as long as possible)

Stay sitting, Concentration *nāsāgra* during more or less 2 minutes.

Example 40

Paścimatāna Āsana - Kapāla Bhāti - 12 breaths followed by Ujjāyi 4 breaths B.K. 5 s

- Repeat 3 times

Bhagīratha Āsana – 3 breaths

Supta Parvata Āsana - 6 breaths, B.K. 5 s

Sarvānga Āsana - 12 breaths

Śīrṣa Āsana - 12 breaths or Supta Pāda Aṅguṣṭa Āsana 6 breaths B.K. 5 s

Dhanura Āsana - 3 times

Marīcya Āsana N°2 - 3 breaths

Ardha Matsyendra Āsana N° 2 - 3 breaths

Bastri - 30 Cycles followed by

Nāḍī Śodhana - 8 Cycles, Concentration *hṛdaya*

Stay sitting, Concentration *hṛdaya* during more or less 2 minutes.

Example 41

Kapāla Bhāti, variation - 12 breaths followed by Samasthiti - 3 breaths B.K. 5 s

- Repeat 3 times

Ūrdhva Prasuta Pāda Āsana and Ardha Setu Bandha Āsana – 6 times

Bhujaṃga Āsana, variation - 3 times

Sarvānga Āsana - 12 breaths, Concentration *kaṇṭha*

Śīrṣa Āsana - 12 breaths B.K. 5 s or, Baddha Koṇa Āsana 12 breaths, Concentration *nābhi*

Ūrdhva Mukha Padma Āsana - 3 breaths

Pinḍa Āsana - 3 breaths

Karṇa Pīḍa Āsana – 3 breaths

Dhanura Āsana, variation - 3 breaths

Marīcya Āsana N°2 - 3 breaths

Bastri - 30 Cycles followed by

Nāḍī Śodhana - 6 Cycles, Inhalation Concentration *mūla to śīrṣa*, Exhalation Concentration *hṛdaya*

Stay sitting, Concentration *hṛdaya* during more or less 2 minutes.

Example 42

Kapāla Bhāti - 16 breaths followed by

Ujjāyi Anuloma - 6 Cycles

Jaṭhara Parivṛtti N° 2 - 3 breaths

Bhujaṃga Āsana - 3 times

Sarvānga Āsana - 12 breaths

Śīrṣa Āsana - 12 breaths; or Viparīta Karaṇi 8 breaths

Variations of Sarvānga Āsana:

- Eka Pāda Ākuñcana Āsana - 1 time alternating
- Dvi Pāda Ākuñcana Āsana - 1 time
- Ākuñcana Āsana Parivṛtti - 1 time
- Prasārita Sarvānga Āsana - 1 time

Viparīta Śalabha Āsana - 3 times

Vasiṣṭha Āsana – 1 breath

Sitting, Concentration *tāraka* more or less 1 minute

Bastri - 30 Cycles followed by

Nāḍī Śodhana - 6 Cycles A.K. 10 s

Example 43

Kapāla Bhāti - 16 breaths followed by

Ujjāyi Anuloma - 3 Cycles A.K. 5 s and B.K. 5 s

- Repeat 2 times

Utthita Pāda Aṅguṣṭa Āsana - 6 breaths

Bhujaṃga Āsana, variation - 3 times

Sarvānga Āsana - 12 breaths

Śīrṣa Āsana - 12 breaths; or Supta Pāda Aṅguṣṭa Āsana - 12 breaths B.K. 5 s

Variations of Sarvānga Āsana:

- Eka Pāda Sarvānga Āsana - 1 time alternating
- Eka Pāda Ākuñcana Āsana - 1 time alternating
- Dvi Pāda Ākuñcana Āsana - 1 time
- Ākuñcana Āsana Parivṛtti - 1 time
- Prasārita Sarvānga Āsana - 1 time
- Pārśva Eka Pāda Sarvānga Āsana - 1 time
- Ardha Padma Ākuñcana Āsana – 1 breath

Dhanura Āsana - 3 breaths

Paścimatāna Āsana - 8 breaths A.K. 5 s, Concentration *kaṇṭha*

Sitting, concentration *lalāṭa* more or less 1 minute followed by

Bastri - 30 Cycles followed by

Nāḍī Śodhana - 6 Cycles B.K. 5 s, Inhalation, Concentration *kaṇṭha*, Exhalation Concentration *hṛdaya*

Stay sitting, Concentration *hṛdaya* during more or less 2 minutes.

Example 44

Sitting Concentration *nāsāgra*
Ujjāyi Viloma - 6 Cycles
Supta Pārśva Eka Pāda Aṅguṣṭa Āsana - 3 breaths
Dhanura Āsana - 3 times
Sarvānga Āsana - 12 breaths
Śīrṣa Āsana - 12 breaths or Utthita Pāda Aṅguṣṭa Āsana 6 breaths B.K. 5 s
Hala Āsana - 3 breaths or 3 times followed by Karṇa Pīḍa Āsana – 3 breaths
Rāja Kapota Āsana - 3 breaths
Parvata Āsana or Vajra Āsana, variations - 2 times each variation
Sitting, Concentration *tāraka* more or less 1 minute followed by
Bastri - 30 Cycles followed by
Nāḍī Śodhana - 6 Cycles, Concentration *hṛdaya*
Stay sitting, Concentration *nāsāgra* during more or less 2 minutes.

Example 45

Kapāla Bhāti - 16 or 24 breaths followed by
Ujjāyi Pratiloma - 4 Cycles
Utthita Pārśva Koṇa Āsana - 3 breaths
Supta Pāda Aṅguṣṭa Āsana - 6 breaths
Adho Mukha Padma Āsana or Adho Mukha Baddha Koṇa Āsana - 3 times or 3 breaths
Sarvānga Āsana - 12 breaths
Śīrṣa Āsana - 12 breaths; or Viparīta Karaṇi 8 breaths, Concentration *kaṇṭha*
Dhanura Āsana - 3 times or 3 breaths
Bhāradvāja Āsana – 3 breaths
Marīcya Āsana N°2 - 3 breaths
Sitting, Concentration *hṛdaya*
Bastri - 30 Cycles followed by
Nāḍī Śodhana - 2 Cycles A.K. 5 s or 10 s Concentration *hṛdaya*
- Repeat 3 times
Stay sitting, Concentration *hṛdaya* during more or less 2 minutes.

Example 46

Bastri - 30 Cycles or more followed by Śītalī B.K. 5 s
Or Kapāla Bhāti - 24 breaths Ujjāyi Anuloma 6 Cycles A.K. 5 s
Nāva Āsana - 3 breaths
Simha Āsana or Adho Mukha Padma Āsana - 3 breaths
Sarvānga Āsana - 12 breaths
Śīrṣa Āsana - 12 breaths; or Utthita Pāda Aṅguṣṭa Āsana - 6 breaths B.K. 5'
Variations of Sarvānga Āsana:
- Eka Pāda Sarvānga Āsana - 1 time alternating
- Eka Pāda Ākuñcana Āsana - 1 time alternating
- Dvi Pāda Ākuñcana Āsana - 1 time
- Prasārita Sarvānga Āsana - 1 time

Upaviṣṭa Koṇa Āsana complete - 2 breaths for each phase
Vimāna Āsana – 1 breath
Bastri - 30 Cycles followed by
Nāḍī Śodhana - 6 Cycles A.K. 5 s, Concentration *hṛdaya*
Stay sitting, Concentration *nāsāgra* during more or less 2 minutes.

Example 47

Ujjāyi Pratiloma - 4 Cycles
Jaṭhara Parivṛtti N°2 - 3 breaths
Sarvānga Āsana - 12 breaths
Śīrṣa Āsana - 12 breaths; or Viparīta Karaṇi - 8 breaths
Ardha Padma Hala Āsana – 3 breaths followed by Karṇa Pīḍa Āsana - 3 breaths
Adho Mukha Padma Āsana or Adho Mukha Baddha Koṇa Āsana - 3 breaths
Vajra Āsana, variations – 3 breaths followed by Uṣtra Āsana - 3 breaths
Ardha Matsyendra Āsana N°2 - 6 breaths
Bastri - 30 Cycles followed by
Nāḍī Śodhana - 6 Cycles, Inhalation Mūla to *kaṇṭha*, Exhalation Concentration *nābhi*
Stay sitting, Concentration *nābhi* during more or less 2 minutes.

Example 48

Kapāla Bhāti - 24 breaths followed by

Ujjāyi Anuloma - 6 Cycles A.K. 5 s

Utthita Pāda Aṅguṣṭa Āsana - 6 breaths B.K. 5 s, Concentration *bhrūmadhya*

Ūrdhva Mukha Śvāna Āsana - 3 breaths, Concentration *kaṇṭha*

Sarvānga Āsana - 12 breaths, Concentration *kaṇṭha*

Śīrṣa Āsana - 12 breaths; or Taṭāka Mudra - 12 breaths B.K. 5 s, Inhalation Concentration *mūla to śīrṣa*, Exhalation Concentration *kaṇṭha*

Sarvānga Āsana – 12 breaths, Concentration *kaṇṭha*

Baddha Koṇa Āsana - 12 breaths, Inhalation Mūla to *kaṇṭha*, Exhalation Mūla

Upaviṣṭa Koṇa Āsana - 6 breaths, Concentration *nābhi*

Bastri - 30 Cycles followed by

Nāḍī Śodhana - 2 Cycles (Sūrya Bhedana) Inhalation 5 or 8 s, Concentration *lalāṭa*, A.K. 10 or 16 s, Concentration *kaṇṭha*, Exhalation 10 s or 16 s, Concentration *hṛdaya*

- Repeat 3 times

Stay sitting, Concentration *hṛdaya* during more or less 2 minutes.

Example 49

Sit in Ananta Āsana

Kapāla Bhāti - 24 breaths followed by

Ujjāyi Viloma - 6 Cycles B.K. 5 s

Vīra Bhadra Āsana – 1 breath and then Garuḍa Āsana - 1 breath

Dhanura Āsana - 3 times

Sarvānga Āsana - 12 breaths

Śīrṣa Āsana - 12 breaths; or Utthita Pāda Aṅguṣṭa Āsana 6 breaths

Variations of Sarvānga Āsana:

- Baddha Koṇa Āsana in Sarvānga Āsana - 3 times
- Pārśva Eka Pāda Sarvānga Āsana - 2 times
- Ardha Padma Ākuñcana Āsana - 3 times

Viparīta Śalabha Āsana - 3 times

Ardha Matsyendra Āsana N° 2 - 3 breaths

Bastri - 30 Cycles followed by

Nāḍī Śodhana - 6 Cycles, A.K. 5 s Concentration *hṛdaya*

Example 50

Kapāla Bhāti - 24 breaths followed by

Ujjāyi Anuloma - 6 Cycles A.K. 5 s

Utthita Pārśva Koṇa Āsana - 3 breaths

Eka Pāda Dhanura Āsana - 3 times

Sarvānga Āsana - 12 breaths

Śīrṣa Āsana - 12 breaths; or Utthita Pāda Aṅguṣṭa Āsana - 6 breaths B.K. 5 s

Variations of Sarvānga Āsana:

- Dvi Pāda Ākuñcana Āsana - 1 time
- Ākuñcana Āsana Parivṛtti - 1 time
- Ardha Padma Ākuñcana Āsana - 3 times

Bheka Āsana - 3 times

Ākarṇa Dhanura Āsana - 3 breaths

Bastri - 30 Cycles or more followed by

Nāḍī Śodhana - 6 Cycles B.K. 5 s Concentration *lalāṭa*

Stay sitting, Concentration *lalāṭa* during more or less 2 minutes.

Example 51

Kapāla Bhāti - 24 Breaths followed by

Ujjāyi Pratiloma - 4 Cycles

Utthita Pārśva Utthāna Āsana - 3 breaths

Utthāna Pāda Āsana - 3 breaths

Sarvānga Āsana - 12 breaths

Śīrṣa Āsana - 12 breaths; or Utthita Pāda Aṅguṣṭa Āsana - 8 breaths B.K. 5 s

Variations of Sarvānga Āsana:

- Eka Pāda Sarvānga Āsana - 1 time alternating
- Eka Pāda Ākuñcana Āsana - 1 time alternating
- Dvi Pāda Ākuñcana Āsana - 1 time
- Ākuñcana Āsana Parivṛtti - 1 time
- Prasārita Sarvānga Āsana - 1 time

Bheka Āsana - 3 breaths

Parivṛtta Paścimatāna Āsana - 3 breaths on each side

Bastri - 30 Cycles or more followed by

Nāḍī Śodhana - 6 Cycles B.K. 5 s Concentration *hṛdaya*

Example 52

Ujjāyi Viloma - 6 Cycles B.K. 5 s, Inhalation Concentration *kaṇṭha*, Exhalation Concentration *nābhi*

Utthita Pāda Aṅguṣṭa Āsana - 6 breaths B.K. 5 s, Concentration *bhrūmadhya*

Dhanura Āsana - 3 breaths

Sarvānga Āsana - 12 breaths, Concentration *kaṇṭha*

Śīrṣa Āsana - 12 breaths, Concentration *kaṇṭha* or Supta Pāda Aṅguṣṭa Āsana - 6 breaths B.K 5 s

Baddha Koṇa Āsana - 8 breaths B.K 5 s Inhalation Concentration *mūla to śīrṣa*, Exhalation Concentration *nābhi*

Ardha Matsyendra Āsana N° 2 - 3 breaths

Bastri - 30 Cycles followed by

Nāḍī Śodhana (Abhyantara Vṛtti) - 6 Cycles, Inhalation 8 or 10 s, Concentration *nāsāgra* to *hṛdaya*, Exhalation 16 or 20 s, Concentration *hṛdaya*

Stay sitting, Concentration *hṛdaya* during more or less 2 minutes.

Example 53

Kapāla Bhāti - 24 breaths followed by

Ujjāyi Anuloma - 6 Cycles A.K. 5 s

Baddha Koṇa Āsana - 6 breaths B.K. 5 s

Eka Pāda Śalabha Āsana - 3 times alternating

Sarvānga Āsana - 12 breaths

Śīrṣa Āsana - 12 breaths B.K. 5 s; or Viparīta Karaṇi 8 breaths

Variations of Sarvānga Āsana:

- All 1 time each

Adho Mukha Padma Āsana – 3 breaths or Adho Mukha Baddha Koṇa Āsana – 3 breaths

Marīcya Āsana N°3 - 3 breaths

Bastri - 30 Cycles followed by

Nāḍī Śodhana - 6 Cycles, Exhalation longer than Inhalation

Stay sitting, Concentration *tāraka* during more or less 2 minutes.

Example 54

Kapāla Bhāti - 24 breaths followed by

Ujjāyi Anuloma - 6 Cycles A.K. 5 s

Matsya Āsana – 3 breaths or Supta Parvata Āsana – 6 breaths

Eka Pāda Dhanura Āsana - 2 times same leg

Sarvānga Āsana - 12 breaths

Śīrṣa Āsana - 12 breaths B.K. 4 s or Supta Pāda Aṅguṣṭa Āsana 6 breaths B.K. 5 s

Variations of Sarvānga Āsana:

- Eka Pāda Ākuñcana Āsana - 1 time alternating
- Dvi Pāda Ākuñcana Āsana - 1 time
- Ākuñcana Āsana Parivṛtti – 1 time
- Baddha Koṇa Āsana in Sarvānga Āsana – 3 times and then 3 breaths
- Pārśva Eka Pāda Sarvānga Āsana – 1 time

Marīcya Āsana N°3 – 3 breaths

Bastri - 30 Cycles followed by

Nāḍī Śodhana (Abhyantara Vṛtti) - 6 Cycles, Inhalation Concentration *nāsāgra* to *hṛdaya*, Exhalation Concentration *hṛdaya*

Stay sitting, Concentration *hṛdaya* during more or less 2 minutes.

Example 55

Taṭāka Mudra - 12 breaths, Inhalation Concentration Pāda *aṅguṣṭa to śīrṣa*, Exhalation Concentration *kaṇṭha*

Supta Parvata Āsana - 6 breaths B.K. 5 s, Concentration *kaṇṭha*

Sarvānga Āsana - 12 breaths, Concentration *kaṇṭha*

Śīrṣa Āsana - 12 breaths; or Mahā Mudra 6 breaths, Concentration *nābhi*

Sarvānga Āsana - 12 breaths, Concentration *kaṇṭha*

Simha Āsana - 3 breaths; or Adho Mukha Padma Āsana - 3 breaths, Concentration *bhrūmadhya*

Bhāradvāja Āsana - 3 breaths, Concentration *nāsāgra*

Ardha Matsyendra Āsana N°2 - 3 breaths, Concentration *kaṇṭha*

Bastri - 30 Cycles followed by

Nāḍī Śodhana (Abhyantara Vṛtti) - 6 Cycles, Inhalation Concentration *nāsāgra* to *hṛdaya*, Exhalation Concentration *hṛdaya*

Stay sitting, Concentration *hṛdaya* during more or less 2 minutes.

Example 56

Sitting in Ananta Āsana, Kapāla Bhāti - 16 breaths followed by Ujjāyi - 4 breaths Inhalation as long as possible

- Repeat 3 times

Vīra Bhadra Āsana - 1 breath followed by Garuḍa Āsana – 1 breath

Śalabha Āsana - 3 times

Śīrṣa Āsana - 12 breaths; or Supta Pāda Aṅguṣṭa Āsana - 12 breaths, Concentration *kaṇṭha*

Variations of Sarvānga Āsana:

- Eka Pāda Sarvānga Āsana - 1 time alternating
- Eka Pāda Ākuñcana Āsana - 1 time alternating
- Dvi Pāda Ākuñcana Āsana - 1 time
- Ākuñcana Āsana Parivṛtti - 1 time
- Pārśva Eka Pāda Sarvānga Āsana - 1 time
- Ardha Padma Ākuñcana Āsana - 3 times

Parivṛtta Paścimatāna Āsana - 3 breaths

Ākarṇa Dhanura Āsana - 3 breaths

Bastri - 30 Cycles or more followed by

Nāḍī Śodhana - 6 Cycles B.K. 5 s or 10 s, Concentration *hṛdaya*

Stay sitting, Concentration *tāraka* during more or less 2 minutes.

Example 57

Kapāla Bhāti - 24 breaths followed by

Ujjāyi Pratiloma - 4 Cycles

Supta Parivṛtta Pārśva Eka Pāda Aṅguṣṭa Āsana - 3 breaths

Sarvānga Āsana - 12 breaths

Śīrṣa Āsana - 12 breaths; or Utthita Pāda Aṅguṣṭa Āsana - 8 breaths B.K. 5 s

Variations de Sarvānga Āsana:

- Dvi Pāda Ākuñcana Āsana - 1 time
- Ākuñcana Āsana Parivṛtti - 1 time
- Prasārita Sarvānga Āsana - 1 time
- Pārśva Eka Pāda Sarvānga Āsana - 1 time
- Ardha Padma Ākuñcana Āsana - 3 times

Vasiṣṭha Āsana - 2 breaths

Ardha Matsyendra Āsana N° 2 - 6 times

Bastri - 30 Cycles or more followed by

Nāḍī Śodhana (Abhyantara Vṛtti) - 6 Cycles, Inhalation Concentration *nāsāgra* to *hṛdaya*, A.K. 5 or 10 s, Exhalation Concentration *hṛdaya*

Stay sitting, Concentration *hṛdaya* during more or less 2 minutes.

Example 58

Sit in Padma Āsana - Kapāla Bhāti - 12 breaths followed by Ujjāyi - 4 breaths B.K. 5 s, Concentration *nābhi*

- Repeat 3 times

Prasārita Pāda Utthāna Āsana - 6 breaths

Sarvānga Āsana - 12 breaths

Śīrṣa Āsana - 12 breaths; or Supta Pāda Aṅguṣṭa Āsana - 12 breaths B.K. 5 s

Sarvānga Āsana - 12 breaths

Uṣṭra Āsana - 3 breaths

Ardha Matsyendra Āsana N° 2 - 3 breaths

Parivṛtta Paścimatāna Āsana – 3 breaths

Bastri - 30 Cycles followed

Nāḍī Śodhana - 8 Cycles, Concentration *hṛdaya*

Stay sitting, Concentration *hṛdaya* during more or less 2 minutes.

8
Life Saving Sessions

For Hindus, the word soul is related and linked to God. To save one's soul is to free it from bondage, and thus achieve liberation from the cycle of rebirth (*Mokṣa*). My father was not sure that Westerners believed in the same notion of the soul. He knew that they were more attached to their lives than to their souls. Among the Hindus, although the fear of death exists, it is the interest for the liberation of the soul that weakens their fear.

Although my father has never imposed his religious beliefs on his students, he had the gift to encourage them to go to the Supreme. To inspire his Western students to discover and pursue their spiritual path, he called some of the practice sessions, **Life Saving Sessions**. For the Hindus, he called these sessions, *Ātma Śuddhi Krama* because Hindus knew the meaning of this Sanskrit expression.

Practice of these sessions helps awaken and develop the concept of the soul in Westerners.

Example 1

Sitting in Ananta Āsana - Concentration *nāsāgra* followed by Ujjāyi Anuloma - 6 Cycles

Baddha Koṇa Āsana - 6 breaths, Concentration *kaṇṭha*

Bhujaṃga Āsana - 3 times

Sarvānga Āsana - 12 breaths

Utthita Pāda Aṅguṣṭa Āsana - 6 breaths, Concentration *kaṇṭha*

Sarvānga Āsana - 6 breaths

Paścimatāna Āsana - 6 breaths, Concentration *kaṇṭha*

Ujjāyi Viloma - 6 Cycles

Example 2

Ujjāyi Viloma - 6 Cycles

Sitting, Concentration *nāsāgra*, normal breaths

Taṭāka Mudra - 8 breaths, Concentration *kaṇṭha*

Bhujaṃga Āsana - 3 breaths

Sarvānga Āsana - 12 breaths

Baddha Koṇa Āsana - 8 breaths, A.K. 5 s, Concentration *nāsāgra*

Sarvānga Āsana - 8 breaths

Paścimatāna Āsana - 8 breaths, Concentration *kaṇṭha*

Sitting, Concentration *tāraka* (more or less 1 minute)

Nāḍī Śodhana - 6 Cycles

Example 3

Śītalī 2nd Technique - 12 breaths, B.K. 5 s

Mahā Mudra - 6 breaths, B.K. 5 s Concentration *kaṇṭha*

Bhujaṃga Āsana - 3 breaths

Sarvānga Āsana - 12 breaths

Śīrṣa Āsana - 12 breaths; or Utthita Pāda Aṅguṣṭa Āsana - 6 breaths, B.K. 5 s

Sarvānga Āsana - 12 breaths

Bhujaṃga Āsana - 3 breaths, Concentration *bhrūmadhya*

Baddha Koṇa Āsana - 6 breaths, Concentration *nābhi*

Nāḍī Śodhana - 6 Cycles, Inhalation as long as possible, Concentration *nābhi*

Stay sitting, Concentration *nābhi* during more or less 2 minutes.

Example 4

Kapāla Bhāti - 24 breaths followed by

Ujjāyi Anuloma - 6 Cycles

Matsya Āsana - 3 breaths; or Supta Parvata Āsana 6 breaths, B.K. 5 s

Bhujaṃga Āsana - 3 breaths, Concentration *tāraka*

Sarvānga Āsana - 12 breaths

Śīrṣa Āsana - 6 or 12 breaths; or Baddha Koṇa Āsana - 12 breaths, Inhalation Concentration *kaṇṭha*, Exhalation Concentration *nābhi*

Sarvānga Āsana - 8 breaths

Mahā Mudra - 6 breaths, Concentration *kaṇṭha*

Paścimatāna Āsana - 8 breaths, Concentration *nābhi*

Khecarī Mudra – 6 breaths

Nāḍī Śodhana - 6 Cycles, A. K. 5 s Concentration *hṛdaya*

Stay sitting, Concentration *nābhi* during more or less 2 minutes.

Example 5

Kapāla Bhāti - 16 or 24 breaths followed by

Ujjāyi Anuloma - 8 Cycles

Matsya Āsana - 3 breaths; or Supta Parvata Āsana - 6 breaths, B.K. 5 s

Bhujaṃgi Mudra - 3 breaths, Concentration *bhrūmadhya*

Sarvānga Āsana - 12 breaths, Concentration *kaṇṭha*

Śīrṣa Āsana - 12 breaths, Concentration *kaṇṭha*; or Utthita Pāda Aṅguṣṭa Āsana - 8 breaths, B.K. 5 s Concentration *bhrūmadhya*

Sarvānga Āsana - 8 breaths, A. K. 3 s Concentration *kaṇṭha*

Khecarī Mudra

Bastri - 30 Cycles or more followed by

Nāḍī Śodhana - 6 Cycles, A. K. 5 s Concentration *hṛdaya*

Stay sitting, Concentration *hṛdaya* during more or less 2 minutes.

Example 6

Bastri - 30 Cycles or more followed by

Śītalī 2nd Technique - 12 Cycles

Taṭāka Mudra - 12 breaths, Inhalation Concentration *Pāda aṅguṣṭa to śīrṣa*, exhalation **Concentration *kaṇṭha***

Mahā Mudra - 6 breaths, B.K. 5 s, Concentration *kaṇṭha*

Bhujaṃgi Mudra - 3 breaths, Concentration *bhrūmadhya*

Sarvānga Āsana - 12 breaths

Śīrṣa Āsana - 12 breaths; or Utthita Pāda Aṅguṣṭa Āsana - 6 breaths, B.K. 5 s

Sarvānga Āsana - 12 breaths

Bhujaṃga Āsana - 3 breaths, Concentration *kaṇṭha*

Paścimatāna Āsana - 6 breaths, Inhalation Concentration *mūla to śīrṣa*, exhalation Concentration *kaṇṭha*

Nāḍī Śodhana - 6 Cycles, Inhalation as long as possible, Concentration *hṛdaya*

Stay sitting, Concentration *hṛdaya* during more or less 2 minutes.

Example 7

Bastri - 30 Cycles followed by

Śītalī 2nd Technique - 6 Cycles, A. K. 5 s

Mahā Mudra - 6 breaths, B. K. 5 s, Concentration *nāsāgra*

Śīrṣa Āsana - 12 breaths; or Baddha Koṇa Āsana (Back against the wall) - 12 breaths, Inhalation Concentration *mūla to śīrṣa*, exhalation Concentration *nābhi*

Sarvānga Āsana - 16 breaths

Bhujaṃgi Mudra - 3 breaths

Paścimatāna Āsana - 6 breaths, Concentration *kaṇṭha kūpa*

Khecarī Mudra - 6 breaths

Bastri - 30 Cycles or more followed by

Nāḍī Śodhana - 6 Cycles, B.K. 5 s, Concentration *hṛdaya*

Stay sitting and maintain mental state.

Example 8

Kapāla Bhāti - 24 breaths followed by

Ujjāyi Anuloma - 6 Cycles A.K. 5 s, Concentration *kaṇṭha*

Mahā Mudra - 6 breaths, B.K. 5 s, Concentration *kaṇṭha*

Bhujaṃga Āsana - 3 breaths

Sarvānga Āsana - 12 breaths

Śīrṣa Āsana - 12 breaths; or Utthita Pāda Aṅguṣṭa Āsana - 6 breaths, B.K. 5 s

Sarvānga Āsana - 12 breaths

Bhujaṃga Āsana - 3 breaths, Concentration *kaṇṭha*

Paścimatāna Āsana - 6 breaths, Inhalation Concentration *mūla to śīrṣa*, exhalation Concentration *kaṇṭha*

Khecarī Mudra - 6 breaths

Sūrya Bhedana (1st Technique) - 6 Cycles, Concentration Inhalation *hṛdaya*, exhalation *nābhi*

Stay sitting, Concentration *nābhi* during more or less 2 minutes.

Example 9

Aśvinī Mudra (First Technique)

Mahā Mudra - 6 breaths, B. K. 5 s, Concentration *nāsāgra*

Śīrṣa Āsana - 12 breaths; or Baddha Koṇa Āsana (back against the wall) - 12 breaths, Inhalation Concentration *mūla to śīrṣa*, exhalation Concentration *nābhi*

Sarvānga Āsana - 16 breaths

Bhujaṃgi Mudra - 3 breaths

Paścimatāna Āsana - 6 breaths, A.K. 5 s, Concentration *kaṇṭha kūpa*

Bastri - 30 Cycles or more followed by

Nāḍī Śodhana - 6 Cycles, B.K. 5 s, Concentration *hṛdaya*

Stay sitting and maintain mental state

Example 10

Mahā Bandha - 24 breaths, followed by

Ujjāyi Anuloma - 6 Cycles, A.K. 5 s (in Baddha Koṇa Āsana)

Paścimatāna Āsana - 6 breaths, A.K. 5 s, Concentration *nābhi*

Bhujaṃgi Mudra - 3 breaths

Sarvānga Āsana - 12 breaths

Śīrṣa Āsana - 12 breaths; or Baddha Koṇa Āsana - 8 breaths, Concentration *nābhi* (back against the wall)

Hala Āsana - 3 breaths

Mahā Mudra - 8 breaths, Concentration *nābhi*

Sit in Ananta Āsana, Concentration *lalāṭa* more or less 1 minute

Bastri - 30 Cycles followed by

Sūrya Bhedana (2nd Technique) - 3 Cycles

Bastri - 30 Cycles followed

Sūrya Bhedana (2ndTechnique) - 3 Cycles

Stay sitting, Concentration *lalāṭa* during more or less 2 minutes.

Example 11

Kapāla Bhāti - 24 breaths followed by

Ujjāyi Anuloma - 3 Cycles A.K. 5 s, Concentration *kaṇṭha*

Kapāla Bhāti - 24 breaths followed by

Ujjāyi Anuloma - 3 Cycles A.K. 5 s, Concentration *kaṇṭha*

Aśvinī Mudra (2nd Technique)

Bhujaṃga Āsana - 3 breaths

Sarvānga Āsana - 12 breaths

Śīrṣa Āsana - 12 breaths; or Baddha Koṇa Āsana - 12 breaths, Concentration *nābhi*

Hala Āsana - 3 breaths

Mahā Mudra - 8 breaths, Concentration *bhrūmadhya*

Khecarī Mudra - 6 breaths

Bastri - 30 Cycles followed by

Sama Vṛtti (Nāḍī Śodhana) - 3 Cycles

Bastri - 30 Cycles followed by

Sama Vṛtti (Nāḍī Śodhana) - 3 Cycles

Stay sitting, Concentration *hṛdaya* during more or less 2 minutes.

9
Examples of Prāṇāyāma Practice Sessions

Example 1

Taṭāka Mudra - 12 breaths, Concentration *kaṇṭha*

Ujjāyi Anuloma - 6 Cycles, Inhalation Concentration *kaṇṭha*

Ujjāyi Viloma - 6 Cycles, Exhalation Concentration *kaṇṭha*

Ujjāyi Viloma - 6 Cycles, Concentration *nābhi*

Nāḍī Śodhana - 6 Cycles, Concentration *nābhi*

Stay sitting, Concentration *nābhi* during more or less 1 minute.

Example 2

Taṭāka Mudra - 12 breaths

Śītalī 2nd Technique – 6 Cycles

Kapāla Bhāti - 24 breaths followed by

Ujjāyi Anuloma - 6 Cycles A.K. 3 s

Kapāla Bhāti - 24 breaths followed by

Ujjāyi Viloma - 6 Cycles B.K. 3 s

Nāḍī Śodhana - 6 Cycles (if possible, 8 Cycles)

Stay sitting, Concentration *kaṇṭha* during more or less 2 minutes.

Example 3

Vajra Āsana - 12 breaths, Concentration *nāsāgra*

Taṭāka Mudra - 12 breaths, Concentration *kaṇṭha*

Kapāla Bhāti - 12 breaths followed by

Ujjāyi Viloma - 6 Cycles, Inhalation Concentration *kaṇṭha*, Exhalation Concentration *nāsāgra*

Baddha Koṇa Āsana - 12 breaths, B.K. 5 s, Inhalation Concentration *bhrūmadhya*, Exhalation Concentration *nābhi*

Sitting in Padma Āsana, Concentration *nāsāgra* more or less 2 minutes. and then

Nāḍī Śodhana - 6 Cycles then,

Stay sitting more or less 2 minutes and maintain mental state.

Example 4

Vajra Āsana or Padma Āsana - 6 breaths, Concentration *nāsāgra*

Taṭāka Mudra - 12 breaths, Inhalation Concentration *mūla* to *kaṇṭha*, Exhalation Concentration *kaṇṭha*

Kapāla Bhāti - 32 breaths followed by

Ujjāyi Anuloma - 6 Cycles, Inhalation Concentration *kaṇṭha*, Exhalation Concentration *nābhi*

Vajra Āsana or Baddha Koṇa Āsana - 12 breaths B. K. 5 s, Inhalation Concentration *mūla* to *kaṇṭha*, Exhalation Concentration *nābhi*

Sitting in Padma Āsana Concentration *tāraka*

Nāḍī Śodhana - 6 Cycles, Inhalation Concentration *nābhi* to *kaṇṭha*, Exhalation Concentration *hṛdaya*

Nāḍī Śodhana - 6 Cycles Concentration *hṛdaya*

Stay sitting, Concentration *hṛdaya* during more or less 2 minutes.

Example 5

Kapāla Bhāti - 24 breaths followed by

Ujjāyi Anuloma - 6 Cycles A.K. 5 s

Sitting in Ananta Āsana - Kapāla Bhāti - 16 breaths followed by

Ujjāyi Viloma - 6 Cycles B.K. 3 s

Baddha Koṇa Āsana - 6 breaths, Concentration *kaṇṭha*

Sitting in Vajra Āsana or Padma Āsana, - 12 breaths Ujjāyi, Concentration *nāsāgra*

Nāḍī Śodhana - 6 Cycles

Sitting in Padma Āsana - 6 breaths Ujjāyi Concentration *bhrūmadhya*

Nāḍī Śodhana - 6 Cycles, Concentration *lalāṭa*

Stay sitting: more or less 2 minutes.

Example 6

Taṭāka Mudra - 12 breaths, B.K. 5 s, Inhalation Concentration *mūla to śīrṣa*, Exhalation Concentration *kaṇṭha*

Śītalī 2nd Technique - 12 breaths

Kapāla Bhāti - 24 breaths followed by

Ujjāyi Anuloma - 6 Cycles A.K. 5 s

Kapāla Bhāti - 24 breaths followed by

Ujjāyi Viloma - 6 Cycles B.K. 5 s, Inhalation Concentration *mūla* to *śīrṣa*, Exhalation Concentration *kaṇṭha*

Nāḍī Śodhana - 6 Cycles, Inhalation Concentration *mūla* to *śīrṣa*, Exhalation Concentration *hṛdaya*

Sitting, Concentration *hṛdaya* during more or less 1 minute.

Example 7

Taṭāka Mudra - 12 breaths, Inhalation Concentration *kaṇṭha*, Exhalation Concentration *nābhi*

Sitting in Padma Āsana or Vajra Āsana, Concentration *nāsāgra*

Kapāla Bhāti - 16 breaths followed by

Ujjāyi Viloma - 6 Cycles, Inhalation Concentration *bhrūmadhya*, Exhalation Concentration *kaṇṭha*

Kapāla Bhāti - 12 breaths followed by

Ujjāyi (Simple) - 4 breaths, Inhalation as long as possible, Concentration *kaṇṭha*

Kapāla Bhāti - 12 breaths followed by

Ujjāyi - 8 breaths, Inhalation as long as possible, Concentration *kaṇṭha kūpa*

Sitting in Padma Āsana, Concentration *lalāṭa*, followed by

Bastri - 30 Cycles followed by

Nāḍī Śodhana - 6 Cycles, Concentration *hṛdaya*

Stay sitting, Concentration *hṛdaya* during more or less 2 minutes.

Example 8

Taṭāka Mudra - 12 breaths, B.K. 5 s, Inhalation Concentration *mūla* to *śīrṣa*, Exhalation Concentration *kaṇṭha*

Kapāla Bhāti - 24 breaths followed by

Ujjāyi Anuloma - 6 Cycles A.K. 5 s

Kapāla Bhāti - 24 breaths followed by

Ujjāyi Viloma - 6 Cycles, B.K. 5 s, Inhalation Concentration *mūla* to *śīrṣa*, Exhalation Concentration *kaṇṭha*

Nāḍī Śodhana (Abhyantara Vṛtti) - 6 Cycles, Inhalation Concentration *nāsāgra* to *hṛdaya*, Exhalation Concentration *hṛdaya*

Sitting, Concentration *hṛdaya* more or less 1 minute

Example 9

Taṭāka Mudra - 12 breaths, B. K. 5 s, Inhalation Concentration *mūla* to *bhrūmadhya*, Exhalation Concentration *kaṇṭha*

Kapāla Bhāti - 24 breaths followed by

Ujjāyi Anuloma - 8 Cycles, A. K. 5 s (add 1 s of A.K. each week, up to 10 s)

Sit in Ananta Āsana,

Kapāla Bhāti - 16 breaths followed by

Ujjāyi Viloma - 8 Cycles B.K. 5 s

Bastri - 30 Cycles or more followed by

Nāḍī Śodhana (Abhyantara Vṛtti) - 6 Cycles, A.K 5 s, Inhalation *nāsāgra* to *hṛdaya*, Exhalation Concentration *hṛdaya*

Stay sitting, Concentration *hṛdaya* during more or less 2 minutes.

Example 10

Sitting in Ananta Āsana or Padma Āsana – 12 breaths Concentration *nāsāgra*

Kapāla Bhāti - 32 or 64 breaths followed by

Ujjāyi Anuloma - 8 Cycles, A.K. 5 s, Inhalation Concentration *kaṇṭha*, Exhalation Concentration *kaṇṭha kūpa*

Ujjāyi Pratiloma - 4 Cycles

Bastri - 30 or 60 Cycles followed by

Nāḍī Śodhana - 8 Cycles, A.K. 5 s or 10 s

Bastri - 30 or 60 Cycles followed by

Nāḍī Śodhana (Sūrya Bhedana) - 6 Cycles, Exhalation 2 times longer than Inhalation, Concentration *hṛdaya*

Nāḍī Śodhana - 6 Cycles

Stay sitting, Concentration *hṛdaya* during more or less 2 minutes.

Example 11

Kapāla Bhāti - 16 or 24 breaths followed by

Ujjāyi Anuloma - 6 Cycles B.K. 5 s

Taṭāka Mudra - 12 breaths, B.K. 5 s Inhalation Concentration *pāda aṅguṣṭa* to *śīrṣa*, Exhalation Concentration *kaṇṭha*

Sitting in Ananta Āsana - Ujjāyi 12 breaths, Inhalation Concentration *mūla* to *śīrṣa*, Exhalation Concentration *nāsāgra*

Sitting Concentration *nāsāgra* (more or less 1 minute)

Bastri - 30 Cycles followed by

Sūrya Bhedana (Nāḍī Śodhana) - 3 Cycles, Inhalation 5 s or 8 s, Concentration *kaṇṭha kūpa*, Exhalation 10 s or 16 s, Concentration *hṛdaya*

- Repeat 2 times

Bastri - 30 Cycles followed by

Nāḍī Śodhana - 6 Cycles, Concentration *hṛdaya*

Stay sitting Concentration *hṛdaya* during more or less 2 minutes.

Example 12

Bastri - 30 Cycles or more followed by

Śītalī - 12 breaths, B.K. 5 s

Taṭāka Mudra - 12 breaths, B.K. 5 s Inhalation Concentration *pāda aṅguṣṭa* to *śīrṣa*, Exhalation Concentration *kaṇṭha*

Sitting in Ananta Āsana, - Ujjāyi 12 breaths, Inhalation Concentration *mūla* to *śīrṣa*, Exhalation Concentration *nāsāgra*

Sitting Concentration *tāraka* (more or less 1 minute)

Bastri - 30 Cycles followed by

Sūrya Bhedana (Nāḍī Śodhana) - 3 Cycles, Inhalation 5 or 8 s, Concentration *kaṇṭha kūpa*, Exhalation 10 or 16 s, Concentration *hṛdaya*

- Repeat 2 times

Bastri - 30 Cycles followed by

Nāḍī Śodhana - 6 Cycles, Concentration *hṛdaya*

Stay sitting, Concentration *hṛdaya* during more or less 2 minutes.

Example 13

Kapāla Bhāti - 16 or 24 breaths followed by

Ujjāyi Viloma - 6 Cycles B.K. 5 s

Taṭāka Mudra - 12 breaths, B.K. 5 s, Inhalation Concentration *pāda aṅguṣṭa* to *śīrṣa*, Exhalation Concentration *kaṇṭha*

Sitting in Vajra Āsana – Ujjāyi 12 breaths, Inhalation Concentration *mūla* to *śīrṣa*, Exhalation Concentration *nāsāgra*

Sitting, Concentration *tāraka* (1 minute)

Bastri - 30 Cycles followed by

Sūrya Bhedana (Nāḍī Śodhana) - 3 Cycles, Inhalation 5 or 8 s, Concentration *kaṇṭha kūpa*, Exhalation 10 or 16 s, Concentration *hṛdaya*

- Repeat 2 times

Bastri - 30 Cycles followed by

Nāḍī Śodhana - 6 Cycles, Concentration *hṛdaya*

Stay sitting, Concentration *tāraka* during more or less 2 minutes.

10
Examples of Practice Sessions on the Full Moon and New Moon days

Note: Do not lie on the back at the end of these sessions.

Example 1 (the day of the New Moon)

Facing the east:
- Bastri - 30 Cycles followed by
- Nāḍī Śodhana - 6 Cycles

Facing the south:
- Bastri - 30 Cycles followed by
- Nāḍī Śodhana - 6 Cycles

Facing the east:
- Bastri - 30 Cycles followed by
- Nāḍī Śodhana - 6 Cycles, Concentration *hṛdaya*

Facing the south:
- Standing and prayer to the ancestors

Example 2 (the day of the New Moon)

Facing the east:
- Bastri - 30 Cycles followed by
- Nāḍī Śodhana - 6 Cycles

Facing the south:
- Bastri - 30 Cycles followed by
- Nāḍī Śodhana - 6 Cycles

Repeat 2 times
Facing the east:
- Bastri - 30 Cycles followed by
- Nāḍī Śodhana - 6 Cycles, Concentration *hṛdaya*

Facing the south
- Prayer to the ancestors

Example 3 (the day of the Full Moon)

Facing the east:
Prayer
Bastri - 30 Cycles followed by
Nāḍī Śodhana - 6 Cycles, Concentration *hṛdaya*
Nāḍī Śodhana 6 Cycles (Sūrya Bhedana 1st Technique), Inhalation 5 s or 8 s, Concentration *nāsāgra*, Exhalation 10 s or 16 s Concentration *hṛdaya*
Bastri - 30 Cycles followed by
Nāḍī Śodhana - 6 Cycles, Concentration *hṛdaya*
Bastri - 30 Cycles followed by
Nāḍī Śodhana - 6 Cycles
Prayer

Example 4 (the day of the full moon)

Facing the east
Prayer
Bastri - 30 Cycles followed
Abhyantara Vṛtti - 6 Cycles
Sama Vṛtti - 6 Cycles
Bastri - 30 Cycles followed by
Nāḍī Śodhana - 6 Cycles, Concentration *lalāṭa*
Bastri - 30 Cycles followed by
Nāḍī Śodhana - 6 Cycles, Concentration *hṛdaya*
Prayer

11
Insight into my father's practice sessions

Kapāla Bhāti - 32 breaths

Ujjāyi Anuloma - 6 Cycles A.K. 5 s, Concentration *kaṇṭha*

Utthita Pāda Aṅguṣṭa Āsana - 6 breaths B.K. 5 s, Concentration *bhrūmadhya*

Supta Parvata Āsana - 6 breaths B.K. 5 s, Inhalation Concentration *mūla* to *kaṇṭha*, Exhalation Concentration *kaṇṭha*

Bhujaṃga Āsana - 3 breaths, Concentration *bhrūmadhya*

Sarvānga Āsana - 12 breaths, Concentration *kaṇṭha*

Śīrṣa Āsana - 12 breaths, Concentration *lalāṭa*

Ardha Padma Hala Āsana – 3 breaths

Hala Āsana – 3 breaths

Karṇa Pīḍa Āsana - 3 breaths

Adho Mukha Padma Āsana - 3 breaths, Concentration *kaṇṭha*

Ardha Baddha Padma Paścimatāna Āsana - 3 breaths, Inhalation Concentration: *nābhi*, Exhalation Concentration *kaṇṭha*

Baddha Koṇa Āsana - 12 breaths, Inhalation Concentration *mūla* to *śīrṣa*, Exhalation Concentration Mūla

Bastri - 60 Cycles

Nāḍī Śodhana - 6 Cycles, Abhyantara Vṛtti

Kapāla Bhāti - 32 breaths
Ujjāyi Anuloma - 6 Cycles, B.K. 5 s, Concentration *nābhi*
Bhagīratha Āsana - 6 breaths, Concentration *nāsāgra*
Ardha Padma Apāna Āsana - 3 breaths B.K. 5 s
Eka Pāda Dhanura Āsana - 3 times
Sarvānga Āsana - 12 breaths, Concentration *kaṇṭha*
Śīrṣa Āsana - 12 breaths, Concentration *lalāṭa*
Ūrdhva Mukha Padma Āsana – 3 breaths
Piṇḍa Āsana - 3 breaths
Dhanura Āsana - 3 breaths, Concentration *kaṇṭha*
Ardha Matsyendra Āsana N° 1 - 3 breaths, Concentration *nāsāgra*
Ākarṇa Dhanura Āsana - 3 breaths, Concentration *tāraka*
Bastri - 60 Cycles
Nāḍī Śodhana - 6 Cycles, Abhyantara Vṛtti

Kapāla Bhāti - 32 breaths
Ujjāyi Viloma - 6 Cycles, B.K. 5 s, Inhalation Concentration *nābhi*, Exhalation Concentration *mūla*
Vīra Bhadra Āsana - 3 breaths, Concentration *tāraka*
Utthāna Pāda Āsana - 3 breaths, Concentration *kaṇṭha*
Śvāna Āsana - 1 breath
Sarvānga Āsana - 12 breaths, Concentration *kaṇṭha*
Śīrṣa Āsana - 12 breaths, Concentration *lalāṭa*
Variations of Sarvānga Āsana
- Eka Pāda Sarvānga Āsana – 1 breath
- Ardha Padma Ākuñcana Āsana – 1 breath
- Pārśva Eka Pāda Sarvānga Āsana – 1 breath
- Ākuñcana Āsana – 1 breath

Śalabha Āsana - 3 breaths
Marīcya Āsana N° 2 - 3 breaths, Concentration *nāsāgra*
Bastri - 60 Cycles
Nāḍī Śodhana - 6 Cycles, Abhyantara Vṛtti

11. INSIGT INTO MY FATHER'S PRACTICE SESSIONS

Kapāla Bhāti - 64 breaths
Ujjāyi Anuloma - 6 Cycles A.K. 10 s
Bastri - 30 Cycles
Nāḍī Śodhana (Sama Vṛtti) - 8 Cycles, Concentration *hṛdaya*
Bastri - 60 Cycles
Sūrya Bhedana (Nāḍī Śodhana) - 6 Cycles, Inhalation 1 *Gāyatrī*[1], Antah Kumbhaka 4 *Gāyatrī* Exhalation 2 *Gāyatrī*, Concentration *hṛdaya*
Bastri - 60 Cycles
Nāḍī Śodhana - 6 Cycles, Concentration *hṛdaya* (mental recitation of *Viṣṇu Gāyatrī*[2] during Nāḍī Śodhana)

Bastri - 60 Cycles
Śītalī 12 Breaths
Utthita Trikoṇa Āsana N° 2 - 3 Breaths
Supta Parivṛtta Pārśva Eka Pāda Āsana - 3 breaths
Bhujaṃga Āsana variation - 3 breaths, Concentration *kaṇṭha*
Sarvānga Āsana - 12 breaths, Concentration *kaṇṭha*
Śīrṣa Āsana - 12 breaths, Concentration *lalāṭa*
Sarvānga Āsana -12 breaths, Concentration *kaṇṭha*
Adho Mukha Padma Āsana - 3 breaths, Concentration *kaṇṭha*
Uṣṭra Āsana - 3 breaths
Bhāradvāja Āsana - 3 breaths, Concentration *kaṇṭha*
Bastri - 60 Cycles
Nāḍī Śodhana - 6 Cycles, Abhyantara Vṛtti

Kapāla Bhāti - 64 breaths
Ujjāyi Anuloma - 8 Cycles A.K. 5 s
Matsya Āsana - 3 breaths, Concentration *kaṇṭha*
Bhujaṃga Āsana - 3 breaths, Concentration *bhrūmadhya*
Sarvānga Āsana - 16 breaths, Concentration *kaṇṭha*
Śīrṣa Āsana - 16 breaths B.K. 5 s, Concentration *lalāṭa*
Sarvānga Āsana - 16 breaths, Concentration *kaṇṭha*
Mahā Mudra - 12 breaths, B.K. 5 s, Concentration *bhrūmadhya*
Paścimatāna Āsana - 12 breaths, B.K. 5 s Inhalation Concentration *bhrūmadhya*, Exhalation Concentration *nābhi*
Nāḍī Śodhana Abhyantara Vṛtti - 6 Cycles, A. K. 5 s

---

[1] *Om bhur bhuva swaha, tat savitur vareṇnyam bhargo devasya dhīmahi, dhiyo yo nah prachodayat.*
[2] *Om Nārāyaṇnāya vidmahe vāsudevaya dhīmahi tanno Viṣṇuh prachodayat, Om Namo Nārāyaṇāya.*

12
The Fruits of Āsanas

The '**fruits**' shown for the *Āsanas* are the result of the observations that my father, made in his teachings from 1936 until his departure from this world in 1989.

I received this teaching from my father and I have used the same instructions since I began to teach, in 1957, instructions that I continue to use today. I also noted that in practising the *Āsanas*, whether in India or Europe, my students benefited from the same '**fruits**' as those that were indicated by my father.

These '**fruits**' are not the result of scientific research, but are the results of a great number of years of experience based on the teachings of the traditional works of Yoga, written in Sanskrit using the terminology of Indian medicine.

I allowed myself some adjustments in this traditional language to favour understanding and make it accessible to 21st century readers who are unfamiliar with the technical terms of the Indian languages.

I offer my apologies in advance for any errors committed in the use of technical terms and I appeal to the understanding of specialists.

The '**fruits**' here revealed are not exhaustive. I am certain the *Āsanas* presented in this work have a much larger ray of action than the technical specifications indicated.

For the good of all, it would be interesting if a scientific study were conducted based on these parameters and made available to all.

Several of my students have voluntarily offered their support in appearing in the photos published in this book. When these photos were taken, some of them suffered disabilities due to their state of health or the result of an accident. My aim is to show to a great number of people that these *Āsanas* are within everybody's reach—men, women, children, young men, young women, elderly people, pregnant women, and those with physical limits.

However, I strongly recommend the readers to seek the advice of their doctor before practising Yoga. I advise against practising Yoga without the counsel of an experienced Yoga teacher.

13
Āsana Sheets

Adho Mukha Baddha Koṇa Āsana

Adha (Adho) = facing down, *mukha* = the face, *baddha* = to tie, *koṇa* = the angle, the pelvis.

Fig. 35 Adho Mukha Baddha Koṇa Āsana (Estelle)

Technique

Lie down on the stomach, forehead on the floor, palms of the hands on the floor at the same level as the lowest ribs, fingers directed forwards, elbows bent as close as possible to the body, legs together and held taut, eyes closed. Spread the two legs completely keeping them taut. Bend the legs and bring the soles of the feet one against the other, keep the feet on the floor or slightly raised.

Inhalation: Taking support on the hands while stretching the arms, raise the head, the shoulders and the chest, pelvis, and the top part of the thighs. Keep the knees on the floor and lower the thighs. Try to put your feet on the floor.

Do 3 *Ujjāyi* breaths.

Exhalation: Bend the arms keeping the elbows together, and progressively lower the thighs, pelvis, chest, shoulders and finally, the forehead to the floor. Stretch your legs, join them, and then turn over on to your back.

Take rest.

Fruits

- Makes supple the spinal, cervical and dorsal columns, helps to Rectifies dorsal kyphosis.
- Makes supple all the pelvis joints and the coxofemoral joints, helps to open the pelvis and helps easy delivery.
- Supports the perineum and tones up the pelvic floor.
- Supports and improves renal functions.
- Lengthens inhalation time, increases respiratory capacity and pulmonary compliance.
- Improves gas exchange at the level of the pulmonary alveolus.
- Improves pulmonary functions.
- Helps digestion, intestinal absorption and intestinal elimination, and prevents constipation.

Adho Mukha Padma Āsana

Adha (Adho) = facing down, *mukha* = the face, *padma* = the lotus.

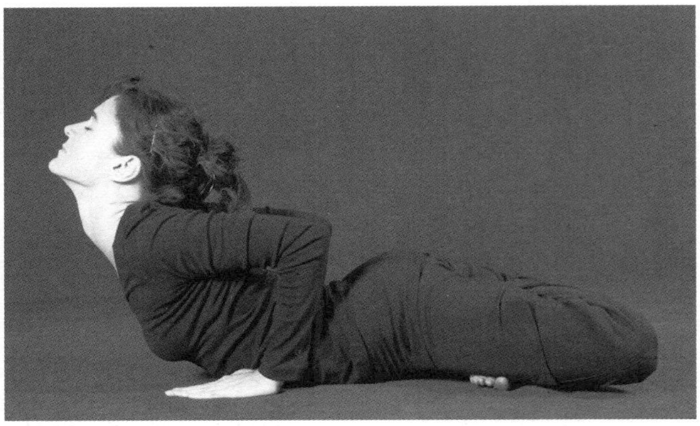

Fig. 36 Adho Mukha Padma Āsana (Stéphanie)

Technique

Do Padma Āsana. Stretch the arms out in front of you and bend the chest in order to place the hands approximately 80 centimetres on the floor in front of the knees, fingers directed forwards. Rise up on the knees then lower the pelvis towards the floor in order to lie on the stomach. Place your forehead and hands on the floor at the level of the lower ribs.

Inhalation: Taking support on the hands and stretching the arms without spreading the elbows, raise the head, the shoulders and the upper part of the chest keeping the navel on the floor and pressing the pelvis to the floor.

Exhalation: Bend the arms keeping the elbows together, and progressively lower the pelvis, the chest, the shoulders and the forehead to the floor.

Do 3 times or 3 *Ujjāyi* breaths.

Taking support on the hands, go back to the sitting position and undo Padma Āsana or undo Padma Āsana while lying on the stomach, then turn over on your back.

Take rest.

Concentration

- *Bhrūmadhya.*

Fruits

- Makes supple the spinal, cervical and dorsal columns, helps to Rectifies dorsal kyphosis.
- Makes supple all the pelvic joints, facilitates delivery and reduces the pain sensation in delivery.
- Stabilizes the hypophysis (pituitary) gland's hormonal secretions.
- Stabilizes the thyroid gland's hormonal secretions.
- Restores the ovarian functions.
- Improves the gas exchange in the pulmonary alveolus.
- Helps the digestion, and intestinal absorption.
- Tones up the muscles of the abdominal organs and prevents their prolapses.
- Improves the arterial circulation of heart and brain.
- Improves venous circulation in the lower limbs, prevents and reduces varicose veins.
- Promotes mental attention.

Adho Mukha Padma Āsana, variation

Adha (Adho) = facing down, *mukha* = the face.

Fig. 37 Adho Mukha Padma Āsana, variation (Heike)

Technique

Lie down on your stomach with your forehead touching the floor, the palms of the hands on the floor at the level of the lowest ribs, fingers directed forwards, the elbows folded and kept as close as possible to the body, legs joined and taut, eyes closed. Spread the legs taut, then flex the legs and cross them. If possible, turn the inner sides of the feet to the floor.

Inhalation: Taking support on the hands and stretching the arms, raise the head, the shoulders and the chest, the pelvis and the upper part of the thighs. Keep the knees on the floor and lower the thighs.

Exhalation: Bend the arms without separating the elbows and progressively lie down the pelvis, the thighs, the chest, the shoulders and finally, the forehead on the floor.

Do 3 times or 3 *Ujjāyi* breaths.

Uncross and stretch your legs, then bring them together. Turn over on your back

Take rest.

Concentration

- *Kaṇṭha, bhrūmadhya.*

Fruits

- Makes supple the spinal, cervical and dorsal columns, helps to Rectifies dorsal kyphosis.
- Makes supple all the pelvic joints, facilitates delivery and reduces the pain sensation in delivery.
- Stabilizes the hypophysis (pituitary) gland's hormonal secretions.
- Stabilizes the thyroid gland's hormonal secretions.
- Restores the ovarian functions.
- Improves the gas exchange in the pulmonary alveolus.
- Helps the digestion, and intestinal absorption.
- Tones up the muscles of the abdominal organs and prevents their prolapses.
- Improves the arterial circulation of heart and brain.
- Improves venous circulation in the lower limbs, prevents and reduces varicose veins.
- Promotes mental attention.

Adho Mukha Śvāna Āsana

Śvāna = the dog, the cat, the feline, *adha (adho)* = facing down, *mukha* = the face.

Fig. 38 Adho Mukha Śvāna Āsana (Françoise)

Fig. 39 Adho Mukha Śvāna Āsana (Muriel)

Technique

Lie down on the stomach, forehead on the floor, the palms of the hands on the floor at the level of the lowest ribs, fingers directed forwards, the elbows bent as close as possible to the body, legs joined and taut, the toes upturned, the eyes closed.

Inhalation: Taking support on the hands and stretching the arms, raise the pelvis and lift the buttocks up. Bend the trunk towards your stretched legs. Place your head between your stretched arms, the neck extended. Keep the legs taut, pressing the heels towards the floor.

Do 3 to 6 *Ujjāyi* breaths.

Exhalation: Raise the head, bring the chest forward again, without moving the elbows apart. Bend the arms and lower the body gently to the floor.

Turn over and rest on your back.

Concentration

- *Kaṇṭha.*

Fruits

- Rectifies the static position of the spine, maintains intervertebral spaces and prevents slipped discs. Strengthens muscles located all along the spinal column. Makes supple the shoulder joints and the entire spinal column. Develops rib cage volume.
- Develops the muscles of the legs and the arms.
- Harmonizes peristaltic movement of the alimentary canal; improves intestinal elimination and prevents constipation.
- Improves the venous and lymphatic circulations.
- Develops respiratory capacity.
- Stimulates diuresis.

Ākarṇa Dhanura Āsana

Karṇa = ear. Prefix 'a' expresses proximity, *dhanus* = bow. In this Āsana, the body looks like an archery.

Fig. 40 Ākarṇa Dhanura Āsana (Claire)

Technique

Sit in Daṇḍa Āsana. Hold the big toes with your thumbs, the index and middle finger of each hand.

Exhalation: With the help of your left hand, raise the left foot. Bring the left foot to the head until the left heel is close to the left ear. At the same time, pull the left elbow backward to the level of the left shoulder. Do not lose hold of the right big toe and keep the right leg stretched out. Keep the head upright and look straight ahead of you.

Do 3 *Ujjāyi* breaths.

Inhalation: Bring the left foot back next to the right foot

Do the Āsana with the right foot the same way.

Take rest.

Concentration

- *Pāda aṅguṣṭa* (the big toe of the stretched leg), *tāraka*.

Fruits

- Develops the muscles of the arms, legs and the lower abdomen. Strengthens the coxofemoral joints.
- Stabilizes all the secretions of the alimentary canal.
- Reduces dispersion due to the hyperactivity of the sense perceptions.
- Improves mental concentration.

Ananta Āsana

Ananta = the infinite: name of the primordial snake. It is the Āsana of prayer and meditation. It is also the Āsana of Vedic rituals.

Fig. 41 Ananta Āsana
(Claire)

Technique

Do Daṇḍa Āsana. Bend the right knee, take the right foot in the hands and place it on the middle of the left thigh. Bend the left knee, take the left ankle in the hands and place the left foot under the right thigh. Lower the chin and straighten the spine so it is perfectly straight. Bend the arms, join the palms of the hands and bring them to the breastbone, put your thumbs against the sternum, fingers directed upwards towards the sky. Lower the elbows.

Do 12 *Ujjāyi* breaths.

Relax the hands, stretch the legs on the floor and bring the feet together. Take rest.

Reminder: If you are using this Āsana for prayer and meditation, do not lie on your back.

Note that there is Yoga another version of Ananta Āsana in Yoga, which will not be described here.

Concentration

- *Nāsāgra, kaṇṭha, bhrūmadhya, tāraka, hṛdaya.*

Fruits

- The perfect Āsana for prayer and meditation.

Apāna Āsana or Pavana Mukta Āsana

Apāna = to reject, eliminate.

In Indian medicine, *Apāna* is a function that manages all the body's eliminations (renal, intestinal, sebaceous, child bearing, death...). This Āsana, therefore, promotes the different elimination functions. It is also named *Pavana Mukta Āsana. Pavana* = wind (or intestinal gas), *mukta* = free. It is an Āsana that facilitates the evacuation of intestinal gas.

Fig. 42 Apāna Āsana
(Stéphanie)

Technique

Lie on the back, legs joined, feet joined, arms along the body, the palms of the hands on the floor, chin lowered, and eyes closed. Bend both knees and fold them on to the stomach. Put your arms around your legs and intertwine your fingers around the legs below the knees.

Do 3 or 6 *Ujjāyi* breaths.

Relax the arms and rest them along the body, palms of the hands on the floor. Stretch out the legs on the floor and join the feet.

Take rest.

Fruits

- Improves intestinal elimination, prevents constipation and reduces intestinal meteorism.

Ardha Baddha Padma Paścimatāna Āsana

Ardha = half, *baddha* = tied, *padma* = lotus, *paścima* = west, *utthāna* = to spread, extension. This is Paścimatāna Āsana with one leg in Padma Āsana.

Fig. 43 Ardha Baddha Padma Paścimatāna Āsana

(Renée)

Technique

Do Daṇḍa Āsana. Bend the right knee, take the right foot in the hands and put it on the high part of the left thigh, with the heel close to the navel. Put your right arm behind the back to hold the right foot with the right hand. To make it easier to hold it, turn the chest towards the right and then hold the right foot. Bring the chest around to face the left leg. Bend the chest forward and hold the big toe of the left foot with the left hand. Straighten up the back, draw in the chin and stretch the neck.

Do 3 or 6 *Ujjāyi* breaths.

Relax the hands, stretch out the right leg. Do the Āsana with the left leg. Relax the hands, stretch out the left leg.

Take rest.

Concentration

- *Kaṇṭha, nāsāgra, nābhi.*

Fruits

- Tones up the muscles of the abdominal organs and prevents their prolapses.
- Improves intestinal absorption and elimination, prevents constipation.
- Stimulates all of the hepatic functions.
- Promotes elimination of gallstones.
- Balances the endocrine secretions of the gonads.
- Stabilizes pancreas endocrine secretions.
- Prevents and reduces prostatic hypertrophy.
- Helps to absorb uterine fibromas.
- Improves the venous and lymphatic circulations.
- Improves renal functions. Stimulates diuresis.
- Supports the functions of spleen.
- Supports and tones up myocardium.
- After delivery, reduces tissue oedema and strengthens the uterine wall.
- Promotes mental attention.

Ardha Candra Āsana

Ardha = half, *candra* = moon. *Ardha Candra Āsana* was also used to prepare the physical body for long-lasting rituals demanding corporal immobility.

Fig. 44 Ardha Candra Āsana

(Pascal)

Technique

Stand up, feet joined, arms along the body. Bend the left knee resting the sole of the left foot, as high as possible on the inside of the right thigh. Put the heel against the perineum. Raise the arms laterally above the head; join the palms of the hands. Gaze at a point in front of you.

Do 3 *Ujjāyi* breaths.

Lower the arms and place your left foot on the floor.

Do the Āsana with the right leg.

Lower the arms and place the right foot on the floor.

Take rest.

Concentration

- *Nāsāgra.*

Fruits

- Increases the sense of balance.
- Promotes mental attention.

Ardha Matsyendra Āsana N° 1

This is one of the most important sitting Āsanas. *Ardha* = half, Matsyendra = proper name. *Matsya* = fish, *Indra* = name of a god. Matsyendra is the father of Hatha Yoga. As Lord Shiva was revealing the secret of yoga to his spouse Pārvathi, without their knowledge, a fish was listening attentively to the teaching of Shiva. This latter got angry and wanted to banish the fish but Pārvathi intervened on its behalf. Shiva blessed the fish granting him the possibility of transmitting the secret of Hatha Yoga to humanity in his next life. So a child with one ear with a hole, who came into the world in Nepal who was called Gorakha Nātha or Goraksha Nātha. *Go* = cow, ear, *rakha* = having hole, *nātha* = devoted to gods. He taught the secret of Hatha Yoga. A clairvoyant yogi passing by looking at him said, 'You are the fish that listened to Shiva,' and he changed his name to Matsyendra.

Fig. 45 Ardha Matsyendra Āsana N° 1

(Chantal)

Fig. 46 Ardha Matsyendra Āsana N° 1

(Brigitte and Renée)

Technique

Do Daṇḍa Āsana. Bend the right knee, hold the right foot in the hands and put it on the high part of the left thigh, heel close to the navel. Turn the chest well to the left, place your left arm behind your back. Hold the right thigh with the left hand. While keeping the chest turned to the left, bend the trunk forward. Stretch the right arm towards the left leg. Turn the forearm and the right wrist in order to have the thumb pointing down towards the floor and the little finger pointing up. Then hold the outer side of the left foot with the right hand. Turn the head to the right and straighten up the back.

Do 3 *Ujjāyi* breaths.

Relax the arms, bring back the chest to the front and stretch the right leg out in front of you.

Do the Āsana on the other side.

Relax the arms, bring back the chest to the front and stretch the left leg out in front of you.

Take rest.

Concentration

- *Kaṇṭha, nāsāgra.*

Fruits

- Makes supple the shoulder joints.
- Rectifies dorsal kyphosis, lumbar hyperlordosis and scoliosis.
- Strengthens coxofemoral joints.
- Promotes digestion, absorption and intestine elimination, prevents constipation.
- Stimulates all hepatic functions.
- Promotes elimination of gallstones.
- Improves respiratory capacity and pulmonary functions.
- Restores the ovarian functions, prevents and helps to reduce ovarian cysts.
- Prevents and reduces signs of menopause.
- Stabilizes hormonal secretions of the pituitary gland.
- Stabilizes pancreas endocrine secretions.
- Helps to absorb uterine fibromas.
- After delivery, reduces oedema of tissue and strengthens the uterine wall.
- Supports and tones up the myocardium.
- Helps to restore the different phases of sleep.
- Stabilizes the vegetative nervous system.
- Helps to dissipate mental confusion, provides clarity of the mind.
- Improves the functions of sense perceptions.

Ardha Matsyendra Āsana N° 2

Fig. 47 Ardha Matsyendra Āsana N° 2, right side

(Estelle)

Technique

Do Daṇḍa Āsana. Tuck up the right leg underneath the left leg, knee on the floor to bring the right foot to the outside of the left buttock. Bend the left knee in order to put the sole of the left foot to the right of the right knee. Hold the left thigh against the chest. Turn the chest to the left in order to take the thorax completely out of the left thigh. Pass your right arm around the outside of the left knee and hold the inner side of the left foot. Straighten the back while still keeping the chest turned to the left. Put your left arm behind your back and hold the right thigh. Turn the head to the right and raise the chin.

Do 3 *Ujjāyi* breaths.

Relax the arms, bring the chest back to the middle and let your legs stretch out straight in front of you.

Do the Āsana on the other side.

Relax the arms, bring the chest back to the middle and let your legs stretch out straight in front of you.

Take rest.

Concentration

- *Nāsāgra, bhrūmadhya.*

Fruits

- Stabilizes all endocrine secretions.
- Supports cardiac functions.
- Improves assimilation and helps tissue construction.
- Helps to establish a conception in utero.

Ardha Nāva Āsana

Ardha = half, *nāva* = boat, ship.

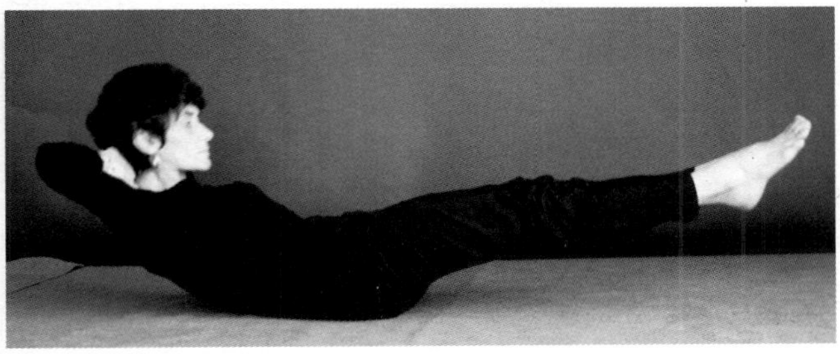

Fig. 48 Ardha Nāva Āsana
(Renée)

Technique

Lie on the back, legs joined, feet joined, arms along the body, the palms of the hands on the floor, chin lowered, and eyes closed. Interlock the fingers, put the hands behind the back of the neck and separate the elbows.

Exhalation: Simultaneously raise the head, the chest and the legs. Keep the lumbar region balanced. Keep the elbows separated.

Do 3 times or 3 *Ujjāyi* breaths.

Inhalation: Rest the legs, the chest and the head on the floor simultaneously.

Take rest.

Fruits

- Rectifies the static position of the spine, maintains intervertebral spaces and prevents slipped discs.
- Strengthens and develops the abdomen and lower abdomen muscles.
- Improves abdominal organ posture and prevents their prolapses.
- Improves intestinal digestion and elimination, prevents constipation and reduces intestinal meteorism.
- Prevents and helps to reduce ovarian cysts.
- Supports venous circulation.

Ardha Padma Apāna Āsana

Ardha = half, *padma* = lotus, *apāna* = reject, get rid of, eliminate.

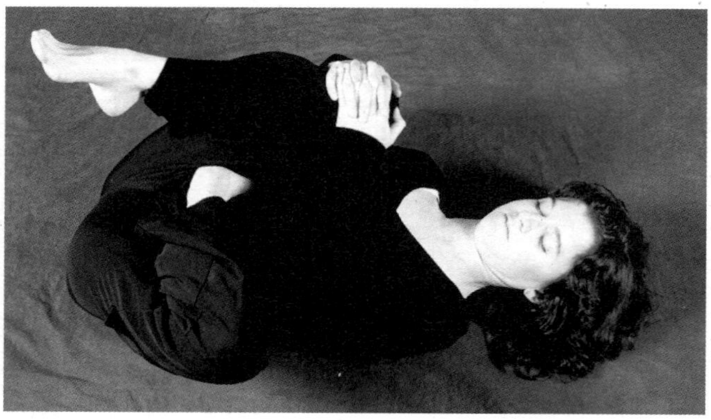

Fig. 49 Ardha Padma Apāna Āsana, left side (Stéphanie)

Technique

Lie on the back, legs joined, feet joined, arms along the body, the palms of the hands on the floor, the chin lowered, and eyes closed. Bend the right knee, hold the right foot in the hands and put it on the high part of the left thigh, the heel close to the navel. Bend the left knee and bring the thigh towards the stomach. Put the arms around the left leg. Interlock the fingers on the left leg or interlock the fingers on the left knee and hold it.

Do 3 Ujjāyi breaths.

Relax the fingers, rest the arms on the floor along the body. Stretch the legs out on the floor and bring the feet together.

Do the Āsana on the other side.

Relax the fingers, rest the arms on the floor along the body. Stretch the legs out on the floor and bring the feet together.

Rest.

Fruits

- Stabilizes all secretions of the alimentary canal.
- Reduces intestinal meteorism. Reduces colic spasms from colitis stress.
- Stimulates diuresis.
- Improves lymphatic circulation of the body.
- Tones up cardiac muscles.
- Stabilizes ovarian functions.
- Strengthens the uterine wall.

Ardha Padma Hala Āsana

Hala = plough. It is also the name of a snake poison, which the Gods Kṛṣṇa and Shiva have drunk to prevent men and animals from being killed.

Fig. 50 Ardha Padma Hala Āsana
(Cornelia)

Technique

Do Sarvānga Āsana. Bend your right knee and place your right foot in the hollow on the left side of your groin. Hold the right foot slightly on the outside of the left thigh.

Exhalation: Lower the taut left leg and place the left foot on the floor behind the head. Keep the left knee well raised.

Inhalation: Lift the left leg held taut.

Do 3 times or 3 Ujjāyi breaths.

Uncross the right leg and bring it back next to the left leg. Do the Āsana on the other side.

Come down from Sarvānga Āsana.

Take rest.

Fruits

- Improves intestinal absorption.
- Improves pulmonary compliance and pulmonary functions.
- Improves renal functions.
- Stabilizes thyroid gland hormonal secretions.

Ardha Padma Paścimatāna Āsana

Ardha = half, *padma* = lotus, *paścima* = west, *utthāna* = to stretch out, extension.

Fig. 51 Ardha Padma Paścimatāna Āsana

(Chantal)

Technique

Do Danḍa Āsana. Bend the right knee, hold the right foot in the hands and put it on the upper part of the left thigh, with the heel close to the navel. Interlock the fingers, turn the palms of the hands out, thumbs towards the interior.

Inhalation: Raise the arms taut over the head. Lower the chin, stretch the back of the neck and close the eyes.

Exhalation: Bend the trunk, lower the arms, turn the hands over and uncross the fingers in order to hold the left foot in both hands. Stretch the arms taut in order to straighten the back (especially the lower part of the back) without raising the shoulders or the chin.

Do 3 or 6 Ujjāyi breaths.

Inhalation: Interlock the fingers, turn out the palms of the hands, thumbs towards the interior. Raise the arms taut over the head stretching the trunk vertically.

Exhalation: Lower the arms, turn the hands over and uncross the fingers.

Stretch the right leg and place it next to the left leg.

Do the Āsana on the other side.

Stretch the left leg and place it next to the right leg.

Take rest.

Concentration

- *Kaṇṭha.*

Fruits

- Makes supple all the pelvic joints.
- Rectifies the static position of the spine, maintains intervertebral spaces and prevents slipped discs.
- Improves intestinal absorption and elimination and prevents constipation.
- Promotes elimination of gallstones.
- Stimulates diuresis.
- Stabilizes prostatic functions.
- Strengthens the uterine wall.
- Reduces tissue oedema and strengthens uterine wall after delivery.
- Improves the venous and lymphatic circulations.
- Improves mental concentration.

Ardha Setu Bandha Āsana

Ardha = half, *setu* = bridge, *bandha* = bound. Bound Half-bridge.

Fig. 52 Ardha Setu Bandha Āsana (Renée)

Fig. 53 Ardha Setu Bandha Āsana (Muriel)

Technique

Lie on the back, legs joined, feet joined, hands along the body, palms of the hands on the floor, chin lowered, and eyes closed. Bend both knees, put the feet on the floor, heels against the buttocks and if possible hold the ankles.

If you cannot take hold of the ankles, spread your legs and feet to the width of your hips and then hold of your ankles.

Inhalation: Lift up the buttocks and the back as high as possible, without raising the shoulders, or spreading the knees.

Do 6 *Ujjāyi* breaths.

Exhalation: Rest the back and the buttocks on the floor. Stretch the legs out on the floor and join the legs and the feet.

Take rest.

Fruits

- Makes supple the dorsal spinal column and the sacrolumbar region.
- Strengthens knee joints.
- Makes supple coxofemoral joints, helps to open the pelvis and reduces pain in delivery.
- Rectifies pelvis posture.
- Tones up cardiac muscles.
- Improves intestinal elimination, prevents constipation.
- Reduces symptoms of premenstrual syndrome.

Ardha Utkaṭa Āsana

Ardha = half, *utkaṭa* = chair.

Fig. 54 Ardha Utkaṭa Āsana

(Pascal)

Technique

Stand up, feet joined, arms along the body.

Inhalation: Interlock the fingers, turn the palms of the hands over. Raise the arms stretched over the head, keep the stretched arms parallel.

Exhalation: Crouch without raising the heels and keep the thighs parallel to the floor. Lower the arms in front to keep them at shoulder height. Straighten the chest, keep the back straight and the head looking forward.

Inhalation: Rise up and raise the arms stretched above the head.

Repeat this movement 3 to 6 times or do 3 breaths.

Exhalation: Lower your arms in front of you.

Take rest.

Fruits

- Rectifies the static position of the spinal column and maintains intervertebral spaces.
- Strengthens the muscles located along the spinal column, especially the ones at the lumbar level. Makes supple all the pelvis joints, more particularly, coxofemoral joints and shoulder joints. Strengthens knee joints. Develops the muscle structure of the abdominals, the lower abdomen and the legs.
- Strengthens the abdominal organs and the kidneys, and prevents their prolapses.
- Increases the sense of balance.
- Improves digestion, intestinal absorption and intestinal elimination and fights against constipation. Reduces the undesirable effects of chronic flatulence, intestinal meteorism and colic spasms of colitis stress.
- Improves venous and lymphatic circulation of the entire body.
- Develops respiratory capacity.
- Stimulates diuresis.

Baddha Koṇa Āsana

Baddha = bound, *koṇa* = angle, in Indian medicine, the pelvis or the shoulders. Bind the pelvis. Can become a *Mudra, Mahā Bandha.* Could be used to do *Prāṇāyāmas*.

Fig. 55 Baddha Koṇa Āsana

(Muriel)

Technique

Do Daṇḍa Āsana. Bring the soles of the feet together the one against the other, heels as close as possible to the perineum, thighs on the floor. Hold the toes, the feet or the ankles. Strengthen the entire back. Lower the chin and close the eyes.

Do 6 or 12 *Ujjāyi* breaths.

Relax the hands, stretch the legs out in front of you and bring the feet together.

Rest.

Concentration

- *Kaṇṭha, nābhi.*

Fruits

- Improves digestion and intestinal elimination, prevents constipation.
- Promotes bile drainage.
- Reduces undesirable signs of chronic flatulence.
- Stimulates production of gastric secretions.
- Stimulates all hepatic functions.
- Improves the venous and lymphatic circulations.
- Improves arterial circulation of the heart.
- Prevents and helps to reduce ovarian cysts.
- Restores the ovarian cycle and reduces symptoms of premenstrual syndrome.
- Reduces menopause symptoms.
- Helps to resorb uterine fibroids.
- Prevents and reduces prostatic hypertrophy.
- Stabilizes the vegetative nervous system.
- Makes supple pelvis joints and helps delivery, reduces pain sensation during the delivery, prevents precocious uterine contractions.
- Reduces dispersion due to the hyperactivity of the sense perceptions and promotes mental attention.

Bhagīratha Āsana

Bhagīratha = the name of a prince. *Bhāgīrathi* is another name for the Ganges.

Fig. 56 Bhagīratha Āsana

(Renée)

Technique

Do Samasthiti. Bend the right knee and put the right foot in the hollow of the left groin. Keep the right foot slightly to the outside of the left thigh.

Inhalation: Raise the arms taut laterally and join the palms of the hands above the head. Gaze at a point in front of you.

Do 3 to 6 *Ujjāyi* breaths.

Exhalation: Lower the arms and place the right foot on the floor.

Do the Āsana with the left leg.

Exhalation: Lower the arms and place the left foot on the floor.

Lie down and take rest.

Concentration

- *Nāsāgra, tāraka and bhrūmadhya.*

Fruits

- Rectifies static position of the spine.
- Makes supple all the pelvis joints.
- Promotes elimination of gallstones.
- Improves intestinal absorption.
- Tones up the muscles of the abdominal organs and prevents their prolapses.
- Improves venous circulation of lower limbs.
- Improves renal functions.
- Stabilizes ovarian functions.
- Stabilizes the mental state.

Bhāradvāja Āsana

Bhāradvāja is the name of a great Indian pharmacopoeia master, famous for his knowledge of the properties of plants.

Fig. 57 Bhāradvāja Āsana 1

(Renée)

Fig. 58 Bhāradvāja Āsana 2

(Renée)

Technique

Do Daṇḍa Āsana. Bend the left knee and place the back of the left foot on the outside of the left buttock. Bend the right knee, hold the right foot in the hands and place it on the upper part of the left thigh with the heel close to the navel. Bring the knees closer together. Put the right arm around behind the back in order to hold the right foot with the right hand. Turn the chest to the right to facilitate the grip and hold the right foot. Bring back the bust facing the left leg. Bring the left hand out in front of you and place it on the floor under the right knee (palms of the hand on the floor and fingers directed to the left.) Then turn the head to the left. Close the eyes.

Do 3 *Ujjāyi* breaths.

Relax the hands, extend the legs on the floor and join the feet.

Do the Āsana on the other side.

Relax the hands, extend the legs along the floor and join the feet.

Take rest.

Note: If you cannot take hold of the foot when putting the arm behind the back: in the same position, interlock the fingers, turn the palms of the hands outward, thumbs towards the interior. Raise the arms taut over the head. Lower the chin and close the eyes.

Exhalation: Bend the chest forward, put the hands on the floor.

Inhalation: Raise the chest straight up, raise the arms over the head.

Repeat 3 times.

Do the Āsana on the other side.

Exhalation: Relax the fingers, lower the arms.

Extend the legs along the floor and join the feet.

Rest.

Concentration

- *Nāsāgra.*

Fruits

- Rectifies static position of the spine.
- Stabilizes all secretions of the alimentary canal. Promotes elimination of gallstones. Improves intestinal elimination, prevents constipation.
- Stabilizes pancreas exocrine and endocrine secretions as well as all adrenal gland secretions.
- Supports the functions of spleen.
- Improves renal functions.
- Develops respiratory capacity.
- Stabilizes endocrinal secretions of the gonads.
- Prevents and reduces prostatic hypertrophy.
- Helps to resorb uterine fibroids.
- Helps to establish a conception *in utero.*

Bheka Āsana

Bheka = frog. In this Āsana, the body takes the shape of a frog.

Fig. 59 Bheka Āsana
(Françoise)

Technique

Lie on the stomach with the forehead on the floor, arms along the body, the back of the hands on the floor, legs joined and taut and eyes closed. Bend the knees then spread the feet. Place the hands on the back of the feet, fingers on the ankles. The fingers pointing towards the ankles. Keep the elbows bent upwards and the feet still spread.

Inhalation: Bending the wrists and the elbows, bring the feet towards the floor in order to pull the head and the chest backwards. It is the traction on the feet that helps to raise the head and the chest.

Exhalation: Lay the chest and the forehead on the floor and relax the pressure on the feet.

Do 3 times or 3 *Ujjāyi* breaths.

Relax the feet, put the arms on the floor, hands back on the floor. Lower the legs along the floor and join the feet.

Turn over and take rest.

Concentration

- *Bhrūmadhya.*

Fruits

- Rectifies dorsal kyphosis and develops ribcage volume.
- Makes supple all the pelvis joints, and strengthens coxofemoral joints.
- Supports the perineum and tones up the pelvic floor. Strengthens the abdominal organs and the kidneys, and prevents their prolapses.
- Stimulates all the hepatic functions.
- Stabilizes the secretions of the alimentary canal.
- Improves renal functions.
- Supports the functions of spleen.
- Stabilizes the vegetative nervous system.
- Tones up cardiac muscles.
- Improves pulmonary compliance and pulmonary functions.
- Helps to maintain Bāhya Kumbhaka.
- Stabilizes all the endocrine secretions of the body.
- Prevents and reduces signs of menopause.
- Helps to resorb uterine fibroids.
- Reduces oedema tissue and strengthens the uterine wall after delivery.
- Provides mental attention and improves mental concentration.
- Helps to restore the different sleeping phases.

Bhujaṃga Āsana

Bhuja = shoulder, *aṁga* = limb. *Bhujaṃga* = snake. In this Āsana, the body takes the shape of a cobra.

Fig. 60 Bhujaṃga Āsana

(Stéphanie)

Technique

Lie on the stomach with the forehead on the floor, arms along the body, the back of the hands on the floor, legs joined and taut, eyes closed. Bend the arms while raising the elbows and put the hands on the floor at the level of the lower ribs, hands close to the body, fingers directed towards the head.

Inhalation: Pressing the hands to the floor, raise the head, the neck, the shoulders, the chest and the stomach. Keep the navel and the abdomen on the floor. Relax the abdomen.

Exhalation: Lower the stomach, the chest and the shoulders to the floor. Put the forehead on the floor.

Do 3 times or 3 *Ujjāyi* breaths.

Turn over and take rest.

Concentration

- *Bhrūmadhya, tāraka.*

Fruits

- Rectifies static position of the spine.
- Rectifies dorsal kyphosis and scoliosis.
- Makes supple the sacrolumbar region.
- Strengthens the muscles located all along the spinal column.
- Improves respiratory capacity and lengthens the Inhalation time.
- Improves intestinal absorption.
- Tones up cardiac muscles.
- Stabilizes blood pressure in case of low blood pressure.
- Improves mental concentration and reduces mental weariness.
- Develops self-confidence, provides courage and increases perseverance.

Bhujaṃga Āsana, variation

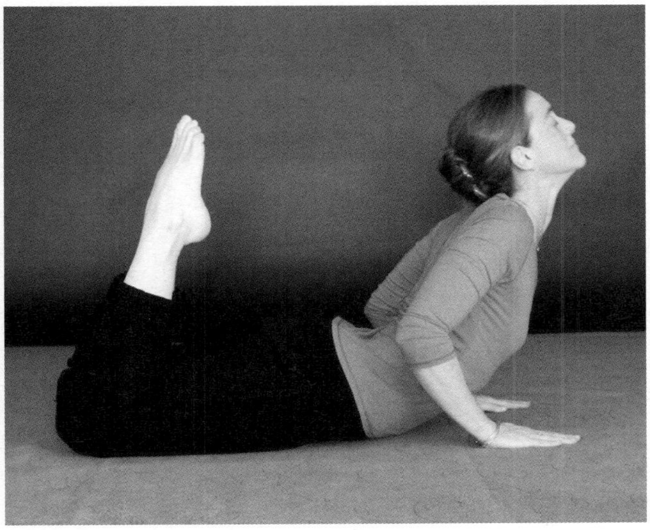

Fig. 61 Bhujaṃga Āsana, variation (Estelle)

Technique

Lie on the stomach with the forehead on the floor, arms along the body, the back of the hands on the floor, legs joined and taut and eyes closed. Bend the arms raising the elbows and put the hands on the floor at the level of the lower ribs, hands close to the body, fingers directed towards the head.

Inhalation: Pressing the hands to the floor, raise the head, the neck, the shoulders, the chest and the abdomen. Keep the navel and the stomach on the floor. Relax the abdomen.

Exhalation: Bend the knees without lowering the chest and keep the feet joined.

Inhalation: Without lowering the chest, stretch out the joined legs and place the feet together on the floor.

Do 3 times.

Exhalation: Lower the stomach, the chest and the shoulders to the floor. Put the forehead on the floor.

Stretch the arms (along the body) out, put the back of the hands on the floor.

Turn over and take rest.

Fruits

- Makes supple all the pelvis joints.
- Improves the venous and lymphatic circulations.
- Relieves ‘restless legs syndrome’ (also known as ‘Wittmaak Ekbom’s syndrome’).
- Stimulates ovulation.
- Strengthens uterine walls and helps to resorb uterine fibroids.
- Tones up the keeping of abdominal organs and prevents their prolapses.
- Stabilizes all adrenal gland secretions.
- Improves pulmonary functions.
- Helps to maintain Antah Kumbhaka.

Catuś Pāda Pīṭam

This is a variation of Pūrvatāna Āsana. *Catuś* comes from *catvāri* = four, *pāda* = foot, *pīṭa* = seat. Catuś Pāda Pīṭam indicates a small, relatively broad bench, with short feet, more particularly used for rituals to allow participants to sit down in Padma Āsana.

Fig. 62 Catuś Pāda Pīṭam 1
(Françoise)

Fig. 63 Catuś Pāda Pīṭam 2
(Muriel)

Fig. 64 Catuś Pāda Pīṭam 3
(Françoise)

Technique

Do Daṇḍa Āsana. Put the hands on the floor, about 50 centimetres behind the buttocks, fingers pointed towards the buttocks. Bend the knees and the elbows and bring the feet to the floor about 50 centimetres from the buttocks. Stretch the back, lower the chin and close the eyes.

Inhalation: Leaning on the hands and the feet, stretch the arms and raise the buttocks as high as possible. Lower the head.

Exhalation: Bend the elbows, rest the buttocks on the floor in the same place, lower the chin and stretch the back.

Do 3 to 6 times or 3 *Ujjāyi* Breaths.

Stretch the legs out on the floor, join the feet and bring the hands close to the buttocks.

Take rest.

Fruits

- The same as Pūrvatāna Āsana.

Daṇḍa Āsana

Daṇḍa = stick, spinal column. *Daṇḍa* (stick) is one of the ten means of persuasion! In this Āsana, the chest remains straight like a stick.

Fig. 65 Daṇḍa Āsana
(Estelle)

Technique

Sit on the floor, legs taut in front of you. Bring the legs and the feet together. Draw in the chin and straighten the entire spinal column so it is perfectly straight. Interlock the fingers, turn over the palms of the hands, thumbs facing inwards and close the eyes. Raise the arms taut over the head.

Do 6 *Ujjāyi* breaths.

Take rest.

Concentration

- *Nāsāgra, kaṇṭha.*

Fruits

- Rectifies the static position of the spine, maintains intervertebral spaces and prevents slipped discs. Makes supple the sacrolumbar region.
- Improves intestinal digestion and absorption, prevents constipation.
- Improves intestine elimination function during pregnancy and prevents haemorrhoids.
- Supports the perineum and averts organ prolapses after delivery.
- Stabilizes the vegetative nervous system.

Daṇḍa Āsana, variations

Fig. 66 Daṇḍa Āsana, variations 1

(Patrice)

Fig. 67 Daṇḍa Āsana, variations 2

(Patrice)

Fig. 68 Daṇḍa Āsana, variations 3

(Patrice)

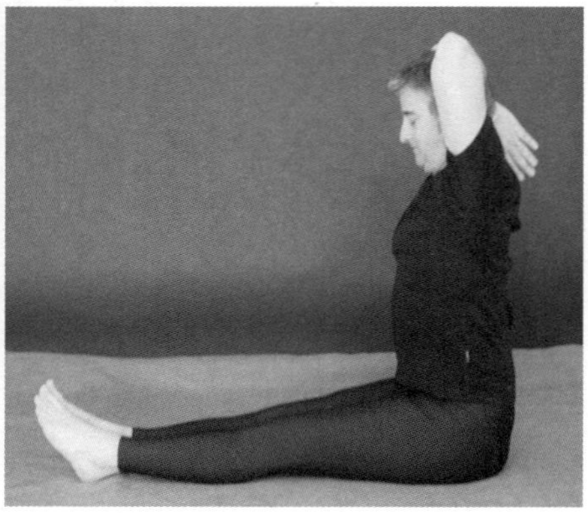

Fig. 69 Daṇḍa Āsana, variations 4

(Patrice)

Technique

Do Daṇḍa Āsana. Lower the chin, stretch the back of the neck.

1st movement

Interlock the fingers and turn the palms of the hands over, thumbs towards the interior.

Inhalation: Raise the arms taut straight up over the head.

Exhalation: Lower the arms taut without bending the back.

Do 2 times. Relax the fingers.

2nd movement

Keep the arms taut along the body, put the hands on the floor, fingers directed forwards.

Inhalation: While turning the arms towards the exterior, raise the arms taut laterally, palms of the hands upwards and join the palms of the hands over the head.

Exhalation: While turning the arms towards the Interior, lower the arms taut, palms of the hands facing down, without bending the back.

Do 2 times.

3rd movement

Keep the arms taut along the body, put the hands on the floor, fingers directed forwards.

Inhalation: Raise the arms taut laterally, palms of the hands facing downwards. Bring the back of the hands together over the head.

Exhalation: Lower the arms taut, without bending the back, palms of the hands directed towards the floor.

Do 2 times.

4th movement

Keep the arms taut along the body, put the hands on the floor, fingers directed forwards.

Inhalation: While turning the arms towards the exterior, raise the arms taut laterally, join the palms of the hands together over the head.

Exhalation: Without bending the back, bend the elbows and bring the forearms towards the back, hands behind the head and thumbs against the back of the neck. Tighten up the elbows and keep them away from the head.

Inhalation: Raise the hands and stretch the arms.

Do 2 times.

Exhalation: While turning the arms towards the interior, lower the arms taut, laterally, palms of the hands directed towards the floor.

Take rest.

Fruits

- Supports cardiac functions.
- Rectifies the static position of the spine, maintains intervertebral spaces and prevents slipped discs. Makes supple the sacrolumbar region.
- Improves intestinal digestion and absorption, prevents constipation.
- Improves intestine elimination function during pregnancy and prevents haemorrhoids.
- Supports the perineum and averts organ prolapses after delivery.
- Stabilizes the vegetative nervous system.

Dhanura Āsana

Dhanus = bow. In this Āsana, the body takes the shape of a bow.

Fig. 70 Dhanura Āsana
(Chantal)

Technique

Lie on the stomach, with the forehead on the floor; arms along the body, the back of the hands on the floor, legs joined and taut and eyes closed. Bend the knees together, hold the ankles and stretch out the feet.

Inhalation: Raise the head, the chest, as well as the thighs joined together at the same time without bending the elbows. Remain on the umbilical region.

Exhalation: Lower the thighs, the chest and the forehead to the floor.

Do 3 times or 3 *Ujjāyi* breaths.

Relax the ankles and stretch the legs, place the feet on the floor and the arms along the body.

Turn over and take rest.

Concentration

- *Kaṇṭha.*

Fruits

- Makes supple the spinal, cervical and dorsal column. Strengthens coxofemoral joints.
- Strengthens the abdominal organs and the kidneys, and prevents their prolapses.
- Improves digestion. Reduces undesirable effects of chronic flatulence.
- Stabilizes all secretions of the alimentary canal. Promotes elimination of gallstones and bile drainage.
- Develops respiratory capacity. Makes Antah Kumbhaka and Bāhya Kumbhaka practice easier.
- Supports cardiac functions.
- Stimulates ovulation.
- Stabilizes all the adrenal gland secretions.
- Stabilizes hormonal secretions of the pituitary gland.
- Stabilizes the vegetative nervous system.
- Helps to dissipate mental confusion, provides clarity of mind and improves mental concentration.

Dhanura Āsana, variation

Fig. 71 Dhanura Āsana, variation
(Stéphanie)

Technique

Lie on the stomach with the forehead on the floor, arms along the body, the back of the hands on the floor, legs joined and taut and eyes closed. Bend the knees together, hold the ankles and stretch out the feet.

Inhalation: Stretch the arms, press your thighs to the floor and draw out the feet backwards as if you wanted to place them on the floor and raise up the head and the chest.

Exhalation: Rest the chest and the forehead on the floor and draw the feet towards the buttocks.

Do 3 times or do 3 *Ujjāyi* breaths.

Release the ankles, stretch the legs and place the arms along the body.

Turn over and take rest.

Fruits

- Makes supple the spinal, cervical and dorsal column. Strengthens coxofemoral joints.
- Strengthens the abdominal organs and the kidneys, and prevents their prolapses.
- Improves digestion. Reduces undesirable effects of chronic flatulence.
- Stabilizes all secretions of the alimentary canal. Promotes elimination of gallstones and bile drainage.
- Develops respiratory capacity. Makes Antah Kumbhaka and Bāhya Kumbhaka practice easier.
- Supports cardiac functions.
- Stimulates ovulation.
- Stabilizes all the adrenal gland secretions.
- Stabilizes hormonal secretions of the pituitary gland.
- Stabilizes the vegetative nervous system.
- Helps to dissipate mental confusion, provides clarity of mind and improves mental concentration.

Eka Pāda Apāna Āsana

Eka = one, *pāda* = foot, leg, *apāna* = reject, eliminate.

Fig. 72 Eka Pāda Apāna Āsana

(Patrice)

Technique

Lie on the back, legs and feet joined, arms along the body, the palms of the hands on the floor, chin lowered, and eyes closed. Bend the left knee and bring the left thigh up to the abdomen. Interlock the fingers around the left leg. Keep the right leg taut on the floor.

Do 3 to 6 *Ujjāyi* breaths.

Relax the fingers and place the arms on the floor along the body placing the left leg held taut on the floor.

Do the Āsana with the right leg.

Relax the fingers and place the arms on the floor along the body placing the right leg held taut on the floor.

Take rest.

Fruits

- Prevents and relieves sciatica. Makes supple the lumbar spinal column.
- Improves intestinal elimination, prevents constipation. Reduces intestinal meteorism and colic spasms of colitis stress.
- Stimulates diuresis.

Eka Pāda Dhanura Āsana

Eka = one, *Pāda* = foot, leg, *dhanus* = bow. In this Āsana, the body looks like a bow.

Fig. 73 Eka Pāda Dhanura Āsana

(Patrice)

Technique

Lie on the stomach, with the forehead on the floor, arms along the body, the back of the hands on the floor, legs joined and taut and eyes closed. Bend the left knee, hold the left ankle with both hands.

Inhalation: Without bending the elbows, raise the head, the bust and the left thigh at the same time. Remain lying on the umbilical region. Keep the right leg held taut on the floor.

Do 3 times or maintain the Āsana while doing 3 *Ujjāyi* breaths.

Exhalation: Lower the thigh, the chest and the forehead to the floor.

Relax the hands, stretch out the left leg, put the foot on the floor next to the right foot and place the arms along the body.

Do the Āsana on the other side.

Relax the hands, stretch out the right leg, put the foot on the floor next to the left foot and place the arms along the body.

Turn over and take rest.

Fruits

- Makes supple the spinal, cervical and dorsal column. Strengthens coxofemoral joints.
- Strengthens the abdominal organs and the kidneys, and prevents their prolapses.
- Improves digestion. Reduces undesirable effects of chronic flatulence.
- Stabilizes all secretions of the alimentary canal. Promotes elimination of gallstones and bile drainage.
- Develops respiratory capacity. Makes Antah Kumbhaka and Bāhya Kumbhaka practice easier.
- Supports cardiac functions.
- Stimulates ovulation.
- Stabilizes all the adrenal gland secretions.
- Stabilizes hormonal secretions of the pituitary gland.
- Stabilizes the vegetative nervous system.
- Helps to dissipate mental confusion, provides clarity of mind and improves mental concentration.

Eka Pāda Śalabha Āsana

Eka = one, *Pāda* = foot, leg, *śalabha* = grasshopper or dragonfly. In this Āsana, the body takes the shape of a dragonfly.

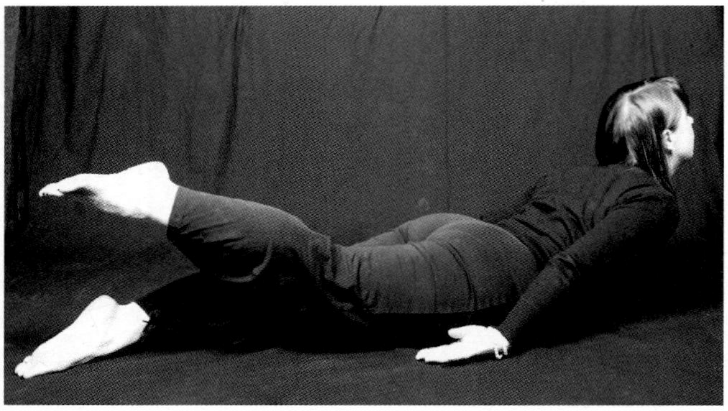

Fig. 74 Eka Pāda Śalabha Āsana

(Cornelia)

Technique

Lie on the stomach, with the forehead on the floor, arms along the body, the back of the hands on the floor, legs joined and taut and eyes closed.

Inhalation: Raise the head, the chest and the left leg held taut, simultaneously. Do not lean the body to the right.

Exhalation: Lower the chest, the left leg and the forehead to the floor.

Do the Āsana with the right leg.

Do 3 times alternately or maintain the Āsana during 1 or 2 *Ujjāyi* breaths on each side.

Turn over and take rest.

Fruits

- Rectifies the static position of the spinal column and maintains intervertebral spaces.
- Strengthens the muscles located all along the spinal column, especially those in the lumbar region.
- Strengthens the coxofemoral joints.
- Prevents kidneys prolapses.
- Stimulates diuresis.
- Restores ovarian cycle and stabilizes ovarian functions.
- Reduces symptoms of premenstrual syndrome.
- Helps to reabsorb uterine fibromas.
- Supports endometrium and promotes conception.
- Promotes elimination of catabolic cellular remnants.
- After delivery, reduces tissue oedema and strengthens the uterine wall.
- Tones up cardiac muscles.
- Improves mental concentration.
- Facilitates holding of *Antah Kumbhaka* and *Bāhya Kumbhaka*.

Eka Pāda Ūrdhva Prasuta Pāda Āsana

Eka = one, *pāda* = foot, leg, *ūrdhva* = upwards, towards the sky, celestial, *prasuta* = to take straight up.

Fig. 75 Eka Pāda Ūrdhva Prasuta Pāda Āsana (Estelle)

Technique

Lie on the back, legs joined, feet joined, arms along the body, the palms of the hands on the floor, chin lowered and eyes closed.

Exhalation: Raise the left leg held taut straight up, without bending the right knee.

Inhalation: Lie the left leg on the floor.

Do the Āsana with the right leg.

Repeat 3 times alternately.

Take rest.

Fruits

- Rectifies the static position of the spine, maintains intervertebral spaces and prevents slipped discs.
- Develops the muscles of the legs.
- Improves venous and lymphatic circulation of the entire body.
- Improves intestinal elimination, prevents constipation. Reduces intestinal meteorism.

Eka Pāda Viparīta Śalabha Āsana

Eka = one, *pāda* = foot, leg, *viparīta* = eccentric, upside down, *śalabha* = grasshopper.

Fig. 76 Eka Pāda Viparīta Śalabha Āsana (Claire)

Technique

Lie on the stomach, with the forehead on the floor, arms along the body, the back of the hands on the floor.

Inhalation: Raise the left leg held taut as high as possible without swinging the body to the right. Keep the right leg taut. Do not raise the head or the shoulders.

Exhalation: Place the leg back on the floor. Do the Āsana with the other leg.

Do 3 times alternately.

Turn over and take rest.

Fruits

- Rectifies the static position of the spinal column and pelvis posture. Makes supple sacrolumbar region and strengthens coxofemoral joints.
- Strengthens the abdominal organs and the kidneys, and prevents their prolapses. Tones up the perineum.
- Tones up sub-umbilical muscle structure.
- Develops rib cage volume.
- Stimulates secretions of the small intestine. Stabilizes exocrine secretion of the pancreas.
- Promotes bile drainage.
- Prevents and reduces haemorrhoids.
- Improves the venous and lymphatic circulations.
- Strengthens cardiac muscles.
- Improves pulmonary functions and pulmonary compliance. Develops respiratory capacity. Helps holding of Antah Kumbhaka and Bāhya Kumbhaka.
- Improves renal functions.
- Stabilizes all the endocrinal secretions.
- Supports endometrium and promotes conception.
- Stabilizes prostatic functions. Prevents and reduces prostatic hypertrophy.
- Stabilizes the vegetative nervous system. Improves nervous resistance to external stimulus such as stress, for example.
- Improves functions of all the organs of the body.
- Provides mental attention. Increases memorising capacity. Develops self-confidence, provides courage and increases perseverance.

Garuḍa Āsana

Garuḍa = eagle. It is also the name of the king of the birds. Garuḍa is lord Viṣṇu's vehicle.

Fig. 77 Garuḍa Āsana 1

(Pascale)

Fig. 78 Garuḍa Āsana 2, right side

(Gabriel)

Technique

Do *Samasthiti*. Put the right leg behind the left leg at a distance of a minimum of one meter, both legs in line. Keep the trunk facing the left leg. Interlock the fingers, turn over the palms of the hands, thumbs towards the interior. Raise the arms taut over the head. Lower the chin and close the eyes.

Exhalation: Without bending the chest forward, bend the left knee in order to bring the thigh parallel to the floor. Keep the right leg taut. Keep the head straight. Lower the arms in front to the level of the shoulders, relax the fingers and turn the palms of the hands towards the sky. Bend the elbows, bring them backwards in order to put the hands at the level of the lower ribs. Draw in your elbows.

Do 1 *Ujjāyi* breath.

Join the hands putting the thumbs against the sternum, fingers pointed towards the sky.

Do 1 *Ujjāyi* breath.

Inhalation: Raise the arms over the head, keeping the hands joined. Stretch the left leg again and lower the arms along the body. Bring the right leg back alongside the left leg.

Do the Āsana on the other side.

Straighten the right leg again and lower the arms along the body. Bring the left leg back alongside the right leg.

Take rest.

Fruits

- Same as Vīra Bhadra Āsana.

Hala Āsana

Hala = plough, poison. It is also the name of the snake's venom drunk by lords Kṛṣṇa and Shiva to prevent men and animals being killed. In this Āsana, the body looks like a plough.

Fig. 79 Hala Āsana 1

(Renée)

Fig. 80 Hala Āsana 2

(Pascal)

Technique

Do Sarvānga Āsana.

Exhalation: Keeping the back straight, lower both legs taut and place the feet on the floor behind the head. Stretch the arms on the floor, interlock the fingers and turn the hands over.

Do 3 *Ujjāyi* breaths. Then relax the hands, bend the elbows and place the hands at the level of the upper ribs.

Inhalation: Raise the legs taut in Sarvānga Āsana.

Exhalation: Lower the legs at right angles, then stretch the arms along the floor.

Inhalation: Unfold the back, then the legs taut on the floor without raising up the head or the shoulders.

Take rest.

Fruits

- Rectifies static position of the spine. Makes supple the cervical spinal column.
- Rectifies lumbar hyperlordosis.
- Stimulates production of gastric secretions.
- Improves renal functions.
- Stabilizes thyroid gland hormonal secretions, ovaries, adrenal gland glands and the pineal gland.
- Tones up cardiac muscles.
- Promotes the elimination of cellular catabolic residue.
- Helps to establish a conception in utero.

Jaṭhara Parivṛtti N° 1

Jaṭhara = stomach, *parivṛtti* = turn round about.

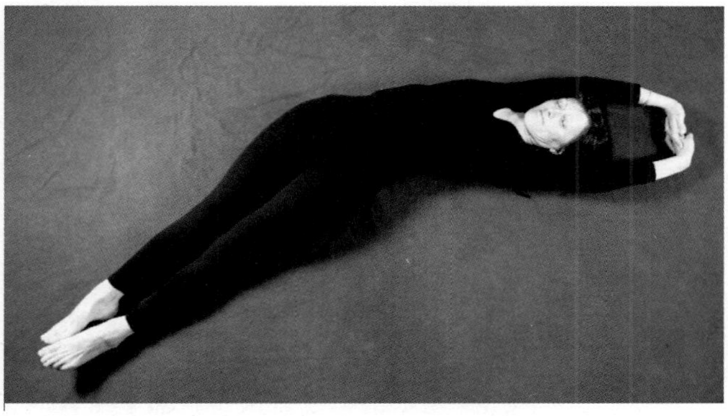

Fig. 81 Jaṭhara Parivṛtti N° 1
(Chantal)

Technique

Lie on the back, legs joined, feet joined, arms along the body, palms of the hands on the floor, chin lowered, and eyes closed. Interlock the fingers, turn over the palms of the hands, thumbs towards the interior. Raise the arms taut over the head. Without moving the pelvis, slide the legs taut towards the left one after the other, in small movements.

Do 3 *Ujjāyi* breaths.

Bring the legs back to the middle in small movements.

Do the Āsana on the other side.

Do 3 *Ujjāyi* breaths.

Bring the legs back to the middle in small movements. Relax the hands and lower the arms along the body, palms of the hands on the floor.

Take rest.

Fruits

- Prevents and relieves sciatica.
- Strengthens coxofemoral joints, Makes supple pelvis joints and makes delivery easier.
- Stimulates all the hepatic functions.

Jaṭhara Parivṛtti N° 2

Fig. 82 Jaṭhara Parivṛtti N° 2
(Gabriel)

Technique

Lie on the back, legs together, feet together, arms along the body, palms of the hands on the floor, chin lowered and eyes closed. Stretch the arms on the side in the axis of the shoulders and put the palms of the hands on the floor.

Exhalation: Raise the legs taut vertically and lay them on the floor on the left side at the height of the left hand. Hold the big toes or the ankle of the right leg with the left hand. Raise the head slightly, turn it to the right and place the right ear on the floor. Keep the cervical vertebrae in the axis of the dorsal column.

Do 3 *Ujjāyi* breaths.

Raise the head slightly again, bring it back to the middle. Put the left hand on the floor.

Inhalation: Raise the legs taut vertically again.

Exhalation: Lay the legs on the right side at the height of the right hand. Hold the big toes or the ankle of the left leg with the right hand. Raise the head slightly again, turn it to the left and put the left ear on the floor. Keep the cervical vertebrae in the axis of the dorsal column.

Do 3 *Ujjāyi* breaths.

Raise the head again slightly, bringing it in the middle. Put the right hand on the floor.

Inhalation: Raise the legs taut vertically again, then rest them back on the floor again in the axis of the body. Lower the arms.

Take rest.

Fruits

- Makes supple the spinal, cervical and dorsal columns.
- Stimulates production of gastric secretions and improves digestion.
- Stimulates diuresis.
- Prevents kidneys prolapses.
- Tones up cardiac muscles.
- Prevents and helps to reduce ovarian cysts.

Karṇa Pīḍa Āsana

Karṇa = ear, *pīḍa* = illnesses, sufferings.

Fig. 83 Karṇa Pīḍa Āsana

(Renée)

Technique

Do Sarvānga Āsana.

Exhalation: Lower both legs, bent, spread the knees and join the feet. Put the toes on the floor behind the head, knees against the ears and the shoulders. Stretch the arms on the floor, interlock the fingers and turn the hands over.

Do 3 *Ujjāyi* breaths.

Inhalation: Relax the hands, bend the elbows and put the hands at the level of the highest ribs. Raise the feet again and bring the legs up again in Sarvānga Āsana.

Exhalation: Lower the legs taut at right angles, stretch the arms.

Inhalation: Lay the back down then the legs taut on the floor without raising the head or the shoulders from the floor.

Take rest.

Fruits

- Rectifies the static position of the spine, maintains intervertebral spaces and prevents slipped discs.
- Stabilizes all secretions of the alimentary canal.
- Stabilizes ovarian functions. Prevents and helps to reduce ovarian cysts.
- Prevents and reduces signs of menopause. Supports endometrium.
- Stabilizes prostatic functions.
- Strengthens the abdominal organs and the kidneys, and prevents their prolapses.
- Supports mental concentration.

Marīcya Āsana N° 1

Marīcya is the name of a Vedic sage.

Fig. 84 Marīcya Āsana N° 1
(Gabriel)

Technique

Do Danḍa Āsana. Bend the left leg to bring the left thigh against the chest with the heel against the left buttock. Bring the left shoulder forward until the armpit touches the left thigh. Bend the left elbow and put your arm and the left elbow around the tibia (shinbone) and the left thigh. Bring the left hand behind the back to the level of the waist. Then bring the right arm behind the back from the right and hold the left hand. Stretch the back, keep the chest and the head forward, look towards the big toe of the right foot, and then close your eyes, and maintain the gazing at the big toe.

Do 3 or 6 *Ujjāyi* Breaths.

Relax the hands, lay the left leg on the floor and join the feet.

Do the Āsana with the right leg.

Relax the hands, lay the right leg down on the floor and join the feet.

Take rest.

Concentration

- *Pāda aṅguṣṭa* (big toe) of the taut leg.

Fruits

- Improves renal functions. Prevents kidney stone formation.
- Restores ovarian cycle and Stabilizes ovarian functions. Supports endometrium and promotes conception.
- Prevents and reduces prostatic hypertrophy.

Marīcya Āsana N° 2

Fig. 85 Marīcya Āsana N° 2, right side (Catherine)

Technique

Do Daṇḍa Āsana. Bend the left knee to bring it against the left shoulder, the heel against the left buttock. Turn the chest to the left while completely freeing the breast. Place the right shoulder forward of the left knee and hold the right arm forward by turning the chest even more to the left. Bend the right elbow and surround the left knee with the right elbow. Bring the right wrist up behind the back to the level of the waist. Bring the left hand behind the back and take hold of the right hand. Straighten the back, turn the head to the right, keep the chin on the shoulder and close your eyes.

Do 3 to 6 *Ujjāyi* breaths.

Relax the hands, extend the left leg along the floor and join the feet.

Do the Āsana with the right leg.

Relax the hands, extend the right leg along the floor and join the feet.

Take rest.

Concentration

- *Nāsāgra, kaṇṭha.*

Fruits

- Develops respiratory capacity.
- Improves renal functions. Prevents kidney stone formation and helps its elimination.
- Stabilizes all the adrenal gland secretions.
- Improves all the functions of the organs of the body.

Marīcya Āsana N° 3

Fig. 86 Marīcya Āsana N° 3, right side

(Estelle)

Technique

Do Daṇḍa Āsana. Bend the right knee, put the upper part of the right foot next to the right buttock. Bend the left knee and put it against the left shoulder, heel against the left buttock. Bring the left shoulder forward until the armpit touches the left knee. With the left elbow, put your arm around the tibia (shinbone) and the left thigh. Bring the left hand behind the back to the level of the waist. Bring the right arm behind the back from the right side and hold the left hand. Straighten the back, keep the chest and the head forward, and close the eyes.

Do 3 to 6 *Ujjāyi* breaths.

Relax the hands, extend the legs along the floor and join the feet.

Do the Āsana on the other side.

Relax the hands, extend the legs along the floor and join the feet.

Take rest.

Concentration

- *Nāsāgra, kaṇṭha.*

Fruits

- Stabilizes endocrine secretions of the gonads.
- Stimulates ovulation and restores ovarian cycle. Reduces symptoms of premenstrual syndrome.
- Stabilizes all the adrenal gland secretions.

Matsya Āsana

Matsya = fish.

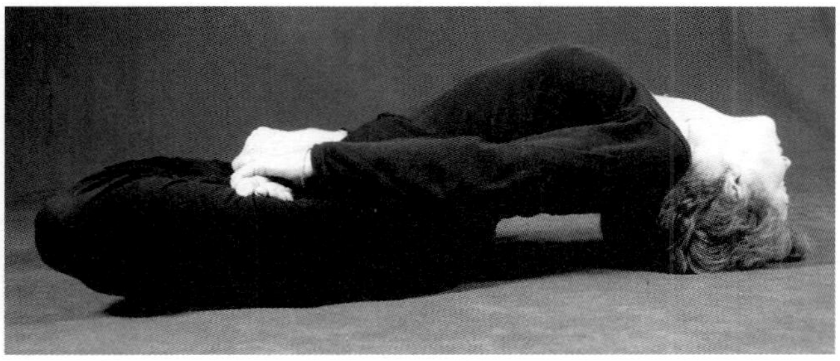

Fig. 87 Matsya Āsana

(Brigitte)

Technique

Lie on the back with the legs together, feet together, arms along the body, palms of the hands on the floor, chin lowered and eyes closed. Cross the legs or put them in Padma Āsana. Lay the thighs on the floor. Pushing on the elbows, raise the head and the chest slightly then stretch the head back in order to rest the top of the head on the floor. Raise the elbows from the floor, stretch the arms and put the hands on the feet or on the thighs.

Do 3 *Ujjāyi* or Śītalī breaths.

Put the elbows on the floor. Pushing on the elbows, raise the head and the chest slightly then hold up the head. Lay the head and the chest on the floor, relax the arms and lay them along the body. Lay the legs on the floor, feet together.

Take rest.

Concentration

- *Bhrūmadhya.*

Fruits

- Makes supple the spinal, cervical and dorsal columns. Rectifies dorsal kyphosis.
- Tones up cardiac muscles.
- Stimulates all the hepatic functions.
- Stabilizes exocrine secretion of the pancreas.
- Stabilizes endocrine secretions of the pancreas.
- Prevents and reduces haemorrhoids.
- Develops respiratory capacity.
- Stabilizes blood pressure in case of low blood pressure.
- Stabilizes all the endocrine secretions of the body.
- Provides mental attention and improves mental concentration. Reduces mental dispersion (unfocused mind) due to hyperactivity of perception senses. Develops self-confidence, provides courage and increases perseverance.

With Śītalī

- Improves digestion.
- Stabilizes blood pressure in case of low blood pressure.
- Prevents and reduces thyroid goitres.
- Reduces menstrual bleeding

Nāva Āsana

Nāva = boat.

Fig. 88 Nāva Āsana

(Pascal)

Technique

Do Daṇḍa Āsana.

Inhalation: Incline the trunk backwards and raise the legs taut at the same time. Keep the feet and the head at the same height. Stretch the arms ahead of you and bring the palms of the hands to the outer side of the legs. Keep the back curved, lower the chin slightly and remain in balance on the sacrolumbar region. Look towards your big toes and close your eyes.

Do 3 *Ujjāyi* breaths.

Exhalation: Lay the legs down on the floor, bring the chest up vertically, lower the arms and put the hands on the floor.

Take rest.

Concentration

- *Kaṇṭha.*

Fruits

- Rectifies the static position of the spine, maintains intervertebral spaces and prevents slipped discs. Strengthens muscles located all along the spinal column.
- Strengthens abdominal muscles. Strengthens the abdominal organs and the kidneys, and prevents their prolapses.
- Improves intestinal digestion and absorption. Stimulates small intestine secretions.
- Strengthens the uterine wall. Restores the ovarian cycle.

Padma Āsana

Padma = lotus, navel. One of the most important Āsanas; it is the Āsana of predilection for meditation.

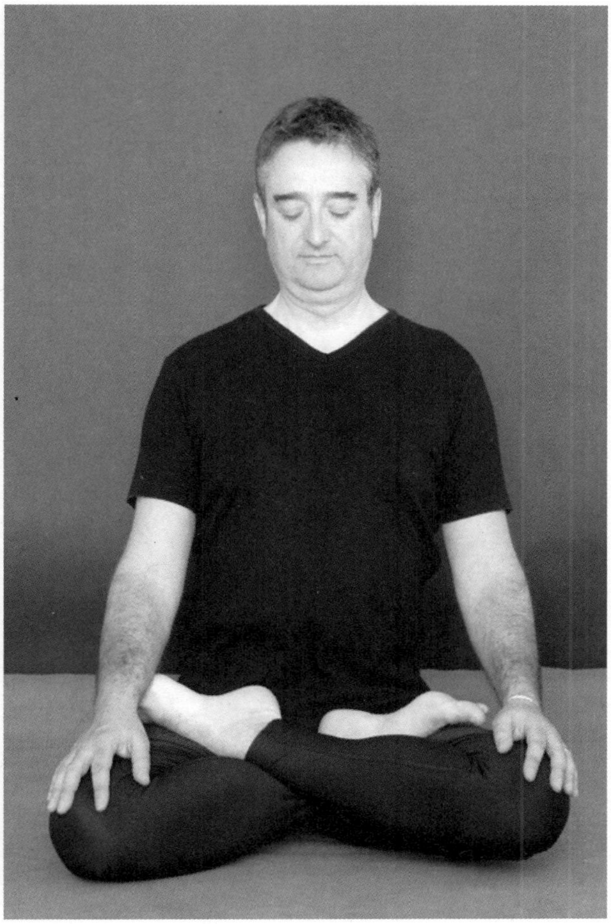

Fig. 89 Padma Āsana
(Patrice)

Technique

Do Daṇḍa Āsana. Bend the right knee, hold of the right foot with the hands and place it on the upper part of the left thigh, the heel close to the navel. Bend the left knee, hold of the left foot with the hands and place it on the upper part of the right thigh, the heel close to navel. Draw in the chin and straighten the entire spinal column so that it is perfectly straight. Stretch the arms, put the palms of the hands on the knees, fingers pointed towards the floor.

Do 6 *Ujjāyi* breaths.

Stretch the legs out on the floor and keep the feet together. Do the Āsana placing first the left foot on the right thigh.

Do 6 *Ujjāyi* breaths.

Stretch the legs out and join the feet together.

Take rest.

Note: If you cannot do this posture, simply cross the legs in 'cross-legged' position.

Concentration

- *Nāsāgra, kaṇṭha, bhrūmadhya, hṛdaya, tāraka.*

Fruits

- Excellent Asana for the practice of Prāṇāyāma and meditation.

Parigha Āsana

Parigha = barrier (fence).

Fig. 90 Parigha Āsana, right side
(Pascal)

Technique

Kneel down keeping the ankles together and the upper part of the feet flat on the floor. Stretch the left leg on the left side within the same line as the right knee. Turn the left foot towards the left.

Inhalation: Interlock the fingers, turn over the palms of the hands, thumbs towards the interior. Raise the arms taut over the head. Lower the chin and close the eyes.

Exhalation: Bend the trunk laterally to the left, keep the head and the chest facing forward.

Inhalation: Bring the trunk up vertically.

Do 3 times.

Exhalation: Relax the fingers, lower the arms and fold the left leg.

Do the Āsana with the right leg.

Lower the arms and fold the right leg, sit on the heels.

Take rest.

Fruits

- Rectifies the static position of the spine, maintains intervertebral spaces.
- Makes supple all the pelvis joints. Develops rib cage volume.
- Strengthens the abdominal organs and the kidneys, and prevents their prolapses.
- Reduces undesirable effects of chronic flatulence.
- Stimulates diuresis.
- Improves venous and lymphatic circulation of the entire body.
- Prevents and helps to reduce ovarian cysts. Helps to resorb uterine fibroids.
- Prevents and reduces prostatic hypertrophy.

Parvata Āsana

Parvata = mountain. In this Āsana, the body takes the shape of a mountain.

Fig. 91 Parvata Āsana 1

(Estelle)

Fig. 92 Parvata Āsana 2

(Estelle)

Fig. 93 Parvata Āsana 3

(Estelle)

Fig. 94 Parvata Āsana 4

(Estelle)

Technique

Do Padma Āsana or sit cross-legged. Draw in the chin and straighten the entire spinal column so it is perfectly straight. Interlock the fingers, turn over the palms of the hands, thumbs facing inwards and close the eyes. Raise the arms taut over the head.

Do 2 *Ujjāyi* breaths.

1st movement

Interlock the fingers, turn over the palms of the hands, thumbs towards the interior.

Inhalation: Raise the arms taut vertically over the head.

Exhalation: Lower the arms taut without letting the back sag.

Do 2 times. Relax the fingers.

2nd movement

Keep the arms taut along the body, put the hands on the floor, fingers pointed forwards.

Inhalation: Raise the arms taut laterally, palms of the hands facing up, join the palms of the hands together over the head.

Exhalation: Lower the arms taut, palms of the hands facing the floor, without letting the back sag.

Do 2 times.

3rd movement

Keep the arms taut along the body, put the hands on the floor, fingers pointed forward.

Inhalation: Raise the arms taut laterally, palms of the hands facing down, join the back of the hands together over the head.

Exhalation: Lower the arms taut, without letting the back sag, palms of the hands facing the floor.

Do 2 times.

4th movement

Keep the arms taut along the body, put the hands on the floor, fingers pointed forward.

Inhalation: Raise the arms taut laterally, palms of the hands facing up, join the palms of the hands together over the head.

Exhalation: Without letting the back sag, bend the elbows, keep the hands joined together and bend the forearms backwards in order to bring the hands behind the head, thumbs against the back of the neck. Tighten up the elbows and keep them away from the head.

Inhalation: Raise the hands and stretch the arms.

Do 2 times.

Exhalation: Lower the arms taut laterally, palms of the hands facing the floor.

Extend the legs out on the floor, feet together.

Take rest.

Fruits

- Rectifies static position of the spine. Strengthens muscles located all along the spinal column. Strengthens abdominal muscles.
- Develops respiratory capacity.
- Stabilizes the vegetative nervous system.
- Reduces symptoms of premenstrual syndrome.

Parvata Āsana, bending

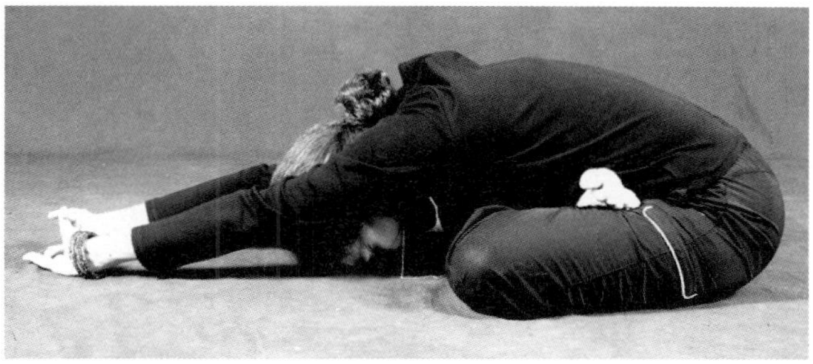

Fig. 95 Parvata Āsana, bending N° 1
(Dominique)

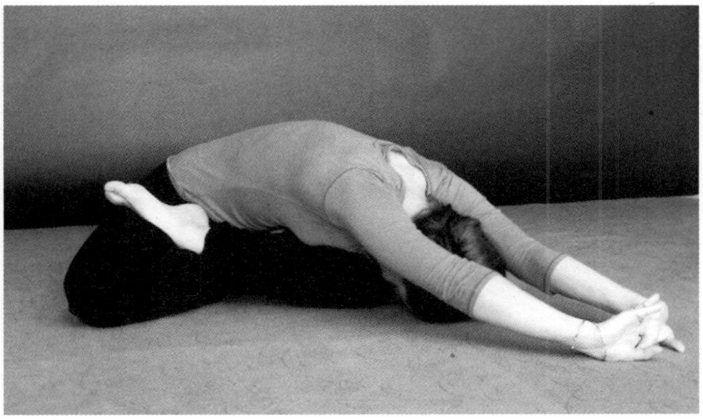

Fig. 96 Parvata Āsana, bending N° 2
(Estelle)

Fig. 97 Parvata Āsana, bending N° 3
(Estelle)

Technique

Do Padma Āsana or sit in cross-legged position. Lower the chin and straighten the entire spinal column so it is perfectly straight. Interlock the fingers, turn over the palms of the hands, thumbs inwards and close the eyes. Raise the arms taut over the head.

Exhalation: With the arms taut, bend forward, put the head and the hands on the floor without raising the buttocks.

Inhalation: Raise up the trunk raising first the hands. Turn the chest completely to the left. Keep it facing the left thigh. Keep the chin against the breastbone.

Exhalation: Bend the trunk on the left thigh, put the hands on the floor without raising the buttocks.

Inhalation: Raise up the trunk raising first the hands. Turn the chest completely to the right. Keep it facing the right thigh. Keep the chin against the breastbone.

Exhalation: Bend the trunk on the right thigh, put the hands on the floor without raising the buttocks.

Inhalation: Raise up the trunk raising first the hands. Turn the chest to the middle again and keep the chin on against the breastbone.

Exhalation: With the arms taut, bend forward, put the head and the hands on the floor without raising the buttocks.

Inhalation: Raise up the chest raising the hands first.

Repeat the three bends 3 times.

Exhalation: Lower the arms and relax the hands.

Extend the legs out along the floor, feet together.

Take rest.

Fruits

- Rectifies static position of the spine. Strengthens muscles located all along the spinal column. Strengthens abdominal muscles.
- Develops respiratory capacity.
- Stabilizes the vegetative nervous system.
- Reduces symptoms of premenstrual syndrome.

Paścimatāna Āsana

Paścima = the west, dorsal region, *utthāna* = extension. In this Āsana, the entire dorsal region is stretched.

Fig. 98 Paścimatāna Āsana

(Estelle)

Technique

Do Daṇḍa Āsana. Interlock the fingers, turn over the palms of the hands, thumbs inwards. Raise the arms taut over the head. Lower the chin and close the eyes.

Exhalation: Bend the trunk forward, lower the arms, relax the hands and hold the big toes, the ankles or the tibias. Without releasing the hands, straighten the back stretching the spinal column. Lower the shoulders and the chin.

Do 6 *Ujjāyi* breaths.

Inhalation: Interlock the fingers, turn the palms of the hands over, raise the arms taut over the head straightening the trunk vertically.

Exhalation: Lower the arms and relax the fingers.

Take rest.

Concentration

- All vital points located between *mūla* and *śīrṣa*.

Fruits

- Rectifies the static position of the spine, maintains intervertebral spaces and prevents slipped discs.
- Lengthens Exhalation time.
- Stabilizes the endocrine secretions of the pancreas.
- Stimulates the production of gastric secretions and improves digestion. Improves intestinal elimination, prevents constipation.
- Stabilizes all endocrine secretions.
- Provides mental calm and improves mental concentration. Stimulates enthusiasm.

Parivṛtta Paścimatāna Āsana

Parivṛtta = turn around, *paścima* = the west, dorsal region, *utthāna* = extension.

Fig. 99 Parivṛtta Paścimatāna Āsana, right side

(Stéphanie)

Technique

Do Daṇḍa Āsana.

Inhalation: Raise the arms laterally in a horizontal position, palms of the hands turned towards the floor.

Exhalation: Turn the trunk to the left and lean the chest on the taut legs. Turn the right arm towards the exterior and bending the arm, bring the right elbow towards the floor on the exterior of the right knee, palm of the right hand against the outer side of the left foot. Hold the left foot. Bring the left arm over the head in order to take hold of the outer side of the right foot, palm of the left hand against the outer side of the right foot. Keep the head between the arms.

Do 1 to 3 *Ujjāyi* breaths.

Inhalation: Relax the hands, place them back in a horizontal position, turn the chest to face forward and straighten the back.

Do the Āsana on the right.

Inhalation: Relax the hands, place them back in a horizontal position, turn the trunk to face forward and straighten the back.

Exhalation: Lower the arms along the body.

Take rest.

Fruits

- Rectifies static position of the spine. Makes supple all the pelvis joints. Strengthens abdominal muscles and muscles of the dorsal region.
- Strengthens the abdominal organs and the kidneys, and prevents their prolapses.
- Develops respiratory capacity.
- Stimulates diuresis.
- Prevents kidney prolapses.

Parivṛtta Paśćimatāna Āsana, variation

Fig. 100 Parivṛtta Paśćimatāna Āsana, variation

(Françoise)

Technique

Do Danḍa Āsana.

Inhalation: Raise the arms laterally in a horizontal position, palms of the hands turned towards the floor.

Exhalation: Turn the trunk to the left and bend the chest slightly on the taut legs. Hold the outer side of the left foot with the right hand, thumb pointed towards the floor. Put the left arm behind the back and hold the right thigh. Turn the head to the left. Straighten the back and close the eyes.

Do 3 *Ujjāyi* breaths.

Inhalation: Relax the hands, without bending the elbows, put them back in a horizontal position, turn the chest round forward and straighten the back.

Do the Āsana on the right side.

Inhalation: Relax the hands, put them back in a horizontal position, turn the chest round forward and straighten the back.

Exhalation: Lower the arms along the body.

Take rest.

Fruits

- Rectifies static position of the spine. Makes supple all the pelvis joints. Strengthens abdominal muscles and muscles of the dorsal region.
- Strengthens the abdominal organs and the kidneys, and prevents their prolapses.
- Develops respiratory capacity.
- Stimulates diuresis.
- Prevents kidney prolapses.

Piṇḍa Āsana

Piṇḍa = meatball, an offering to the ancestors in the shape of meatballs, foetus. In this Āsana the body takes the foetus position.

Fig. 101 Ūrdhva Mukha Padma Āsana

(Claire)

Fig. 102 Piṇḍa Āsana

(Claire)

Technique

Do Sarvānga Āsana. Put the legs in Padma Āsana, or lie on the back, put the legs in Padma Āsana and do Sarvānga Āsana.

Inhalation: Straighten the knees.

This called is called Ūrdhva Mukha Padma Āsana.

Exhalation: Lower the legs in order to bring the knees against the shoulders. Relax the hands. While keeping balance on the shoulders, put the arms around the legs. See Fig. 15.

Do 3 *Ujjāyi* breaths in this position. Relax the hands, rest the arms on the floor and place the hands behind the back again.

Inhalation: Raise the legs again to return to Sarvānga Āsana.

Exhalation: Lower the legs on a right angle, then put the arms on the floor.

Inhalation: Lay the back down, then the legs on the floor without detaching the head or the shoulders from the floor.

Take rest.

Fruits

- Improves nervous resistance to external stimuli such as stress, for example.

Prasārita Pāda Utthāna Āsana

Prasārita = spread, *pāda* = foot, leg, *utthāna* = extend, extension.

Fig. 103 Prasārita Pāda Utthāna Āsana 1

(Muriel)

Fig. 104 Prasārita Pāda Utthāna Āsana 2

(Stéphanie)

Technique

Do Samasthiti. Spread the legs apart a minimum of one metre fifty, keeping the feet parallel. Raise the arms over the head, arms parallel, keeping the palms of the hands facing forward.

Exhalation: Bend the trunk forward, place the hands on the floor between the feet, in line with the shoulders, and spread the feet apart even more. Put the head on the floor between the hands and relax the abdomen. Close the eyes.

Do 3 to 6 *Ujjāyi* breaths.

Inhalation: Bring the feet a bit closer and raise the chest to the vertical position raising the arms taut over the head. Lower the arms and join the feet together.

Take rest.

Fruits

- Strengthens the abdominal organs and the kidneys, and prevents their prolapses.
- Prevents kidney prolapses.
- Improves the venous and lymphatic circulations. Improves arterial circulation of the heart and the brain.
- Improves intestinal absorption.
- Tones up cardiac muscles.
- Stimulates diuresis.
- Strengthens the linings of the womb.
- At the beginning of the pregnancy, supports the functions of digestion and assimilation.
- Avoids early contractions due to exhaustion or poor assimilation. Reduces labour pains.

Pūrvatāna Āsana

Pūrva = east, frontal region, *utthāna* = extension. This Āsana is practiced after Paścimatāna Āsana. In this Āsana, the entire frontal region is stretched.

Fig. 105 Pūrvatāna Āsana
(Françoise)

Technique

Do Daṇḍa Āsana. Put the hands on the floor behind the buttocks, spread apart at least 50 centimetres, fingers directed towards the buttocks. Close the eyes.

Inhalation: While keeping the legs and the arms taut and pushing on the hands and the heels, raise the pelvis and the chest, head backwards. Point the feet (toes on the floor).

Exhalation: Lay the buttocks down on the floor in the same place, lower the head and straighten the back.

Repeat 3 times. Come back to Daṇḍa Āsana.

Take rest.

Fruits

- Rectifies the static position of the spine, maintains intervertebral spaces.
- Makes supple all the pelvis joints and coxofemoral joints.
- Relieves the syndrome of 'restless legs' (also called 'Wittmaak Ekborns' syndrome').
- Improves the venous and lymphatic circulations.
- During pregnancy, improves the functions of intestinal elimination and prevents haemorrhoids.
- Supports perineum and avoids organ prolapses after delivery.

Pūrvatāna Āsana in Upaviśṭa Koṇa Āsana

Pūrva = east, the frontal part of the body. *Utthāna* = stretch. *Upaviśṭa Koṇa* = obtuse angle. This Āsana is practiced after Upaviśṭa Koṇa Āsana.

Fig. 106 Pūrvatāna Āsana in Upaviśṭa Koṇa Āsana

(Muriel)

Technique

Do Danḍa Āsana. Spread the legs with the feet spread apart at least one-meter fifty. Put the hands on the floor behind the buttocks, spread apart at least 50 centimetres, fingers directed towards he buttocks. Close the eyes.

Inhalation: While keeping the legs and arms taut and pushing on the hands and the heels, raise the pelvis and the chest, head backwards. Point the feet (the toes) to the floor.

Exhalation: Place the buttocks back on the floor to the same place, bring in the head and straighten the back.

Repeat 3 times. Go back into Danḍa Āsana.

Take rest.

Fruits

- Rectifies the static position of spinal column and maintains intervertebral spaces.
- Makes supple all the pelvis and coxofemoral joints.
- Relieves 'restless leg' syndrome (also called 'Wittmaak Ekborns' syndrome').
- Improves the venous and lymphatic circulation of the body.
- During pregnancy, improves the functions of intestinal elimination and prevents haemorrhoids.
- Supports the perineum and avoids prolapsed organs after delivery

Rāja Kapota Āsana

Rāja = the king, *Kapota* = pigeon, *Rāja Kapota* = dove. In this Āsana, the body forms the shape of a dove.

Fig. 107 Rāja Kapota Āsana right side (Brigitte)

Technique

Kneel down sitting on the heels. Put your hands on the floor next to the knees. Using your hands for support, stretch the left leg backwards. Turn the right foot in order to put the upper part of the foot on the floor. Sit on the internal side of the heel of the right foot. Put your hands on the right thigh. Straighten the chest.

Inhalation: Pushing on the right thigh, bring the chest and the head backwards. Close the eyes.

Do 1 to 3 *Ujjāyi* breaths.

Exhalation: Without bending the chest forward or raising the pelvis, bend the left leg and bring the left foot towards the head.

Do 1 to 3 *Ujjāyi* breaths.

Stretch the left leg and put the foot on the floor. Bring the head down. Put the hands again back on the floor next to the right knee. Turn the right foot and put the upper part of the foot on the floor. Bend the left leg again and sit on the heels.

Do the Āsana with the right leg.

Stretch the right leg and put the foot on the floor. Lower the head. Put the hands again back on the floor next to the left knee. Turn the left foot and put the upper part of the foot on the floor. Bend the right leg again and sit on the heels.

Stretch the legs out in front of you.

Take rest.

Concentration

- *Kaṇṭha*.

Fruits

- Makes supple the spinal, cervical and dorsal column. Rectifies dorsal kyphosis.
- Strengthens the coxofemoral joints.
- Strengthens the abdominal organs and the kidneys, and prevents their prolapses.
- Improves renal functions.
- Stabilizes all the adrenal gland secretion.
- Stimulates secretions of the small intestine, and improves intestinal absorption.
- Improves respiratory capacity and pulmonary compliance.
- Stabilizes ovarian functions. Reduces symptoms of premenstrual syndrome.
- Prevents and lessens signs of menopause.
- Supports the endometrium and promotes conception.
- Prevents and reduces prostatic hypertrophy.
- Stabilizes vegetative nervous system.
- Supports blood pressure in cases of hypotension.
- Tones up cardiac muscles.
- Improves the functions of sense perceptions. Improves mental concentration.

Samasthiti

Sama = equal, *sthiti* = stable.

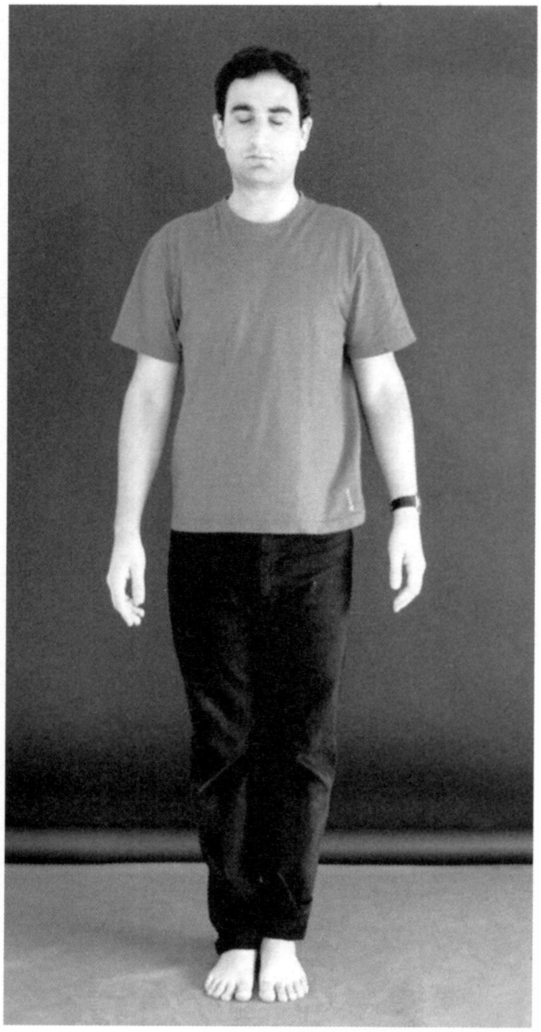

Fig. 108 Samasthiti

(Satya)

Technique

Stand up with feet and big toes together. Lay the arms down alongside the body, palms of the hands facing the thighs, draw in the chin and fully stretch the back of the neck. Keep the body vertical without leaning either forward, backward or to the side.

Do 6 *Ujjāyi* breaths.

Take rest.

Concentration

- *Nāsāgra, kaṇṭha, tāraka.*

Fruits

- Increases the sense of balance.

Sarvānga Āsana

Sarva = all, *aṁga* = limb. In this Āsana, the entire body benefits from this Āsana, hence the name.

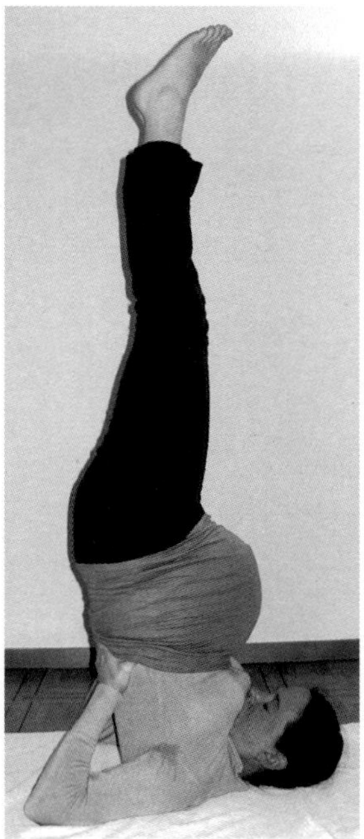

Fig. 109 Sarvānga Āsana

(Muriel)

Fig. 110 Sarvānga Āsana

(William)

Technique

Lie flat on the back, legs together, feet together, arms along the body, palms of the hands on the floor, chin down and eyes closed.

Exhalation: Raise both legs keeping them together; raise the pelvis and the chest vertically in order to support yourself on the shoulders. Bring the sternum against the chin. Bend the elbows and put the palms of the hands on the back at the level of the ribs as close as possible to the shoulder blades. Keep the feet vertical in line with the eyes. Close the eyes.

Do 6, 8 or 12 *Ujjāyi* breaths.

Exhalation: Draw the legs down backwards at a right angle, and then put the arms on the floor, palms of the hands on the floor.

Inhalation: Supporting yourself on your hands, gently lie down again on your back, then put your legs on the floor without raising your head or your shoulders.

Take rest.

Concentration

- *Kaṇṭha.*

Fruits

- Makes supple the spinal, cervical and dorsal column.
- Provides a sensation of lightness throughout the body.
- Improves lymphatic circulation of the body.
- Improves venous circulation of lower limbs, prevents and reduces varicose veins.
- Improves blood circulation between a pregnant mother and foetus.
- Relieves 'restless leg' syndrome (also called 'Wittmaak Ekborns' syndrome').
- Tones up cardiac muscles.
- Reduces and helps to stabilise high blood pressure. Stabilizes blood pressure in case of low blood pressure.
- Improves respiratory capacity and pulmonary compliance.
- Improves renal functions.
- Improves the endocrine secretions of the body.
- Stabilizes thyroid hormone function, which promotes the harmonious growth of young children. Prevents and reduces goitre of the thyroid.
- Supports perineum and avoids organ prolapses after delivery.
- During pregnancy, prevents precarious uterine contractions.
- Supports endometrium and promotes conception.
- Prevents and helps to reduce ovarian cysts.
- Stabilizes the vegetative nervous system.
- Helps to restore the different phases of sleep.
- Improves the functions of all the organs of the body.
- Strengthens the abdominal organs and the kidneys, and prevents their prolapses.
- Supports all the elimination functions of the body.
- Stabilizes all the secretions of the alimentary canal, including salivary glands. Improves intestine elimination, prevents constipation.
- Provides mental attention and improves mental concentration.
- Reduces mental excitement.
- Improves the functions of sense perceptions. Increases nervous resistance to external stimuli such as stress, for example.

Variation of Sarvānga Āsana, Eka Pāda Sarvānga Āsana

Note: These variations can be practiced either one by one or several at a time, as long as you do not exceed a total of 12 breaths. At the end of the variation, come down from Sarvānga Āsana.

Eka = one, *pāda* = foot or leg.

Fig. 111 Eka Pāda Sarvānga Āsana (Renée)

Technique

Do Sarvānga Āsana.

Exhalation: Bring the taut left leg down behind the head and place the foot on the floor. Keep the right leg taut and vertical.

Inhalation: Move the taut left leg back into position beside the right leg. Join the feet together.

Do the Āsana with the right leg.

Repeat two times alternately.

You can do this variation holding the position for 1 to 3 *Ujjāyi* breaths.

Fruits

- Strengthens the abdominal muscles.
- Tones up the muscular structure located under the navel region.
- Strengthens the abdominal organs and the kidneys, and prevents their prolapses.
- Improves digestion.
- Improves the venous and lymphatic circulations.
- Tones up cardiac muscles.
- Facilitates holding of Antah Kumbhaka and Bāhya Kumbhaka.

Variation of Sarvānga Āsana: Eka Pāda Ākuñcana Āsana

Eka = one, *pāda* = foot or leg, *ākuñcana* = contraction, compression.

Fig. 112 Eka Pāda Ākuñcana Āsana

(Renée)

Technique

Do Sarvānga Āsana.

Exhalation: Bend the left knee bringing the heel close to the left buttock, thigh against the stomach and knee beside the head without turning the head. Keep the right leg taut and vertical.

Inhalation: Bring the left leg taut next to the right leg. Join the feet together.

Do the Āsana with the right leg.

You can do this variation maintaining the position for 1 to 3 *Ujjāyi* breaths.

Fruits

- Improves digestion.
- Improves intestinal elimination, prevents constipation.
- Develops respiratory capacity.
- Tones up cardiac muscles.
- Prevents and helps to reduce ovarian cysts.

Variation of Sarvānga Āsana: Dvi Pāda Ākuñcana Āsana

Dvi = two, *pāda* = foot, leg, *ākuñcana* = compression, contraction.

Fig. 113 Dvi Pāda Ākuñcana Āsana (Cornelia)

Technique

Do Sarvānga Āsana.

Exhalation: Bend both knees bringing the heels close to the buttocks, thighs against the stomach and knees at the forehead. Keep the feet and knees together. Press the hands on the back in order to stretch it.

Inhalation: Raise both legs together vertically.

Repeat 3 times.

You can do this variation maintaining the position for 1 to 3 *Ujjāyi* breaths.

Fruits

- Improves digestion.
- Improves intestinal elimination and prevents constipation.
- Develops respiratory capacity.
- Tones up cardiac muscles.
- Prevents and helps to reduce ovarian cysts.

Variation of Sarvānga Āsana: Prasārita Sarvānga Āsana

Prasārita = spread, spread apart.

Fig. 114 Prasārita Sarvānga Āsana (Patrice)

Technique

Do Sarvānga Āsana.

Inhalation: Set both legs apart laterally as much as possible without bending them forward.

Exhalation: Bring both legs together again vertically.

Repeat 3 times or do 3 *Ujjāyi* breaths.

Fruits

- Strengthens the lumbar region.
- Makes supple coxofemoral joints.
- Makes supple the hip joints.
- Makes supple all pelvic joints.
- Helps to open the pelvis and helps easy delivery.
- Supports the perineum and prevents the descent of the pelvic floor.
- Supports perineum and avoids organ prolapses after delivery.
- Strengthens the uterine wall.
- Strengthens the abdominal organs and the kidneys, and prevents their prolapses.

Variation of Sarvānga Āsana: Baddha Koṇa Āsana in Sarvānga Āsana

Baddha = tied up, *koṇa* = angle.

Fig. 115 Baddha Koṇa Āsana in Sarvānga Āsana

(Cornelia)

Technique

Do Sarvānga Āsana.

Exhalation: Bend the knees bringing the soles of the feet together and draw the heels towards the perineum. Spread the knees laterally.

Inhalation: Bring both legs back up vertically and join the feet together.

Repeat 3 times.

You can do this variation maintaining the position for 1 to 3 *Ujjāyi* breaths.

Fruits

- Makes supple coxofemoral joints.
- Makes supple all the pelvic joints.
- Helps to open the pelvis and helps easy delivery.
- Supports the perineum and prevents the descent of the pelvic floor.
- Improves intestinal absorption and elimination, prevents constipation.
- Prevents and reduces haemorrhoids.
- Stimulates diuresis.
- Supports perineum and avoids organ prolapses after delivery.
- Strengthens the uterine wall.
- Prevents and reduces prostatic hypertrophy.
- Strengthens the abdominal organs and the kidneys, and prevents their prolapses.

Variation in Sarvānga Āsana: Ākuñcana Āsana Parivṛtti

Ākuñcana = contraction, compression. *Parivṛtti* = turn round about.

Fig. 116 Ākuñcana Āsana Parivṛtti (Cornelia)

Technique

Do Sarvānga Āsana.

Exhalation: Bend both knees and bring them to the forehead, heels close to the buttocks.

Inhalation: Raise both legs together vertically. Turn the pelvis and the chest to the left. Push with the right hand to turn the chest to the left even more.

Exhalation: Without turning the head, bend both knees and bring them against the left shoulder, heels close to the buttocks.

Inhalation: Raise the legs again while maintaining the twisting action. Turn the pelvis and the chest to the right. Push with the left hand in order to turn the chest even further to the right.

Exhalation: Without turning the head, bend both knees and bring them against the right shoulder, heels close to the buttocks.

Inhalation: Raise the legs again while keeping the twist, and then turn the pelvis forward.

Exhalation: Bend both knees and bring them to the forehead, heels close to the buttocks.

Inhalation: Raise both legs together vertically.

Repeat 3 times.

Fruits

- Rectifies the static position of the spine, maintains intervertebral spaces.
- Strengthens the abdominal organs and the kidneys, and prevents their prolapses.
- Improves intestinal elimination, prevents constipation.
- Prevents and reduces haemorrhoids.

Variation of Sarvānga Āsana: Pārśva Eka Pāda Sarvānga Āsana

Pārśva = side, *eka* = one, *pāda* = foot, leg.

Fig. 117 Pārśva Eka Pāda Sarvānga Āsana (Cornelia)

Technique

Do Sarvānga Āsana.

Exhalation: Turn the left leg out to the left. Bring the left leg down laterally to the left posing the toes on the floor. Keep the left leg in Sarvānga Āsana.

Inhalation: Raise the left leg again and turn it round so it faces forward.

Do the Āsana with the right leg.

Repeat 2 times alternately.

Fruits

- Makes supple all the pelvis joints and rectifies pelvis position.
- Strengthens coxofemoral joints.

Variation of Sarvānga Āsana: Ardha Padma Ākuñcana Āsana

Ardha = half, *Padma* = lotus, *ākuñcana* = contraction, compression, reduction.

Fig. 118 Ardha Padma Ākuñcana Āsana (Cornelia)

Technique

Do Sarvānga Āsana.

Bend the right knee and place the right foot against the hollow of the left groin. Keep the right foot slightly on the outside of the left thigh.

Exhalation: Bend the left knee, keeping the left foot close to the left buttock.

Inhalation: Straighten the left leg while raising the right knee.

Repeat 3 times or do 3 breaths *Ujjāyi*.

Straighten the right leg again.

Do the Āsana with the left leg in Padma Āsana.

Fruits

- Strengthens the abdominal organs and the kidneys, and prevents their prolapses.
- Improves intestinal elimination, prevents constipation.
- Stimulates diuresis.

Śalabha Āsana

Śalabha = grasshopper or dragonfly.

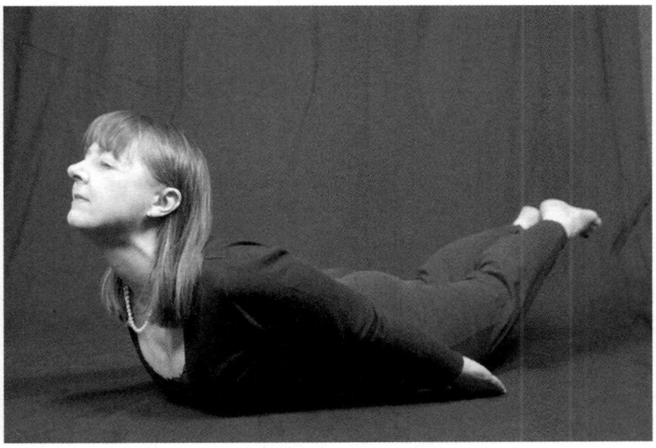

Fig. 119 Śalabha Āsana

(Cornelia)

Technique

Lie down on the stomach, legs and feet together, forehead on the floor, eyes closed, arms alongside the body and the back of the hands on the floor.

Inhalation: Support yourself on the back of the hands and at the same time raise the head, chest and both legs taut. Open up the shoulders.

Exhalation: Bring the chest, legs and forehead down again on the floor.

Repeat 3 times or do 3 *Ujjāyi* breaths.

Turn over and take rest.

Fruits

- Rectifies the static position of the spinal column and maintains intervertebral spaces. Strengthens the muscles located all along the spinal column, especially those in the lumbar region. Strengthens the coxofemoral joints.
- Prevents kidney prolapses.
- Stimulates diuresis.
- Restores ovarian cycle and Stabilizes ovarian functions. Reduces symptoms of premenstrual syndrome. Supports endometrium and promotes conception. Helps to absorb uterine fibromas.
- Promotes elimination of catabolic cellular remnants.
- After delivery, reduces tissue oedema and strengthens the uterine wall.
- Strengthens cardiac muscles.
- Improves mental concentration.
- Facilitates holding of *Antah Kumbhaka* and *Bāhya Kumbhaka*.

Śīrṣa Āsana (Viparīta Karaṇi Mudra)

Śīrṣa = fontanel, *viparīta* = eccentric, upside down, *karaṇi* = small intestine. Posture on the head. Considered as a *Mudra* (Viparīta Karaṇi Mudra). King of the Āsanas, therefore the most important Āsana. No other Āsana can replace it.

Fig. 120 Śīrṣa Āsana

(Muriel)

Fig. 121 Śīrṣa Āsana

(Renée)

Technique (against a wall)

Put a blanket folded in four in front of a wall. Kneel down in front of the blanket. Interlock the fingers. Bend the chest forward in order to put the forearms on the blanket, hands vertical and the back of the fingers against the wall. Make sure that the spacing between the elbows is the same as the width between the shoulders.

Put the top of the head on the blanket in order to have the palms of the hands touching the back of the head; the thumbs should be separated and follow the outline of the head. Press the toes on the floor in order to raise the knees. Move the feet forward with small steps.

Inhalation: Take a little push with both legs together and raise them with both knees bent, without pivoting the head. Immediately, stretch your legs against the wall. Move the back and buttocks away from the wall so they can remain in line with the back of the neck. The back of the fingers and heels should be the only parts of the body in contact with the wall. Raise the shoulders so they are away from the ears. Close the eyes.

Do 6, 8 or 12 *Ujjāyi* breaths.

Exhalation: Bend the knees bringing the thighs against the abdomen, put the feet back on the floor and then the knees.

Lie flat on the back, legs together, feet together, arms along the body, palms of the hands on the floor, chin lowered, eyes closed.

Remark: If there is a painful sensation in the back while resting, do Taṭāka Mudra or Śvāna Āsana.

Concentration

- *Kaṇṭha, nāsāgra, nābhi, hṛdaya.*

Fruits

- Increases sense of balance.
- Improves all the functions of the organs of the body.
- Provides a sensation of lightness throughout the body.
- Improves digestion, intestinal absorption and elimination, fights against constipation.
- Harmonizes the peristaltic movement of the alimentary canal.
- Reduces colic spasms.
- Improves the venous and lymphatic circulations as well as cerebral circulation.
- Supports cardiac functions.
- Improves respiratory capacity and pulmonary compliance.
- Strengthens the abdominal organs and the kidneys, and prevents their prolapses.
- Prevents kidney prolapses.
- Improves renal functions.
- Stabilizes the endocrine secretions of the body as well as the hypothalamus activity on the pituitary gland.
- Supports endometrium.
- Helps to establish a conception in utero.
- Improves blood circulation between a pregnant mother and foetus.
- Improves intestinal elimination function during pregnancy.
- Prevents haemorrhoids.
- Supports perineum and avoids organ prolapses after delivery.
- Prevents precarious womb contractions.
- Stabilizes prostatic functions.
- Prevents and reduces prostatic hypertrophy.
- Helps to restore the different phases of sleep.
- Relieves 'restless leg' syndrome, (also called 'Wittmaak Ekborns' syndrome').
- Stabilizes the vegetative nervous system.
- Improves mental concentration.
- Increases memory and intellectual capacities.
- Provides mental calm, reduces excitement and mental strain.
- Improves nervous resistances to external stimuli such as stress, for example.

Śvāna Āsana

Śvāna = dog, cat, feline. *Ūrdhva* = high, *adha (adho)* = downwards, *mukha* = face, look.

Fig. 122 Ūrdhva Mukha Śvāna Āsana (Cornelia)

Fig. 123 Adho Mukha Śvāna Āsana (Françoise)

Technique

Lie on the stomach. Forehead on the floor, palms of the hands on the floor at the level of the lower ribs, fingers pointing towards the head, elbows bent as close as possible to the body, legs together and taut, toes turned up, chin down and eyes closed.

Inhalation: With the support of the hands and stretching the arms, raise the head, chest and stomach. Keep the legs taut. Raise the knees in order to keep the legs parallel to the floor. Pull the chest backwards. Raise the head backwards. (This Āsana is called Ūrdhva Mukha Śvāna Āsana).

Exhalation: Raise the pelvis and bend the chest forward. Place the head between the arms and bring the chin down. Keep the legs taut and press the heels towards the floor. This Āsana is called Adho Mukha Śvāna Āsana.

Inhalation: Without bending the elbows, lower the pelvis and the legs and raise the upper body again. Bring the head backward in order to get back into Ūrdhva Mukha Śvāna Āsana.

Exhalation: Bend the elbows without opening them and place the legs, abdomen, chest and forehead back on the floor.

Repeat 3 times.

Turn over and take rest.

Fruits

- Rectifies the static position of the spine, maintains intervertebral spaces and prevents slipped discs. Strengthens muscles located all along the spinal column. Makes supple the shoulder joints and the entire spinal column. Develops rib cage volume.
- Develops the muscles of the legs and the arms.
- Harmonizes peristaltic movement of the alimentary canal; improves intestinal elimination and prevents constipation.
- Improves the venous and lymphatic circulations.
- Develops respiratory capacity.
- Stimulates diuresis.

Simha Āsana

Simha = lion.

Fig. 124 Simha Āsana

(Renée)

Technique

Do Padma Āsana. Stretch your arms out in front of you and bend the chest forwards in order to put the hands on the floor approximately 80 centimetres in front of the knees with fingers pointing forward. Rise up on your knees, then lower the pelvis towards the floor in order to place yourself on your stomach. Place the forehead on the floor and the hands at the level of the lower ribs.

Inhalation: Supporting yourself on your hands and stretching the arms without opening the elbows, raise the head, shoulders and chest. Remain on your hands and knees and press your pelvis to the floor. Head up. Open the mouth and stick out the tongue. Direct your gaze between the eyebrows.

Do 3 *Ujjāyi* breaths (through the nose).

Exhalation: Relax your gaze and bring in the tongue. Bend the elbows without opening them and progressively place the thighs, chest and forehead on the floor.

Supporting yourself with your hands, go back into the seated position and undo Padma Āsana.

Take rest.

Concentration

- *Bhrūmadhya.*

Fruits

- Strengthens the coxofemoral joints. Tones up the perineum.
- Prevents and reduces haemorrhoids.
- Stimulates the small intestine secretions.
- Stabilizes exocrine and endocrine secretions of the pancreas.
- Improves arterial circulation of the heart.
- Improves compliance and pulmonary functions.
- Develops respiratory capacity. Lengthens the duration of Inhalation.
- Facilitates holding of Antah Kumbhaka and Bāhya Kumbhaka.
- Improves renal functions.
- Stabilizes hormonal secretions of the pituitary gland and the adrenal gland glands.

- Stabilizes ovarian function. Prevents and helps to reduce ovarian cysts. Promotes resorption of uterine fibromas and helps to establish a conception in utero. Reduces oedema of tissue and strengthens the uterine wall after delivery.
- Stabilizes testicular secretions.
- Calms excitement and stabilizes the vegetative nervous system.
- Supports the functions of spleen.
- Promotes elimination of catabolic cellular remnants.
- Improves mental concentration. Reduces dispersion caused by the hyperactivity of the sense perceptions. Helps to clear up mental confusion, provides a clear mind.
- Improves nervous resistance to external stimuli such as stress, for example.
- Stimulates enthusiasm.
- Develops self-confidence, provides courage and increases perseverance.

Supta Pāda Aṅguṣṭa Āsana

Supta = lying, *pāda* = foot, leg, *aṅguṣṭa* = toe, *pāda aṅguṣṭa* = big toe.

Fig. 125 Supta Pāda Anguṣṭa Āsana
(Renée)

Technique

Lie flat on the back, legs and feet together, arms along the body, palms of the hands on the floor, chin down and eyes closed.

Exhalation: Raise both taut legs vertically without raising the chin. Take hold of the big toes, the ankles or the knees. Relax the abdomen.

Do 6 to 12 *Ujjāyi* breaths.

Inhalation: Put the arms back along the body and put the legs down together on the floor.

Take rest.

Concentration

- *Kaṇṭha.*

Fruits

- Makes supple lumbar spinal column.
- Rectifies the static position of the spine, maintains intervertebral spaces and prevents slipped discs.
- Makes supple the lumbar spinal column, prevents and relieves sciatica. Improves venous circulation of lower limbs, prevents and reduces varicose veins.
- Improves digestion.
- Harmonizes peristaltic movement of the alimentary canal, improves intestinal elimination and prevents constipation.
- Reduces intestinal meteorism and colic spasms of the colitis due to stress. Reduces the undesirable effects of chronic flatulence.
- Stimulates diuresis.

Supta Parivṛtta Pārśva Eka Pāda Aṅguṣṭa Āsana

Supta = lying, *parivṛtta* = turned, *pārśva* = Side, *eka* = one, *pāda* = foot, *aṅguṣṭa* = toe, *pāda aṅguṣṭa* = big toe.

Fig. 126 Supta Parivṛtta Pārśva Eka Pāda Anguṣṭa Āsana

(Renée)

Technique

Lie flat on the back, legs together, feet together, arms along the body, palms of the hands on the floor, chin down and eyes closed. Stretch the arms out to the sides on the same axis as the shoulders and put the palms of the hands on the floor.

Exhalation: Raise the left leg and the right hand vertically. Keep the arm turned inwards. Take hold of the big toe of the left leg with the thumb, index finger and middle finger of the right hand. Failing that, take hold of the external side of the left knee with the right hand. Keep the head on the floor. Without bending the right elbow, place the tautened left leg on the floor to the right. Turn the head to the left. Keep both legs taut.

Do 3 *Ujjāyi* breaths. Bring the head back to the centre.

Inhalation: Raise the taut left leg vertically without releasing the hold of the right hand. Relax the hand and put the right arm on the floor at shoulder level. Put the left leg back on the floor.

Do the Āsana with the right leg.

Bring the arms back along the body.

Take rest.

Fruits

- Makes supple the sacrolumbar region.
- Strengthens the muscles located along the spinal column and the abdominal muscles.
- Strengthens the abdominal organs and the kidneys, and prevents their prolapses.
- Prevents kidneys prolapses.
- Improves digestion, absorption and intestinal elimination, prevents constipation.
- Stabilizes exocrine secretions of the pancreas.
- Promotes bile drainage.
- Develops respiratory capacity.
- Stimulates diuresis.

Supta Pārśva Eka Pāda Aṅguṣṭa Āsana

Supta = lying, *pārśva* = side, *pāda* = foot, *aṅguṣṭa* = toe, *pāda aṅguṣṭa* = big toe.

Fig. 127 Supta Pārśva Eka Pāda Anguṣṭa Āsana

(Stéphanie)

Technique

Lie flat on the back, legs together, feet together, arms along the body, palms of the hands on the floor, chin down and eyes closed. Stretch the arms out to the sides on the same axis as the shoulders and put the palms of the hands on the floor.

Exhalation: Raise the left leg and the left hand vertically. Keep the left arm turned inwards. Take hold of the big toe of the left leg with the thumb, the index finger and the middle finger of the left hand. Failing that, take hold of the inner side of the left knee with the left hand. Keep the head on the floor. Place the taut left leg out to the left. Turn the head to the right. Keep both legs taut on the floor.

Do 3 *Ujjāyi* breaths. Bring the head back to the centre.

Inhalation: Raise the tightened left leg vertically without releasing the hold of the left hand. Relax the hand and put the left arm on the floor at shoulder level. Place the left leg back on the floor.

Do the Āsana with the right leg.

Bring the arms back alongside the body.

Take rest.

Fruits

- Strengthens the muscles located along the spinal column and the abdominal muscles.
- Makes supple the sacrolumbar region.
- Strengthens the abdominal organs and the kidneys, and prevents their prolapses.
- Improves digestion, absorption and intestinal elimination, prevents constipation.
- Stimulates diuresis.

Supta Parvata Āsana

Supta = lying, *parvata* = mountain. The lying mountain.

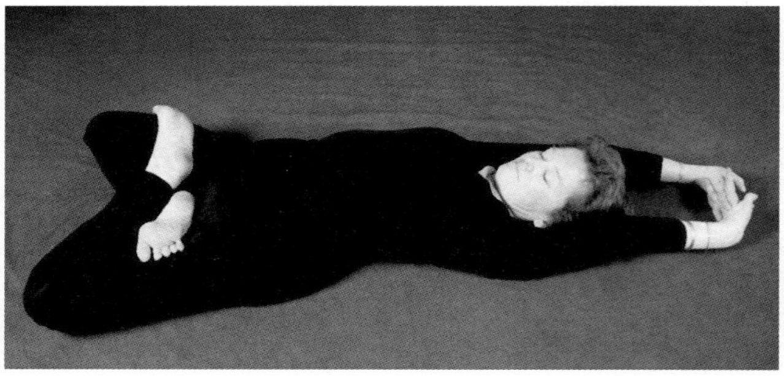

Fig. 128 Supta Parvata Āsana 1

(Brigitte)

Fig. 129 Supta Parvata Āsana 2

(Pascal)

Technique

Lie flat on your back, legs together, feet together, arms along the body, palms of the hands on the floor. Do Padma Āsana with your legs, or simply cross your legs, then put the thighs on the floor. Interlock the fingers, turn the palms of the hands, thumbs facing inwards.

Inhalation: Raise the arms taut above the head. Bring in the chin and close the eyes.

Do 6 *Ujjāyi* breaths.

Exhalation: Bring the arms again in front of you, release the fingers, put the arms back on the floor alongside the body. Uncross the legs and place them straight on the floor.

Take rest.

Concentration

- *Kaṇṭha.*

Fruits

- Makes supple the sacrolumbar region, all the pelvis and coxofemoral joints.
- Facilitates the opening of the pelvis.
- Reduces sensation of pain during delivery.
- Tones up the perineum.
- Strengthens the abdominal organs and the kidneys, and prevents their prolapses.
- Develops ribcage volume.
- Stabilizes all the secretions of the alimentary canal and improves digestion.
- Harmonizes peristaltic movement of the alimentary canal. Stabilizes biological rhythms of the different secretions of the alimentary canal.
- Prevents and reduces haemorrhoids.
- Tones up cardiac muscle and improves arterial circulation of the heart.
- Develops respiratory capacity and lengthens the duration of Inhalation.

- Improves compliance and pulmonary functions.
- Stimulates diuresis.
- Stabilizes hormonal secretions of the thyroid gland.
- Stabilizes hormonal secretions of the pituitary gland.
- Restores the harmony of the ovarian cycle. Prevents and helps to reduce ovarian cysts. Helps to establish a conception in utero. Reduces oedema of tissue and strengthens the uterine wall after delivery.
- Stabilizes prostatic functions. Prevents and reduces prostatic hypertrophy.
- Supports all the elimination functions of the body.

Tāḍa Āsana

Tāḍa = trunk of a tree (coconut tree, palm tree), therefore, a long trunk.

Fig. 130 Tāḍa Āsana
(Dominique)

Technique

Do Samasthiti. Interlock the fingers and turn the palms of the hands over, thumbs pointing inwards. Stretch the arms vertically over the head.

Inhalation: Raise the heels and stand on the top of the toes, stretch the arms upwards without raising the shoulders and fix your gaze on a point straight ahead of you.

Exhalation: Lower the heels.

Repeat 3 times or do 3 *Ujjāyi* breaths.

Lower the arms. Relax the hands.

Take rest.

Fruits

- Increases sense of balance.
- Rectifies scoliosis.
- Provides a sensation of lightness throughout the body.
- Improves the venous and lymphatic circulation of the body.
- Promotes mental attention.
- Reduces mental excitement.

Tāḍa Āsana Parivṛtti

Tāḍa = trunk of a tree (coconut tree, palm tree), therefore, a long trunk, *parivṛtti* = Turn round.

Fig. 131 Tāḍa Āsana Parivṛtti
(Françoise)

Technique

Do Samasthiti.

Inhalation: Raise the arms laterally and horizontally, palms of the hands pointing towards the floor.

Exhalation: Pivot the chest to the left and turn the head to the left. Keep the pelvis facing forward. Keep the arms horizontally. Turn the head to the left. Direct your gaze to the left hand.

Do 1 *Ujjāyi* breath.

Inhalation: Come back to the centre and bring the head back to the front.

Exhalation: Pivot the chest to the right. Turn the head to the right. Keep the pelvis facing forward. Keep the arms horizontally. Turn the head to the right. Direct your gaze to the right hand.

Do 1 *Ujjāyi* breath.

Inhalation: Come back to the centre and bring the head back to the front.

Repeat 3 times alternately.

Exhalation: Lower the arms.

Take rest.

Fruits

- Increases sense of balance.
- Rectifies scoliosis.
- Provides a sensation of lightness throughout the body.
- Improves the venous and lymphatic circulation of the body.
- Promotes mental attention.
- Reduces mental excitement.

Upaviśṭa Koṇa Āsana

Upaviśṭa = obtuse, *koṇa* = angle.

Fig. 132 Upaviśṭa Koṇa Āsana (Pascale)

Technique

Do Daṇḍa Āsana. Spread the legs approximately one metre thirty centimetres apart. Interlock the fingers, turn over the palms of the hands, thumbs facing inwards. Draw in the chin and close the eyes.

Inhalation: Raise the arms taut vertically over the head.

Exhalation: Bend forward, lower the arms, relax the hands and take hold of the big toes, the ankles or the tibias. Without releasing the hands, straighten the back stretching the spinal column. Lower the shoulders and draw in the chin.

Do 6 breaths *Ujjāyi.*

Inhalation: Interlock the fingers, turn over the palms of the hands, thumbs facing inwards, stretch the arms and raise them over the head straightening the upper body vertically.

Exhalation: Keep the back straight, lower the arms and relax the fingers, bring the legs together again.

Take rest.

Concentration

- *Nābhi, kaṇṭha.*

Fruits

- Rectifies lumbar hyperlordosis and pelvic posture.
- Facilitates pelvis opening and prepares for delivery.
- Lessens sensation of pain during delivery.
- Strengthens the coxofemoral joints.
- Improves intestinal digestion and absorption.
- During pregnancy, promotes intestinal elimination and in this way prevents constipation and haemorrhoids.
- Develops respiratory capacity. Lengthens duration of inhalation.
- Facilitates holding of Antah Kumbhaka and Bāhya Kumbhaka.
- Improves renal functions.
- Improves blood circulation between the pregnant mother and foetus.
- Stimulates ovulation.
- Reduces symptoms of premenstrual syndrome.
- Stabilizes prostatic functions.
- Reduces mental excitement.
- Provides concentration and mental attention.
- Improves nervous resistance to external stimuli such as stress, for example.

Upaviśṭa Koṇa Āsana, complete

Fig. 133 Upaviśṭa Koṇa Āsana, complete

(Claire)

Fig. 134 Upaviśṭa Koṇa Āsana, complete

(Claire)

Technique

Do Daṇḍa Āsana. Spread the legs approximately one metre thirty centimetres apart. Interlock the fingers, turn the palms of the hands over, thumbs facing inwards. Draw in the chin and close the eyes.

Inhalation: Raise the arms taut vertically over the head.

Exhalation: Bend the chest between the legs and lower the arms.

Inhalation: Raise the arms erecting the upper body vertically.

Turn the chest to the left, keep the chest facing the left leg and the chin against the breastbone (sternum). Straighten the back.

Exhalation: Bend the chest towards the left leg, put the hands on the foot and keep the legs taut. Keep the right leg and the right buttock on the floor. Without releasing the hands, straighten the back stretching the spinal column. Lower the shoulders and draw in the chin.

Inhalation: Raise the chest and the arms vertically keeping the chest facing the left leg.

Turn the chest completely to the right, keep the chest facing the right leg and the chin against the sternum. Straighten the back.

Exhalation: Bend the chest towards the right leg, put the hands on the foot, keep the legs taut. Keep the left leg and the left buttock on the floor. Without releasing the hands, straighten the back stretching the spinal column. Lower the shoulders and draw in the chin.

Inhalation: Raise the chest and arms vertically keeping the chest facing the right leg.

Come back to the centre, the chest facing forward.

Exhalation: Bend the chest between the legs and lower the arms.

Inhalation: Raise the chest and arms vertically.

Repeat each of the bending actions 3 times.

Lower the arms, relax the fingers, bring the legs together again on the floor, feet together.

Take rest.

Fruits

- Same as Upaviśṭa Koṇa Āsana.

Ūrdhva Mukha Āsana

Ūrdhva = celestial, towards the top, *mukha* = face. In this Āsana, the face and the upper part of the trunk are facing the sky.

Fig. 135 Ūrdhva Mukha Āsana

(Dominique)

Technique

Do *Samasthiti*. Place the arms taut behind the back, hands against the muscles of the buttocks. Interlock the fingers, stretch the shoulders backwards and turn the hands over so that the palms are facing the buttocks.

Inhalation: Stretch the arms towards the floor while bending the upper part of the trunk backwards. While stretching the neck bring the head backwards. Close the eyes. Do not bend the lumbar region.

Exhalation: Bring the chest back vertically releasing the arms. Relax the hands and put them alongside the body.

Do 3 times or hold the Āsana during 3 *Ujjāyi* breaths.

Take rest.

Fruits

- Rectifies static position of the spine.
- Makes supple the cervical spinal column.
- 'Opens' and makes supple the shoulder joints.
- Develops respiratory capacity.
- Stabilizes hormonal secretions of the thyroid gland.
- Strengthens cardiac muscles.
- Improves arterial circulation of the heart and brain.

Ūrdhva Mukha Śvāna Āsana

Śvāna = dog, cat, feline, *ūrdhva* = high, celestial, *mukha* = face, look.

Fig. 136 Ūrdhva Mukha Śvāna Āsana (Cornelia)

Technique

Lie on the stomach, forehead on the floor, palms of the hands facing the floor at the level of the inferior ribs, fingers pointing towards the head, elbows bent as close as possible to the body, taut legs together, toes turned up, chin down and eyes closed.

Inhalation: Supporting yourself on the hands and stretching the arms, raise the head, chest and stomach. Keep the legs taut. Stretch the chest backwards. Raise the head backwards.

Do 3 *Ujjāyi* breaths.

Exhalation: Bend the elbows without opening them and progressively place the knees, pelvis, chest and forehead on the floor.

Turn over and take rest.

Concentration

- *Kaṇṭha.*

Fruits

- Stabilizes the static position of the spinal column, maintains intervertebral spaces and prevents slipped discs.
- Makes supple the cervical and dorsal spinal column.
- Rectifies dorsal kyphosis.
- Rectifies pelvic posture and strengthens coxofemoral joints.
- Makes supple the shoulder joints.
- Develops ribcage volume.
- Strengthens abdominal muscles.
- Strengthens cardiac muscles.
- Improves digestion.

Ūrdhva Prasuta Pāda Āsana

Ūrdhva = upwards, towards the sky, celestial, *prasuta* = bring vertically, *pāda* = foot, leg.

Fig. 137 Ūrdhva Prasuta Pāda Āsana

(Pascale)

Technique

Lie flat on the back, legs together, feet together, arms along the body, palms of the hands on the floor, chin down and eyes closed.

Exhalation: Raise both taut legs vertically, without bending the knees keeping the shoulders and the head on the floor.

Inhalation: Put both taut legs back on the floor.

Repeat 3 or 6 times.

Take rest.

Fruits

- Rectifies the static position of the spinal column and maintains intervertebral spaces.
- Develops the muscles of the legs.
- Tones up sub-umbilical muscles.
- Improves the venous and lymphatic circulations.
- Harmonizes the peristaltic movement of the alimentary canal.
- Improves intestinal absorption and elimination and prevents constipation.

Ūrdhva Prasuta Pāda Āsana and Ardha Setu Bandha Āsana

Ūrdhva = upwards, towards the sky, celestial, *prasuta* = bring vertically, *pāda* = foot, leg, *ardha* = half, *setu* = bridge, *bandha* = Bound. Half-bound bridge.

Fig. 138 Ūrdhva Prasuta Pāda Āsana and Ardha Setu Bandha Āsana 1

(Pascale)

Fig. 139 Ūrdhva Prasuta Pāda Āsana and Ardha Setu Bandha Āsana 2

(Renée)

Technique

Lie flat on the back, legs and feet together, arms along the body, palms of the hands on the floor, chin down and eyes closed.

Exhalation: Raise both legs taut vertically without raising the chin, bend both knees and put the feet on the floor, heels close to the buttocks.

Inhalation: Supporting yourself on your feet, raise the buttocks and the back as high as possible. Keep the heels and the shoulders on the floor, bring the chin in.

Exhalation: Put the back and the buttocks on the floor again.

Inhalation: Raise the feet, stretch the legs vertically and place the taut legs on the floor again.

Repeat 4 or 6 times.

Take rest.

Fruits

- Same as Ūrdhva Prasuta Pāda Āsana and Ardha Setu Bandha Āsana.

Uṣṭra Āsana

Uṣṭra = camel, ostrich. In this Āsana the body looks like the neck of a camel when it is sitting.

Fig. 140 Uṣṭra Āsana
(Stéphanie)

Fig. 141 Uṣṭra Āsana
(Chantal)

Technique

Kneel down on the floor keeping the feet stretched out or toes turned up. Put the palms of the hands on the hips.

Inhalation: Bend the upper part of the back backwards slightly pushing the pelvis and the thighs forwards, without raising the feet. Relax the arms, take hold of the heels with the hands and close the eyes. Distribute the weight of the body between the feet and knees pushing the pelvis forwards.

Do 1 to 3 breaths *Ujjāyi*.

Expiration: Release the hands and straighten up. Place your hands on your hips and sit on heels.

Take rest.

Fruits

- Makes supple cervical, dorsal and sacrolumbar spinal columns.
- Strengthens the muscles located all along the spinal column.
- Makes supple the pelvis joints, especially the coxofemoral joints. Strengthens knee joints.
- Strengthens the abdominal organs and the kidneys, and prevents their prolapses.
- Tones up the perineum.
- Develops ribcage volume.

- Stimulates digestive functions of the liver and the secretions of the small intestine. Promotes drainage of the bile.
- Prevents and reduces haemorrhoids.
- Strengthens cardiac muscles.
- Supports cardiac functions.
- Supports blood pressure in case of hypotension.
- Improves arterial circulation of the heart and the brain.
- Improves pulmonary functions.
- Develops respiratory capacity and lengthens the duration of exhalation and inhalation.
- Facilitates holding of Antah Kumbhaka and Bāhya Kumbhaka.
- Improves renal functions.
- Stabilizes all the endocrinal secretions of the body.
- Promotes harmonious growth of young children.
- Reduces symptoms of premenstrual syndrome.
- Supports endometrium and promotes conception.
- Stabilizes prostatic functions.
- Stabilizes the vegetative nervous system.
- Improves functions of all the organs of the body.
- Promotes elimination of catabolic cellular remnants.
- Reduces mental excitement and promotes mental attention.
- Increases mental concentration.
- Reduces fear, anxiety and depression.
- Improves the sense perceptions.
- Develops nervous resistance to external stimuli such as stress, for example.

Utkaṭa Āsana

Utkaṭa = chair. In this posture, the body takes the sitting position of the Indians.

Fig. 142 Utkaṭa Āsana
(Pascal)

Technique

Do Samasthiti. Interlock the fingers, turn the palms of the hands over, thumbs towards the interior.

Inhalation: Raise the arms taut over the head.

Exhalation: Squat (crouch down) without raising the heels and keep the arms taut over the head. Straighten the chest.

Do 3 times or 3 *Ujjāyi* breaths.

Inhalation: Get up again.

Exhalation: Lower the arms, relax the hands.

Take rest.

Fruits

- Rectifies the static position of the spinal column and maintains intervertebral spaces.
- Strengthens the muscles located along the spinal column, especially the ones at the lumbar level. Makes supple all the pelvis joints, more particularly, coxofemoral joints and shoulder joints. Strengthens knee joints. Develops the muscle structure of the abdominals, the lower abdomen and the legs.
- Strengthens the abdominal organs and the kidneys, and prevents their prolapses.
- Increases the sense of balance.
- Improves digestion, intestinal absorption and intestinal elimination and fights against constipation. Reduces the undesirable effects of chronic flatulence, intestinal meteorism and colic spasms of colitis stress.
- Improves venous and lymphatic circulation of the entire body.
- Develops respiratory capacity.
- Stimulates diuresis.

Utthāna Āsana

Utthāna = extension.

Fig. 143 Utthāna Āsana

(Renée)

Technique

Do Samasthiti. Interlock the fingers, turn the palms of the hands over, thumbs facing inwards.

Inhalation: Raise the arms taut over the head. Bring the chin in.

Exhalation: Without bending the knees, bend forward, release the hands and put them on the floor next to the feet. Bring the forehead against the knees and close the eyes.

Repeat 3 times or do 3 to 6 *Ujjāyi* breaths.

Keep the fingers interlocked while doing the Āsana 3 times.

Interlock the fingers, turn over the palms of the hands, thumbs facing inwards.

Inhalation: Raise the arms and chest vertically keeping the head facing forward.

Exhalation: Lower the arms and relax the hands.

Take rest.

Fruits

- Makes supple and strengthens the lumbar region.
- Develops the muscles of the legs.
- Increases the sense of balance.
- Stimulates diuresis.
- Reduces intestinal meteorism.
- Reduces colic spasms of the colitis due to stress.

Utthāna Pāda Āsana

Utthāna = stretched, *pāda* = foot, leg. Utthāna Pāda is also the name of a Philosophy master.

Fig. 144 Utthāna Pāda Āsana
(Stéphanie)

Technique

Lie flat on the back, legs together, feet together, arms alongside the body, palms of the hands on the floor, chin down and eyes closed. Supporting yourself on the elbows, raise the head and chest slightly then lower the head backwards in order to place the crown of the head on the floor.

Exhalation: Raise the taut legs so that they are at 45° from the floor. Bring the arms up vertically until they are in line with the shoulders and parallel to the legs. Join the hands, fingers pointing towards the sky.

Do 1 to 3 *Ujjāyi* breaths.

Inhalation: Lower the arms and place them alongside the body. Bring the legs back down to the floor. Pushing on the elbows, raise the head and chest slightly and hold up the head. Place the head and chest on the floor, stretch the back of the neck, relax the hands and put them alongside the body.

Take rest.

Fruits

- Makes supple the cervical spinal column.
- Strengthens the muscles located along the spinal column.
- Strengthens abdominal muscles.
- Develops ribcage volume.
- Strengthens the abdominal organs and the kidneys, and prevents their prolapses.
- Increases sense of balance.
- Harmonizes the peristaltic movement of the alimentary canal.
- Strengthens cardiac muscles and improves arterial circulation of the heart.
- Improves respiratory capacity and pulmonary compliance.
- Stabilizes hormonal secretions of the pituitary gland and adrenal gland glands.
- Stimulates ovulation and reduces symptoms of premenstrual syndrome.
- Stabilizes prostatic functions and prevents or reduces prostatic hypertrophy.
- Stabilizes the vegetative nervous system.
- Promotes elimination of the cellular catabolic remnants.
- Helps to dispel mental confusion, provides mental clarity and develops mental concentration.
- Improves the sense perception functions and reduces dispersion arising from hyperactivity.

Utthita Pāda Aṅguṣṭa Āsana

Utthita = standing, *pāda* = foot, leg, *aṅguṣṭa* = toe, *pāda aṅguṣṭa* = big toe.

Fig. 145 Utthita Pāda Anguṣṭa Āsana (Stéphanie)

Technique

Do Samasthiti. Spread the legs approximately 30 to 50 centimetres apart. Interlock the fingers, turn the palms of the hands over, thumbs facing inwards.

Inhalation: Raise the arms taut over the head.

Exhalation: Bend the chest forwards, bring the arms down and relax the hands. Take hold of the big toes or the ankles, keep the arms and the legs taut. Raise the head and the chin, stretch the back.

Do 3 to 6 *Ujjāyi* breaths.

Relax the hands, interlock the fingers and turn the hands over, thumbs facing inwards.

Inhalation: First raise the taut arms vertically then raise the upper body vertically keeping the head facing forward.

Exhalation: Lower the arms, relax the arms and join the feet.

Take rest.

Concentration

- *Kaṇṭha, bhrūmadhya.*

Fruits

- Rectifies the static position of the spinal column and maintains intervertebral spaces.
- Strengthens muscles located along the spinal column.
- Strengthens abdominal muscles.
- Increases sense of balance.
- Improves digestion and stimulates the secretion of the small intestines. Reduces the undesirable effects of chronic flatulence.
- Harmonizes the peristaltic movement of the alimentary canal, improves intestine elimination and prevents constipation.
- Prevents and reduces haemorrhoids.
- Improves lymphatic circulation of the body.
- Strengthens cardiac muscles.
- Improves pulmonary compliance.
- Lengthens exhalation time and facilitates holding of Bāhya Kumbhaka.
- Supports renal functions.
- Stabilizes hormonal secretions of the thyroid gland.
- Stabilizes hormonal secretions of the pineal gland and the parathyroid glands.
- Prevents precarious uterine contractions in case of pregnancy.
- Reduces symptoms of premenstrual syndrome.
- Prevents and helps to reduce ovarian cysts as well as uterine fibromas.
- Strengthens the uterine wall.
- Stabilizes prostatic functions.
- Prevents and reduces prostatic hypertrophy.
- Stimulates all the elimination functions of the body.
- Reduces mental excitement and increases mental attention.
- Improves the sense perceptions.

Utthita Pārśva Koṇa Āsana

Utthita = standing, *pārśva* = side, *koṇa* = angle.

Fig. 146 Utthita Pārśva Koṇa Āsana (Claire)

Technique

Do Samasthiti. Spread the legs approximately 1 metre apart. Turn the left foot towards the left, toes facing outwards. Raise the taut arms laterally into a horizontal position, palms of the hands turned downwards, facing the floor.

Exhalation: Bend the left knee in order to bring the left thigh parallel to the floor. Bend the trunk laterally to the left, put the left hand flat on the floor, on the outer side of the left foot, fingers pointing forward. Bring the right arm taut up to the right ear. Keep the head facing forward, right leg taut with the sole of the foot on the floor.

Do 1 to 3 *Ujjāyi* breaths.

Inhalation: Supporting yourself on the feet, raise the trunk vertically, bring the arms horizontally to shoulder level. Stretch the left leg and bring back the left foot parallel to the right foot.

Do the Āsana on the right side. Join the feet again and lower the arms.

Take rest.

Fruits

- Rectifies scoliosis. Makes supple the sacrolumbar region and all the pelvic joints. Strengthens knee joints.
- Develops the muscles of the legs and the arms.
- Strengthens abdominal muscles.
- Prevents kidney prolapses.
- Stimulates production of gastric secretions and reduces the unfavourable effects of chronic flatulence.
- Harmonizes the peristaltic movement of the alimentary canal, improves intestinal elimination and prevents constipation.
- Promotes elimination of pancreatic and biliary calculus.
- Improves venous and lymphatic circulation of the entire body.
- Strengthens cardiac muscles.
- Develops respiratory capacity.
- Stimulates diuresis.

Utthita Pārśva Utthāna Āsana

Utthita = standing, *pārśva* = side, *utthāna* = spread, stretch, extension.

Fig. 147 Utthita Pārśva Utthāna Āsana (Claire)

Technique

Do Samasthiti. Place the right foot 1 meter behind and in line with the left foot. Interlock the fingers, turn the palms of the hands over, thumbs facing inwards. Raise the arms taut over the head. Bring in the chin.

Exhalation: Bend the trunk forward to the left leg taut and put the hands on the floor on either side of the left foot, place the forehead on the left leg. Close the eyes.

Do 1 to 3 *Ujjāyi* breaths. Interlock the fingers, turn over the palms of the hands, thumbs facing inwards.

Inhalation: First raise the taut arms then raise the upper body vertically keeping the head facing forwards. Lower the arms and relax the hands. Place the right foot back next to the left.

Do the Āsana with the left leg behind.

Lower the arms and release the hands. Bring the left foot back next to the right.

Take rest.

Fruits

- Rectifies the static position of the spinal column and maintains intervertebral spaces.
- Rectifies scoliosis and pelvic posture.
- Strengthens knee joints.
- Develops the muscles of the legs.
- Tones up sub-umbilical muscle structure.
- Prevents kidneys prolapses.
- Increases sense of balance.
- Stimulates digestive functions of the liver and promotes bile drainage. Harmonizes the peristaltic movement of the alimentary canal, improves intestinal elimination and prevents constipation.
- Improves venous and lymphatic circulation of the entire body.
- Develops respiratory capacity.
- Stimulates diuresis.

Utthita Trikoṇa Āsana N° 1

Utthita = standing, *trikoṇa* = three angles, triangle.

Fig. 148 Utthita Trikoṇa Āsana N° 1
(Muriel)

Technique

Do Samasthiti. Spread the legs approximately 1 metre apart, keeping the feet parallel. Raise the arms laterally into a horizontal position at the same height as the shoulders, palms of the hands facing downwards towards the floor. Turn the left foot to the left without turning the pelvis.

Exhalation: Bend the chest laterally to the left. Put the left hand on the floor on the outer side of the left foot, fingers pointing forward, keep the legs taut. Keep the right arm in line with the left arm. Turn the head to the right and keep the chest as close as possible to the left leg. Close the eyes.

Do 1 or 3 *Ujjāyi* breaths.

Inhalation: Raise the chest vertically and come back up facing forward. Bring the left foot back inwards. Turn the right foot to the right.

Do the Āsana to the right.

Lower the arms, join the legs again.

Take rest.

Fruits

- Makes supple the sacrolumbar region and the pelvic joints.
- Rectifies scoliosis.
- Strengthens abdominal muscles.
- Strengthens the abdominal organs and the kidneys, and prevents their prolapses.
- Increases sense of balance.
- Stimulates production of gastric secretions and improves digestion.
- Harmonizes peristaltic movements of the alimentary canal; improves intestinal elimination and prevents constipation.
- Reduces the undesirable effects of gastro-oesophageal reflux.
- Develops respiratory capacity.
- Stimulates diuresis.
- Prevents kidney stone formation.

Utthita Trikoṇa Āsana N° 2

Utthita = standing, *trikoṇa* = three angles, triangle.

Fig. 149 Utthita Trikoṇa Āsana N° 2, back view

(Stéphanie)

Fig. 150 Utthita Trikoṇa Āsana N° 2, front view

(Stéphanie)

Technique

Do Samasthiti. Spread the legs approximately 1 metre apart, keeping the feet parallel. Raise the arms laterally into a horizontal position at the same height as the shoulders, palms of the hands facing downwards towards the floor. Turn the left foot to the left.

Exhalation: Turn the chest to the left and bend the trunk towards the left leg. Put the right hand on the floor on the external side of the left foot, fingers pointing forward, keep the legs taut. Raise the left arm in line with the right arm. Turn the head to the left and keep the chest as close as possible to the leg. Close the eyes.

Do 1 to 3 *Ujjāyi* breaths.

Inhalation: Raise the chest vertically and come back up facing forward. Bring the left foot back inwards.

Do the Āsana to the right.

Lower the arms, join the legs again and take rest.

Fruits

- Makes supple the sacrolumbar region and all the pelvic joints.
- Rectifies scoliosis.
- Strengthens abdominal muscles.
- Strengthens the abdominal organs and the kidneys, and prevents their prolapses.
- Increases the sense of balance.
- Stimulates production of gastric secretions and improves digestion.
- Harmonizes the peristaltic movement of the alimentary canal, which promotes intestinal elimination and prevents constipation.
- Develops respiratory capacity.
- Stimulates diuresis.
- Prevents kidney stone formation.

Vajra Āsana

Vajra = God *Indra*'s weapon, the spinal column.

Fig. 151 Vajra Āsana
(Pascal)

Technique

Kneel down on the floor, sit on your joined heels, feet stretched out. You can put a cushion or a folded blanket under the ankles if necessary. Keep the back straight, chin down. Bend the elbows slightly and place the palms of the hands on the thighs. Close the eyes.

Do 6 or 12 *Ujjāyi* breaths.

Sit on the floor, stretch the legs on the floor and join the feet.

Take rest.

Concentration

- *Nāsāgra, kaṇṭha, bhrūmadhya, tāraka.*

Fruits

- Rectifies the static position of the spine, maintains intervertebral spaces and prevents slipped disc. Rectifies scoliosis.
- Reduces and stabilizes high blood pressure.
- Improves pulmonary compliance.
- Improves blood circulation between the pregnant woman and foetus.
- Improves nervous resistance to external stimuli such as stress, for example.
- Reduces mental excitement. Improves mental attention and improves mental concentration.

Vajra Āsana, variations

Fig. 152 Vajra Āsana, variations 1

(Estelle)

Fig. 153 Vajra Āsana, variations 2

(Estelle)

Technique

Kneel down on the floor, sit on your joined heels, feet stretched out. You can put a cushion or a folded blanket under the ankles if necessary. Keep the back straight, chin down. Interlock the fingers, turn the palms of the hands over, thumbs towards the interior. Raise the arms taut over the head. Draw in the chin and close the eyes.

1st Variation

Inhalation: Raise the pelvis and rest on the knees. Bend the chest backward, without bringing up the feet, raise the head backwards.

Exhalation: Sit down on the heels, set your back straight again, bring the head down, bend the arms, keep the palms of the hands upward, bring the hands behind the neck, spread the elbows.

Repeat 2 times.

Inhalation: While sitting on the heels, raise the arms vertically.

2nd Variation

Exhalation: Bend the chest and the arms taut forward, put the hands and the forehead on the floor.

Inhalation: Raise the arms and the chest vertically while keeping the chin down. Straighten up the back.

Repeat 2 times.

Exhalation: Bend the chest and the arms forward, put the hands and the forehead on the floor.

Do 3 *Ujjāyi* breaths.

Inhalation: Raise the arms and the chest vertically while keeping the chin down. Straighten the back.
Exhalation: Lower the arms, relax the fingers.
Sit on the floor, stretch the legs on the floor and join the feet.
Take rest.

Fruits

- Rectifies the static position of the spine, maintains intervertebral spaces and prevents slipped discs. Rectifies scoliosis.
- Improves digestion and stimulates the secretion of the small intestines. Harmonizes peristaltic movement of the alimentary canal. Reduces intestinal meteorism.
- Promotes elimination of biliary calculus and kidney stone.
- Reduces and helps to stabilize high blood pressure.
- Improves respiratory capacity and pulmonary compliance.
- Strengthens cardiac muscles.
- Improves venous and lymphatic circulation of the entire body.
- Improves nervous resistance to external stimuli such as stress, for example. Reduces mental excitement, provides mental attention and improves mental concentration.

Vasiṣṭha Āsana

Vasiṣṭha is a great Vedic sage.

Fig. 154 Vasiṣṭha Āsana

(Catherine)

Technique

Do Adho Mukha Śvāna Āsana.

Inhalation: Raise the right side of your body and hold your balance on the left hand and the left foot. Put the right leg on the left leg. Keep the left arm taut. Raise the right arm in line with the left arm. Turn the head to the right, direct your gaze to the right hand.

Do 1 *Ujjāyi* breath.

Exhalation: Lower the right arm, pivot on the feet and the left arm, put the right hand on the floor in line with the left one. Return to Adho Mukha Śvāna Āsana.

Do the Āsana on the right side.

Inhalation: Do Ūrdhva Mukha Śvāna Āsana.

Exhalation: Bend the elbows without spreading them and place the legs, the abdomen, the chest and forehead on the floor.

Turn over and take rest.

Concentration

- *Kaṇṭha.*

Fruits

- Rectifies the static position of the spinal column and maintains intervertebral spaces.
- Strengthens the muscles located along the spinal column, especially the ones on the lumbar level. Strengthens abdominal muscles. Makes supple shoulder joints.
- Rectifies the posture of the pelvis.
- Increases sense of balance.
- Harmonizes peristaltic movement of the alimentary canal. Improves intestinal elimination function during pregnancy.
- Prevents haemorrhoids.
- Stimulates all the hepatic functions.
- Stabilizes exocrine secretion of the pancreas.
- Strengthens cardiac muscles.
- Improves the venous and lymphatic circulations.
- Improves pulmonary compliance.
- Prevents precarious uterine contractions in case of pregnancy. Restores ovarian cycle.
- Stabilizes prostatic functions. Prevents and reduces prostatic hypertrophy.
- Calms excitement and stabilizes vegetative nervous system. Improves nervous resistance to external stimuli such as stress, for example.
- Improves the functions of all the organs of the body.
- Reduces mental excitement, improves concentration and functions of sense perceptions.

Vimāna Āsana

Vimāna = plane.

Fig. 155 Vimāna Āsana 1
(Estelle)

Fig. 156 Vimāna Āsana 2
(Estelle)

Technique

Do Garuḍa Āsana.

Exhalation: Stretch the left leg, bend the chest forward and raise the right leg. Keep the trunk and the right leg parallel to the floor, then stretch the arms forward, hands together. Raise the head. Hold your balance on the left leg.

Do 1 *Ujjāyi* breath.

Inhalation: Spread the arms horizontally, palms of the hands towards the floor.

Do 1 *Ujjāyi* breath.

Inhalation: Put the right leg back on the floor behind the left leg, at the starting position, and raise the chest. Place the right foot by the left foot again and lower the arms.

Do the Āsana with the right leg.

Take rest.

Concentration

- *Tāraka*.

Fruits

- Increases sense of balance.
- Makes supple the pelvis joints. Strengthens the muscles located along the spinal column, abdominal muscles and the muscles of the lower limbs.
- Strengthens the abdominal organs and the kidneys, and prevents their prolapses.
- Improves the venous and lymphatic circulations.
- Improves respiratory capacity and pulmonary compliance.
- Stabilizes hormonal secretion of the pineal gland.
- Supports endometrium and promotes conception.
- Calms excitement and stabilizes the vegetative nervous system.
- Reduces mental excitement and promotes concentration. Improves the functions of sense of perception and reduces mental dispersion coming from their hyperactivity.

Viparīta Karaṇi

Viparīta = upside down, eccentric, *karaṇi* = small intestine.

Fig. 157 Viparīta Karaṇi

(Pascal)

Technique

Lie flat on the back, feet together, legs together, arms along the body, palms of the hands on the floor and chin down.

Exhalation: Raise the legs, the buttocks and the lower part of the back. Bend the knees and put the hands at the level of the buttock muscles, bring the feet in line with the head without arching the back then close the eyes. Keep the entire back rounded. Lower the chin.

Do 6 or 12 *Ujjāyi* breaths.

Exhalation: Bend the knees, feet close to the buttocks, put the arms on the floor.

Inhalation: Bring the back down again, then the feet on the floor without stretching the legs and without raising the head. Lie down the legs on the floor.

Take rest.

Concentration

- *Kaṇṭha.*

Fruits

- Rectifies static position of the spine. Strengthens abdominal muscles.
- Supports the perineum and avoids the prolapses of the organs after delivery.
- Improves digestion, intestinal absorption, intestinal elimination and fights against constipation. Prevents and reduces haemorrhoids as well as intestinal meteorism.
- Improves venous and lymphatic circulation of the entire body. Improves coronary artery and cerebral circulation. Helps maintain blood circulation between the pregnant woman and foetus.
- Improves respiratory capacity and lengthens Inhalation time.
- Helps to maintain Antah Kumbhaka.
- Stabilizes hormonal secretions of the pineal gland.
- Supports endometrium, helps to establish a conception in utero. Reduces premenstrual symptoms. Reduces pain sensation during delivery.
- Prevents and reduces prostatic hypertrophy.
- Relieves 'restless leg' syndrome (also called 'Wittmaak Ekborns' syndrome').
- Reduces mental excitement. Improves the functions of sense perceptions and reduces dispersion coming from their hyperactivity.

Viparīta Śalabha Āsana

Viparīta = upside down, eccentric, *śalabha* = grasshopper, dragonfly.

Fig. 158 Viparīta Śalabha Āsana

(Patṟice)

Technique

Lie down on the stomach, forehead on the floor, arms along the body, back of the hands on the floor.

Inhalation: Taking support on the back of the hands, raise both legs taut as high as possible. Keep the forehead and the shoulders on the floor.

Exhalation: Put the legs back on the floor.

Do 3 times or 3 *Ujjāyi* breaths.

Turn over and take rest.

Fruits

- Rectifies the static position of the spinal column and pelvis posture. Makes supple sacrolumbar region and strengthens coxofemoral joints.
- Strengthens the abdominal organs and the kidneys, and prevents their prolapses. Tones up the perineum.
- Tones up sub-umbilical muscle structure.
- Develops rib cage volume.
- Stimulates secretions of the small intestine. Stabilizes exocrine secretion of the pancreas.
- Promotes bile drainage.
- Prevents and reduces haemorrhoids.
- Improves the venous and lymphatic circulations.
- Strengthens cardiac muscles.
- Improves pulmonary functions and pulmonary compliance. Develops respiratory capacity. Helps holding of Antah Kumbhaka and Bāhya Kumbhaka.
- Improves renal functions.
- Stabilizes all the endocrinal secretions.
- Supports endometrium and promotes conception.
- Stabilizes prostatic functions. Prevents and reduces prostatic hypertrophy.
- Stabilizes the vegetative nervous system. Improves nervous resistance to external stimulus such as stress, for example.
- Improves functions of all the organs of the body.
- Provides mental attention. Increases memorising capacity. Develops self-confidence, provides courage and increases perseverance.

Vīra Bhadra Āsana

Vīra = hero, *bhadra* = firm, stable.

Pārvathi, the wife of Shiva, was the daughter of the king of the mountains. This king, on the occasion of a ritual, forgot to invite Shiva. Shiva then got angry and created a son with his 3rd eye in order to destroy his father in law. This son, Vīra Bhadra, went to war and challenged the king of the mountains. Pārvathi understood that this child was none other than Shiva's son, therefore, her son as well! She asked Vīra Bhadra to cite his family tree. Considering his ignorance, Pārvathi introduced herself as the spouse of Shiva, therefore, his mother. Getting angry, Vīra Bhadra went back to Shiva to destroy him. In order to protect Shiva and protect the world, Pārvathi intervened and reduced Vīra Bhadra to nothing.

Fig. 159 Vīra Bhadra Āsana

(Estelle)

Technique

Do Samasthiti. Place the right leg behind the left leg to a minimum of 1 meter. Keep the right foot in line with the left foot. Bring the pelvis facing forward. Interlock the fingers, turn the palms of the hands over, thumbs towards the interior.

Inhalation: Raise the arms taut over the head.

Exhalation: Without bending the chest forward, bend the left knee in order to bring the left thigh parallel to the floor. Keep the right leg taut. Keep the head facing forward and direct your gaze straight ahead.

Do 1 *Ujjāyi* breath.

Inhalation: Straighten the left leg. Pivot the chest and the legs to the right at 180°. Maintain the legs apart. Keep the chest facing towards the right leg.

Exhalation: Without bending the chest forward, bend the right knee in order to bring the right thigh parallel to the floor. Keep the left leg taut. Keep the head facing up forward.

Do 1 *Ujjāyi* breath.

Inhalation: Straighten the right leg.

Exhalation: Bring the left leg together with the right leg, left foot next to the right one. Lower the arms.

Take rest.

Concentration

- *Tāraka.*

Fruits

- Rectifies scoliosis.
- Strengthens knee joints.
- Develops the muscles of the legs and the arms.
- Increases sense of balance.
- Rectifies the static position of the spinal column and maintains intervertebral spaces.
- Strengthens abdominal muscles.
- Tones up sub-umbilical muscle structure.
- Develops respiratory capacity.
- Strengthens cardiac muscles.
- Provides sensation of lightness of the body.
- Strengthens abdominal muscles. Tones up the keeping of abdominal organs and prevents their prolapses.
- Stimulates diuresis. Prevents kidney stones formation.
- Prevents kidney prolapses.
- Improves venous and lymphatic circulation of the entire body.
- Stimulates the production of gastric secretions. Harmonizes peristaltic movement of the alimentary canal, improves intestinal elimination and prevents constipation.
- Reduces mental excitement.
- Promotes mental attention.

14
Mudra Sheets

Aśvinī Muḍra

Aśvinī = twin gods of Indian medicine.

Fig. 160 Aśvinī Mudra

(Estelle)

First Technique

Do Danḍa Āsana. Interlock the fingers, turn the palms of the hands over, thumbs towards the interior. Raise the arms over the head. Draw in the chin and close the eyes. Bend the trunk forward, lower the arms, relax the hands and take hold of the big toes. Without releasing the hands, stretch the back, straightening the spinal column. Lower the shoulders and the chin.

Do 32 or 64 Kapāla Bhāti breaths.

Inhalation: Interlock the fingers, turn the palms of the hands over, stretch the arms and raise them over the head, straightening the trunk vertically.

Exhalation: Lower the arms and relax the fingers.

Take rest.

Second Technique

Do Danḍa Āsana. Interlock the fingers, turn the palms of the hands over, thumbs towards the interior. Raise the arms taut over the head. Draw in the chin and close the eyes. Bend the trunk forward, lower the arms, relax the hands and take hold of the big toes. Without releasing the hands, stretch the back, straightening the spinal column. Lower the shoulders and the chin.

Do 12 *Ujjāyi* breaths, taking an equal time during Inhalation, retention of breath after Inhalation, Exhalation, and retention of breath after Exhalation.

Concentration: **Inhalation**: From *mūla* to *kaṇṭha*, **Anath Kumbhaka**: *bhrūmadhya*, **Exhalation**: *nābhi*, and **Bāhya Kumbhaka**: *mūla.*

Inhalation: Interlock the fingers, turn the palms of the hands over, stretch the arms and raise the arms, straightening the trunk vertically.

Exhalation: Lower the arms and relax the fingers.

Take rest.

Bhujaṃgi Mudra

Bhuja = shoulder, *aṁga* = limb. *Bhujaṃga* = snake. In this Āsana, the body takes the shape of a cobra. *Bhujaṃgi* is the son of Cobra who inherited the spiritual power of Ananta (the Primordial Serpent).

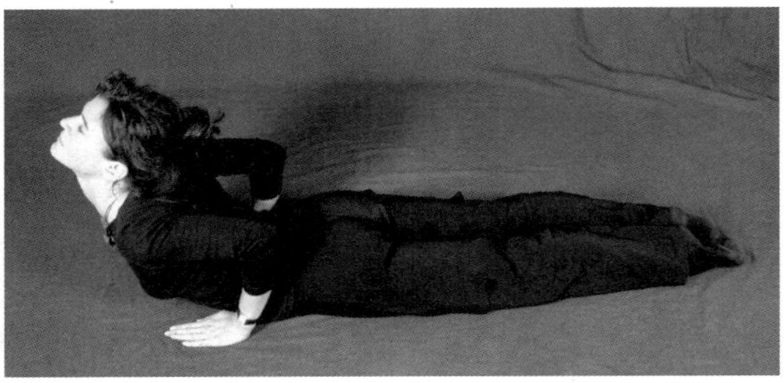

Fig. 161 Bhujaṃgi Mudra

(Stéphanie)

Technique

Lie on the stomach, forehead on the floor, arms along the body, back of the hands on the floor, legs taut together and eyes closed. Bend the elbows and raise them, put the palms of the hands on the floor at the level of the lower ribs, fingers directed towards the head.

Inhalation: Supporting yourself on the hands, raise the head, the neck, the shoulders, the thorax and the stomach. Keep the navel on the floor. Relax the stomach.

Kumbhaka

Antah Kumbhaka: 5 s.

Concentration

Tāraka or bhrūmadhya.

Do 3 *Ujjāyi* breaths.

Exhalation: Lower the stomach, the chest and the shoulders to the floor. Put the forehead on the floor.

Turn over and take rest.

Khecarī Mudra

Kha = sky, *cara* = to move oneself.

Technique

Sit down in Padma Āsana or in Ananta Āsana. Draw in the chin and straighten the entire spinal column so it completely straight. Stretch out the arms place the palms of the hands on the knees, fingers pointed towards the floor. Turn the arms around in order to keep the palms of the hands towards the sky. Fold the forefingers and the thumbs, the extremities of the thumbs and the forefingers touching each other. Bend the elbows. Close the eyes. Open the mouth, stick the tongue out and turn it backward and bring the extremity of the tongue towards the glottis. Close the mouth. Direct your gaze towards the root of uvula (*lalāṭa*) or between the eyebrọws (*bhrūmadhya*), while keeping the eyes closed.

See Fig. 33

Do Nāḍī Śodhana 12 breaths.

Open the eyes and release the tongue. Extend the legs out on the floor, feet together.

Take rest.

Mahā Bandha

Mahā = great, *bandha* = tie, bond.

Fig. 162 Mahā Bandha
(Dominique)

Technique

Do Daṇḍa Āsana. Bring together the soles of the feet, one against the other in order to place the heels as close as possible to the perineum, thighs on the floor. Hold the feet or the ankles. Raise the lower part of the back and straighten the entire back. Draw in the chin and close the eyes.

Do 32 to 64 Kapāla Bhāti breaths.

Relax the hands, extend the legs on the floor, and join the feet.

Take rest.

Mahā Mudra

Mahā = great. *Mudra* = seal. That which removes suffering. In Yoga, the word *mudra* is used in its second sense.

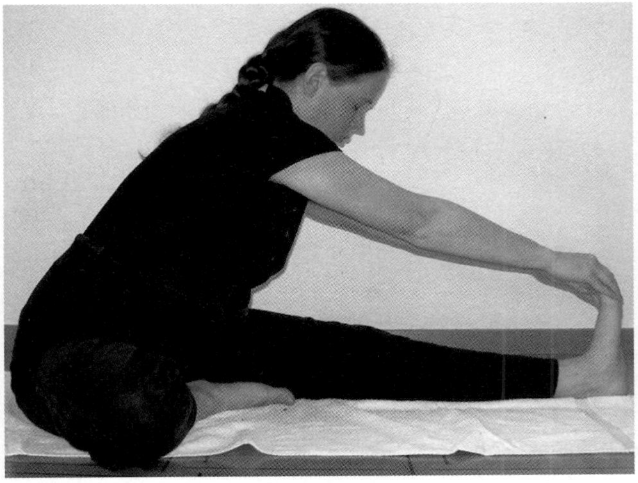

Fig. 163 Mahā Mudra, right side (Muriel)

Fig. 164 Mahā Mudra (William)

Technique

Do Daṇḍa Āsana. Without raising the left knee, bend the left knee and bring the heel against the perineum. Put the sole of the foot against the right thigh. The left thigh making a right angle with the right leg.

Interlock the fingers, turn the palms of the hands over, thumbs towards the interior. Raise the arms taut over the head. Draw in the chin and close the eyes.

Exhalation: Bend the trunk forward, lower the arms, relax the hands and take hold of the big toe or the ankle. Without releasing the hands, straighten the back, stretching the spinal column. Lower the shoulders and the chin.

Do 6 *Ujjāyi* breaths.

Inhalation: Interlock the fingers, turn the palms of the hands over, stretch the arms and raise the arms, straightening the trunk vertically.

Exhalation: Lower the arms and relax the fingers. Extend the left leg and join the feet.

Do the Mudra with the right leg.

Extend the right leg and join the feet.

Take rest.

Concentration

- *Mūla, nābhi, kaṇṭha, lalāṭa, nāsāgra, bhrūmadhya.*

Taṭāka Mudra or Tāḍagi Mudra

Taṭāka, Tāḍagi = pond, jug, stomach.

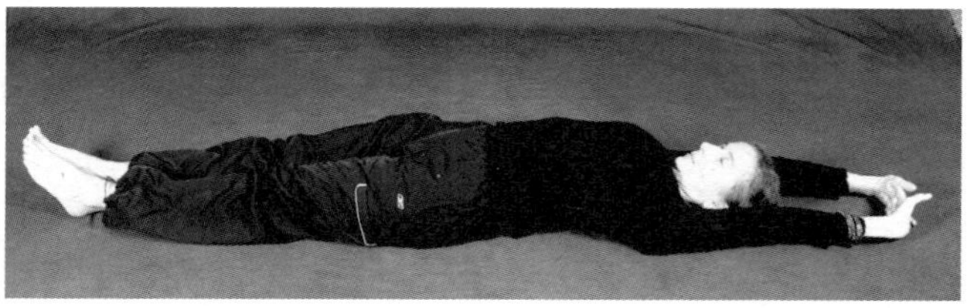

Fig. 165 Taṭāka Mudra

(Dominique)

Technique

Lie on the back, legs together, feet together, arms along the body, palms of the hands on the floor, chin down and eyes closed. Interlock the fingers, turn the palms of the hands over, thumbs towards the interior. Draw in the chin and close the eyes.

Inhalation: Raise the arms taut and bring them behind the head.

Concentration: **Inhalation**: From *pāda aṅguṣṭa* (big toe) to *śīrṣa*; **Exhalation**: *kaṇṭha*, *nābhi* or *mūla*.

Kumbhaka: Bāhya Kumbhaka: 5 s

Do 12 *Ujjāyi* Breaths.

Exhalation: Lower the arms, relax the hands and bring the arms to the sides of the body, palms of the hands on the floor.

Take rest.

Viparīta Karaṇi Mudra

Viparīta = upside down, eccentric, *karaṇi* = small intestine.

Fig. 166 Viparīta Karaṇi Mudra (Gabriel)

Technique (against a wall)

Put a blanket folded in four in front of a wall. Kneel down in front of the blanket. Interlock the fingers. Bend the chest forward in order to put the forearms on the blanket, hands vertical and the back of the fingers against the wall. Make sure that the spacing between the elbows is the same as the width between the shoulders.

Put the top of the head on the blanket in order to have the palms of the hands touching the back of the head; the thumbs should be separated and follow the outline of the head. Press the toes on the floor in order to raise the knees. Move the feet forward with small steps.

Inhalation: Take a small run up with both legs together and raise them with both knees bent, without pivoting the head. Immediately, stretch your legs against the wall. Move the back and buttocks away from the wall so they can remain in line with the back of the neck. The back of the fingers and heels should be the only parts of the body in contact with the wall. Raise the shoulders so they are away from the ears. Close the eyes.

Do 6, 8 or 12 *Ujjāyi* breaths.

Exhalation: Bend the knees bringing the thighs against the abdomen, put the feet back on the floor and then the knees.

Lie flat on the back, legs together, feet together, arms along the body, palms of the hands on the floor, chin lowered, eyes closed.

Concentration

- *Kaṇṭha, nāsāgra, nābhi, hṛdaya.*

15
Prāṇāyāma Sheets

General instructions

Prāṇāyāmas are presented in alphabetical order. For the learning order or for practice protocol, refer to the examples of the General Sessions, or "Life Saving Sessions' or *Prāṇāyāmas*.

*Prāṇāyāma*s are practiced in sitting position, either in Padma Āsana, or Ananta Āsana or in Vajra Āsana. It is possible to do them in Daṇḍa Āsana.

Padma Āsana, Ananta Āsana, Vajra Āsana and Daṇḍa Āsana techniques are described in the *Āsana*s records.

Put the hands on the knees or on the thighs.

For *Prāṇāyāma*s with Inhalation or Exhalation with only one nostril, use *Mṛgī Mudra* with the right hand. *Mṛgī* = deer head.

Mṛgī Mudra Technique

Fold the middle finger and index fingers of the right hand, bringing the tips of those fingers onto the palm of the hand. Straighten the other fingers.

Fig. 167 Mṛgī Mudra

(Sumitra)

Technique for breathing exercise with one nostril

Note: the breathing exercise with one nostril does not use the *Ujjāyi* breathing technique.

Inhalation with the left nostril: With the right hand in *Mṛgī Mudra,* bend the right elbow and bring the right hand to the front of the nose. Place the right thumb on the wing of the right nostril and the right ring finger on the wing of the left nostril. Push the wing of the right nostril in order to completely block the passage through the right nostril. With the ring finger of the right hand, partially push the wing of the left nostril. Inhale through the partially blocked left nostril.

Exhalation with the right nostril: Push the wing of the left nostril in completely. Release the thumb of the right hand slightly to partially free the wing of the right nostril. Exhale through the right nostril.

In case of nasal obstruction (cold, rhinitis, etc.), preventing an easy inhalation, do not inhale with one nostril. Then do *Ujjāyi Anuloma Prāṇāyāma.*

At the end of each inhalation and exhalation, you may replace the right hand on the right thigh or right knee.

Counting the number of breaths:

Count the number of breaths with the left hand.

At the end of the first Exhalation, point the thumb on the first joint of the little finger.

At the end of the second Exhalation, point the thumb on the second joint of the little finger.

At the end of the next Exhalation, point the thumb on the third joint of the little finger.

Follow the same procedure with the ring finger, the middle finger and the index finger.

Thumb pointing on the third joint of the index finger will indicate the twelfth breathing (or the 6th cycle).

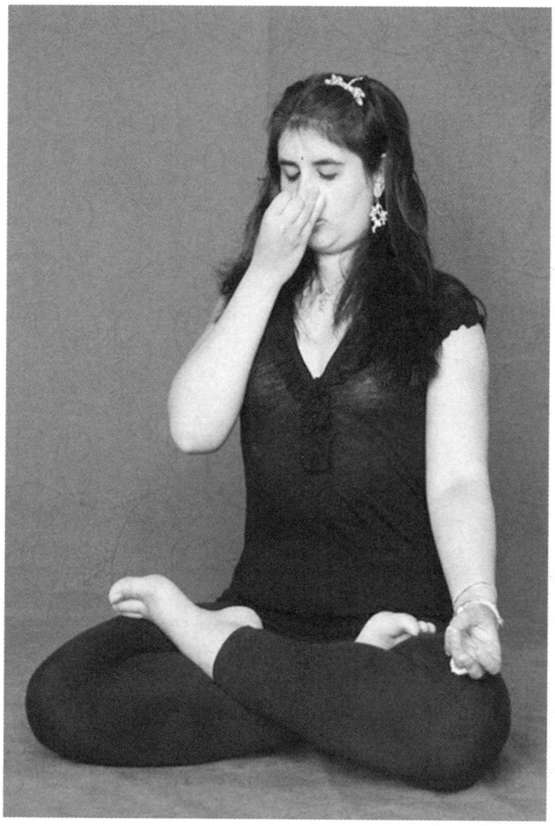

Fig. 168 Prāṇāyama

(Sumitra)

Abhyantara Vṛtti

Abhyantara = towards the interior, *vṛtti* = movement. *Abhyantara Vṛtti* is a Prāṇāyāma that helps to focus the mind towards the soul, located in *hṛdaya*.

Basic Prāṇāyāma: Nāḍī Śodhana.

Technique

Inhalation: left nostril. **Concentration**: *nāsāgra* to *hṛdaya* (i.e., *nāsāgra*, *bhrūmadhya*, *lalāṭa*, *kaṇṭha*, *kaṇṭha kūpa* and *hṛdaya*).

Exhalation: right nostril. **Concentration**: *hṛdaya*.

Inhalation: right nostril. **Concentration**: *nāsāgra* to *hṛdaya* (i.e., *nāsāgra*, *bhrūmadhya*, *lalāṭa*, *kaṇṭha*, *kaṇṭha kūpa* and *hṛdaya*)

Exhalation: left nostril. **Concentration**: *hṛdaya*.

Do 12 breaths (6 Cycles).

Kumbhaka

Antah Kumbhaka: 5 to 10 seconds.

Take rest.

Bāhya Vṛtti

Bāhya = towards the exterior; *vṛtti* = movement. *Bāhya Vṛtti* is a *Prāṇāyāma* that helps direct the mind of the practicing towards the soul, located in *hṛdaya*.

Basic Prāṇāyāma: Nāḍī Śodhana.

Technique

This Prāṇāyāma can only be practiced after having practiced *Abhyantara Vṛtti*.

Practice method: Do *Abhyantara Vṛtti* before the next stages.

First stage

Inhalation: left nostril. **Concentration**: *hṛdaya*.

Exhalation: right nostril. **Concentration**: *nābhi*.

Inhalation: right nostril. **Concentration**: *hṛdaya*.

Exhalation: left nostril. **Concentration**: *nābhi*.

Do 12 breaths (6 Cycles).

Second stage

Inhalation: left nostril. **Concentration**: *hṛdaya*.

Exhalation: right nostril. **Concentration**: *anāhata*.

Inhalation: right nostril. **Concentration**: *hṛdaya*.

Exhalation: left nostril. **Concentration**: *anāhata*.

Do 12 breaths (6 Cycles)

Third stage

Inhalation: left nostril. **Concentration**: *hṛdaya.*

Exhalation: right nostril. **Concentration**: *kaṇṭha.*

Inhalation: right nostril. **Concentration**: *hṛdaya.*

Exhalation: left nostril. **Concentration**: *kaṇṭha.*

Do 12 breaths (6 Cycles).

Fourth stage

Inhalation: left nostril. **Concentration**: *hṛdaya.*

Exhalation: right nostril. **Concentration**: *bhrūmadhya.*

Inhalation: right nostril. **Concentration**: *hṛdaya.*

Exhalation: left nostril. **Concentration**: *bhrūmadhya.*

Do 12 breaths (6 Cycles).

Kumbhaka

Antah Kumbhaka: 5 to 10 seconds.

Take rest.

Bastri

Bastri = small bellows of the goldsmith.

Basic Prāṇāyāma: Nāḍī Śodhana.

Technique

To practice this *Prāṇāyāma*, keep the nostril through which you are breathing (Inhalation or Exhalation) completely free, while keeping the other one completely blocked. Adjust the blocking and the opening of the nostril according to the speed of the breath.

Inhalation: left nostril.

Exhalation: right nostril.

Inhalation: right nostril.

Exhalation: left nostril.

Inhale and exhale rapidly and fully, alternating left nostril and right nostril. Keep a rhythm of one cycle, that is, two breaths per second.

Do 60 breaths (30 Cycles).

Without resting, continue with Śītalī or Nāḍī Śodhana.

Take rest.

Kapāla Bhāti or Bhastrikā

Kapāla = skull, *Bhāti* = open, *bhastrikā* = big bellows of a blacksmith.

According to Indian thinking, when the soul is leaving the body by the fontanel, it does not come back, it escapes the cycle of rebirth. It is not concerned with the Cycles of rebirth. When it does not leave the body by the fontanel, that is to say, when it comes out by other openings, it means that the soul will be reborn. A free being is a being from which the fontanel opens up (in the literal meaning of the word) at the time of the death.

Kapāla Bhāti is a *Prāṇāyāma* that allows the fontanel (*Kapāla Randhra*) to open up at the moment of death.

Technique

Do quick and vigorous nasal breaths to a rhythm of one breath per second.

Inhalation: Push out the abdomen without pushing the chest.

Exhalation: Briskly pull in the abdomen without pulling the chest.

Do 16 to 60 breaths.

Take rest.

Advice: After Kapāla Bhāti do Ujjāyi Anuloma, Ujjāyi Viloma or Ujjāyi Pratiloma.

Kapāla Bhāti can be done in Vajra Āsana, in Baddha Koṇa Āsana or in Paścimatāna Āsana. This last one then becomes Aśvinī Mudra (refer to *Mudra*s records).

Practical advice: 60 Kapāla Bhāti breaths are followed by 6 Cycles of Ujjāyi Anuloma or Ujjāyi Viloma, or 4 Cycles of Ujjāyi Pratiloma.

It is possible to increase the number of Kapāla Bhāti breaths as long as you respect the following principle:

You can add 20 Kapāla Bhāti breaths for 2 Cycles of Ujjāyi Anuloma, Ujjāyi Viloma or Ujjāyi Pratiloma. For example, 80 Kapāla Bhāti breaths are followed by 8 Cycles of Ujjāyi Anuloma or Ujjāyi Viloma, or 6 Cycles of Ujjāyi Pratiloma.

Note: Kapāla Bhāti is recommended in the fall and in the winter.

Kapāla Bhāti, variation

Technique

Stand up, feet spread, bend the knees slightly bringing them forward. Put the hands on the thighs, elbows bent, fingers towards the interior, back rounded, abdomen relaxed, eyes closed.

Do 12 *Kapāla Bhāti* breaths.

Then, do Samasthiti and do 4 *Ujjāyi* breaths.

Repeat 3 times.

Take rest.

Nāḍī Śodhana

Nāḍī = nerve, physical or not. *Śodhana* comes from *śuddhi* = purify. That which purifies the nerves. Nāḍī Śodhana is the most important *Prāṇāyāma*; it is the *Prāṇāyāma* for rituals and meditation, the only one in existence since the Veda.

Technique

Sit in Padma Āsana or cross-legged, keep the back straight, chin down. Bend the elbows slightly and place the palms of the hands on the thighs. Close the eyes.

Inhalation: left nostril.

Exhalation: right nostril.

Inhalation: right nostril.

Exhalation: left nostril

Do 12 breaths (6 Cycles).

Take rest.

Concentration

Nāsāgra, bhrūmadhya, lalāṭa, nābhi, mūla, hṛdaya.

Kumbhaka

Antah Kumbhaka, Bāhya Kumbhaka.

Note: This is a Pranayama with slow breathings without *Ujjāyi*.

Sama Vṛtti

Sama = equal, *vṛtti* = turn around. This *Prāṇāyāma* helps the practicing to reach contemplation beyond the solar disc. Facilitates meditation on the Creator (*Prajāpati*).

Basic Prāṇāyāma: Nāḍī Śodhana.

The length of each breathing phase can be more than 5 seconds but should not exceed 10 seconds.

Technique

Inhalation: left nostril 5 s. **Concentration**: *bhrūmadhya* or *lalāṭa.*

Antah Kumbhaka: 5 s. **Concentration**: *bhrūmadhya* or *lalāṭa.*

Exhalation: right nostril 5 s. **Concentration**: *hṛdaya.*

Bāhya Kumbhaka : 5 s. **Concentration**: *hṛdaya.*

Inhalation: right nostril 5 s. **Concentration**: *bhrūmadhya* or *lalāṭa.*

Antah Kumbhaka: 5 s. **Concentration**: *bhrūmadhya* or *lalāṭa.*

Exhalation: left nostril 5 s. **Concentration**: *hṛdaya.*

Bāhya Kumbhaka: 5 s. **Concentration**: *hṛdaya.*

Do 12 breaths (6 Cycles).

Take rest.

Note: It is possible to increase the number of each stage of this Prāṇāyāma as long as you maintain an equal length for each phase.

Precaution: This *Prāṇāyāma* can only be practiced under the advice and observation of your yoga teacher.

Śītalī

Śīta = cold, freshness. *Śītalī* = that which provides freshness.

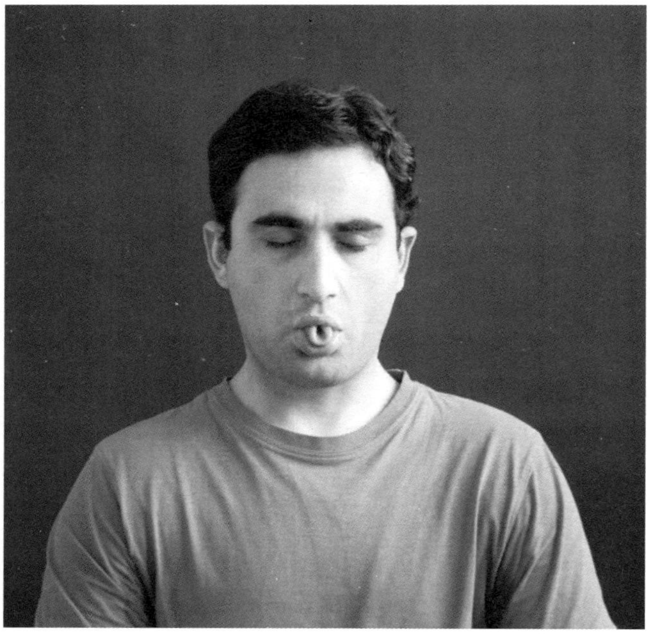

Fig. 169 Śītali
(Satya)

First Technique

Stick the tongue out of the mouth, fold it lengthwise.

Inhalation: Suck the air with the tongue out, lean the head backwards.

At the end of the Inhalation, pull in the tongue, close the mouth and lower the head.

Exhalation: *Ujjāyi.*

Do 12 breaths.

Take rest.

Second Technique

Stick the tongue completely out of the mouth, fold it lengthwise.
Inhalation: Suck the air with the tongue out, raising the head backwards.
At the end of the inhaling, pull in the tongue, close the mouth and lower the head.
Exhalation: Left nostril.
Inhalation: Suck the air with the tongue, raising the head backwards.
At the end of the inhaling, pull in the tongue, close the mouth and lower the head. (chin down).
Exhalation: Right nostril.
Do 12 breaths (that is to say 6 Cycles).
Rest.
Kumbhaka
Antah Kumbhaka 5 s

Reminder: There is no Ujjāyi breathing when exhalation is performed by a single nostril.
Note: Śītalī Prāṇāyāma is recommended in spring and summer.

Stambha Vṛtti

Stambha = exterior, *vṛtti* = movement. *Stambha Vṛtti* is a *Prāṇāyāma* that helps to focus the mind of the practicing towards the soul, located in the *hṛdaya*.
Basic Prāṇāyāma: Nāḍī Śodhana.

Technique

This Prāṇāyāma can only be practiced after having practiced the fourth stage of *Bāhya Vṛtti.*
Indications for Practicing Stambha Vṛtti: Do *Bāhya Vṛtti* before the next stages. Do 12 breaths (6 cycles) at each staga).

First Stage
Inhalation: left nostril. **Concentration**: *nābhi.*
Exhalation: right nostril. **Concentration:** *nābhi.*
Inhalation: left nostril. **Concentration**: *nābhi.*
Exhalation: right nostril. **Concentration:** *nābhi.*

Second Stage
Inhalation: left nostril. **Concentration**: *anāhata.*
Exhalation: right nostril. **Concentration:** *anāhata.*
Inhalation: right nostril. **Concentration:** *anāhata.*
Exhalation: left nostril. **Concentration:** *anāhata.*

Third Stage
Inhalation: left nostril. **Concentration:** *bhrūmadhya.*
Exhalation: right nostril. **Concentration:** *bhrūmadhya.*
Inhalation: right nostril. **Concentration:** *bhrūmadhya.*
Exhalation: left nostril. **Concentration:** *bhrūmadhya.*

Fourth Stage
Inhalation: left nostril. **Concentration**: *śīrṣa.*
Exhalation: right nostril. **Concentration:** *śīrṣa.*
Inhalation: right nostril. **Concentration:** *śīrṣa.*
Exhalation: left nostril. **Concentration**: *śīrṣa.*

Kumbhaka
Antah Kumbhaka 5 to 10 seconds.
Take rest.

Sūrya Bhedana

Sūrya = Sun, *bhedana* = break, open. This *Prāṇāyāma* helps the practitioner to attain a contemplation beyond the solar disc. Facilitates meditation on the Creator (*Prajāpati*).

Basic Prāṇāyāma: Nāḍī Śodhana.

1st Technique

Inhalation: left nostril.
Exhalation: right nostril. (2 times longer than Inhalation).
Inhalation: right nostril.
Exhalation: left nostril. (2 times longer than Inhalation).
Do 12 breaths (6 Cycles).
Rest.

2nd Technique

Inhalation: left nostril 8s. **Concentration**: *nāsāgra.*
Antah Kumbhaka: 32 s. **Concentration**: *kaṇṭha kūpa.*
Exhalation: right nostril 16s. **Concentration**: *hṛdaya.*
Inhalation: right nostril 8s. **Concentration**: *nāsāgra.*
Antah Kumbhaka : 32s. **Concentration**: *kaṇṭha kūpa.*
Exhalation: left nostril 16s. **Concentration:** *hṛdaya.*
Do 12 breaths (6 Cycles).
Take rest.

Precaution: This *Prāṇāyāma* can only be practiced under the advice and the supervision of your yoga teacher.

Ujjāyi Anuloma

Uj = fly, transcend. *Ujjāyi* = feeds and awakens *ojas*, the spiritual element which is in us; the strength of the Creator that helps us to know him.

Technique

Inhalation: *Ujjāyi* (both nostrils open).

Exhalation: left nostril.

Inhalation: *Ujjāyi* (both nostrils open).

Exhalation: right nostril.

Do 12 breaths (6 Cycles).

Take rest.

Concentration

Nāsāgra, bhrūmadhya, lalāṭa, nābhi, mūla, hṛdaya.

Kumbhaka

Antah Kubhaka and Bāhya Kumbhaka

Ujjāyi Pratiloma

Technique

Inhalation: *Ujjāyi* (both nostrils opened).

Exhalation: left nostril.

Inhalation: left nostril.

Exhalation: *Ujjāyi.*

Inhalation: *Ujjāyi.*

Exhalation: right nostril.

Inhalation: right nostril.

Exhalation: *Ujjāyi* (both nostrils opened).

Do 16 breaths (4 Cycles).

Take rest.

Concentration

Nāsāgra, bhrūmadhya, lalāṭa, nābhi, mūla, hṛdaya.

Kumbhaka

Antah Kubhaka and Bāhya Kumbhaka

Ujjāyi Viloma

Technique

Inhalation: left nostril.
Exhalation: *Ujjāyi* (both nostrils open).
Inhalation: right nostril.
Exhalation: *Ujjāyi* (both nostrils open).
Do 12 breaths (6 Cycles).
Rest

Concentration

Nāsāgra, bhrūmadhya, lalāṭa, nābhi, mūla, hṛdaya.

Kumbhaka

Antah Kubhaka and Bāhya Kumbhaka

Glossary of medical terms

Aerophagy, spasmodic swallowing of air, a habit that can lead to belching and stomach pain.

Colic spasm, convulsive contraction of smooth muscles of the colon.

Colitis, swelling (inflammation) of the large intestine (colon).

Constipation, infrequent bowel movements.

Cysts, a closed sac, having a distinct membrane and division on the nearby tissue. It may contain air, fluids, or semi-solid material.

Diuresis, Urinary elimination in its totality, in quantity or in its composition.

Dorsal kyphosis, extreme curvature of the upper back also known as a hunchback.

Fibroma, benign tumours that are composed of fibrous or connective tissue.

Gallstones, kidney stones, hard, pebble-like deposits that form inside the gallbladder. Solid mass made up of tiny crystals in the kidney or ureter.

Haemorrhoids, painful, swollen veins in the lower portion of the rectum or anus.

Hypotension, low blood pressure.

Intervertebral hernia, abnormal protrusion of the intervertebral disc into the spinal canal.

Intestinal bloating, swelling of the abdomen with gas in the intestine.

Lumbar hyperlordosis, accentuated lumbar curve, anterior concavity.

Menstrual haemorrhage, menstrual periods.

Premenstrual syndrome, all the symptoms that occur regularly, in some women before menstruation.

Prostatic hypertrophy, enlargement of the prostate of a benign nature due to benign prostatic hyperplasia causing more or less important obstructions at the time of emptying of the bladder.

Prolapse, a condition where an organ falls down or slips out of place.

Pulmonary compliance, a measure of the ability of the lung to distend in response to pressure without disruption.

Sciatica, a set of symptoms, including pain that may be caused by general compression and/or irritation of one of five spinal nerve roots.

Scoliosis, curvature of the spine from side to side.

Thyroid goitre, the abnormal enlargement of the thyroid gland.

Tissue oedema, increase in the amount of water in the extravascular spaces.

Varicose veins, permanent dilatation of a vein.

Glossary of Sanskrit terms

Adharma, contrary to Dharma, actions to be avoided.

Adhi Ātmika, suffering coming from oneself.

Adhi Bhautika, suffering coming from others.

Adhi Daivika, suffering of the celestial origin.

Adho Gati, downward movement.

Āditya, the Sun.

Agni Hotra, the rituals that enable man to go beyond the seven worlds.

Agni, the Fire.

Ahimsa, not creating suffering in others.

Ākāśa, 'ether' element, one of the five elements that constitutes the created world.

Amāvasya, new moon, the new moon day.

Aṁśa, residual.

Anāhata, the centre of the heart.

Anantā, the primordial Serpent.

Pāda Aṅguṣṭa, the big toes.

Anjaneya, spiritual son of God of wind, a character in Rāmāyaṇa.

Antastrāṭaka, directing the eyes towards an object with sustained attention, eyes shut.

Ap, 'water' element, one of the five elements that constitutes the created world.

Apāna, 'what leaves us.' One of the two functions of *prāṇa*; exhalation.

Āraṇyaka, a treatise of the forest.

Ārjava, the consideration of every path to the Creator as equal.

Artha, balance in material comfort.

Aruṇa, the rising sun.

Aṣṭāṅga Yoga, The eight limbs of Yoga.

Aśva, Golden horse.

Asteya, transmission of the principles taught by the *ṛśis*.

Āstikya, respect for the principles of *dharma* and *adharma,* always in accordance with social and family status.

Atharvaṇa Veda, one of the four Veda-s.

Ātma Śuddhi, act of purifying the soul.

Ātma, the spiritual element in us.

Āyurveda, Indian medical science.

Bahistrāṭaka, directing the eyes towards an object with sustained attention, eyes open.

Bandha, stranglehold of matter.

Bhagavad Gītā, 'The Song of the Lord ', the philosophical teaching of Sri Kṛṣṇa to Arjuna on the battlefield.

Bṛhadāraṇyaka Upaniṣad, one of the major Upaniṣads.

Bhrūmadhya, point between the eyebrows.

Brahma Randhra, the ninth door situated above the fontanel.

Brahma Ratha, Yājñyavalkya's father.

Brahma Rathi, son of Brahma Ratha, Yājñyavalkya's first name.

Brahmacārin, one who moves freely in the soul of any being.

Brahmacarya, the fact of interrupting the interaction between the sense perceptions and the world of experience.

Brāhmaṇa, the philosophical section of Veda.

Brāhmin, Category of people dedicated to the philosophical teaching.

Buddhi, intellect.

Chāndogya Upaniṣad, one of the major Upaniṣads.

Candra, the Moon, a Vedic divinity.

Chāya, shadow, wife of Sun.

Dāna, act of respectfully giving what was earned with one's own efforts.

Darśana, philosophical interpretation.

Darśapūrna, Vedic rites conducted on the New Moon and Full Moon days.

Dayā, protection of all that surrounds us.

Deva, Vedic divinities, God.

Deva aṁśa, the divine 'residue' that is in us.

Deva ṛna, debt of gratitude towards the Creator.

Dhara, to dress.

Dhāraṇa, concentration on a vital point.

Dharma, observance of rules keeping the created world from being destroyed.

Dhṛti, stability of mind, free from any influence.

Dhyāna, meditation

Dhyāna mantra, *mantra* recited before an invocation of a Vedic God.

Dhyāna Śloka, prayer recited to invoke God.

Draupadi, wife of the Pāṇḍavas.

Duḥkha, suffering.

Duḥkhatraya, the three types of sufferings that affect the created beings.

Ekāgrata, concentration, one pointed mental attention.

Gārgi, (f) disciple of Yājñyavalkya.

Gāyatrī, the most important Vedic *mantra.*

Gulpha, ankles.

Hatha Yoga Pradīpika, a reference book on Hatha Yoga.

Hiraṇyagarbha, golden egg or, form of the Creator in the form of a golden egg.

Hita Nāḍī, nerve current that links the heart to the fontanel.

Hrīmatī, attitude one must have towards women, she should not be put in a situation of shame.

Hṛdaya, centre of the heart.

Indra, a Vedic God.

Indriya Śuddhi, purification of sense perceptions.

Īśvara Pūjana, the offering of prayers in total sincerity to the supreme God, according to one's capacity.

Janaka, a great king and a great philosopher.

Jangha, top of the thighs.

Jānu, the knees.

Japa, repetition of a *mantra* or repetition of God's name.

Jīva, individual soul.

Kāla, time (a metaphysical concept).

Kālāhasti, a pilgrim centre in south India.

Kāma, desire to respect the rules of *Dharma,* sensual desire.

Kaṇṭha kūpa, back of the throat.

Kaṇṭha, throat.

Kātyāyana, wife and disciple of Yājñyavalkya.

Khanḍa, chapter of a book.

Kleśa, afflictions that affect our daily life.

Kṛṣṇa Yajur Veda, Black Yajur Veda.

Kṛṣṇa, incarnation of Viṣṇu.

Krodha, anger.

Kṣama, acceptance of pleasure and unhappiness with an equal state of mind.

Kumbhaka, traditional name to designate a Prāṇāyāma. Holding of breath between the two phases of breathing.

Lakṣmī, consort of Lord Viṣṇu.

Lalāṭa, base of the uvula.

Lobha, miserliness.

Mada, passion.

Mahā Bhārata, One of the two Indian epics, the Rāmāyaṇa being the other.

Mahābhūta, the five elements that constitute the created world.

Maitreyī, (f) disciple of Yājñyavalkya.

Manas, mind.

Mantra, sacred formula of the Vedas.

Manuśya ṛna, debt of gratitude towards other human beings.

Marma Sthāna, vital point.

Mātsarya, jealousy.

Mitha Āhāra, feed the body and mind without excess.

Moha, mental confusion.

Mokṣa, liberation.

Mukhya Prāṇa, main Prāṇa.

Mūla, perineum.

Mūrdhna, middle of the forehead.

Nābhi, navel.

Nāsāgra, extreme point of the nose.

Nigarbha, sterile.

Nivṛtti Dharma, path of no-return.

Nivṛtti Mārga, path of no-return, a way to liberation.

Niyama, *Yama* and *Niyama* are ethical and moral principles with regards to oneself and others.

Nyāsa, gestures of purification that precede a ritual or a prayer.

Ūrdhva Gati, upward movement, transcendental path.

Pāda, foot, rhythmic unity in a *mantra*, syllable in poetry.

Pāṇḍava, principle characters in Mahā Bhārata.

Pāpa, that which takes away from God, sin.

Parjanya, water, a Vedic God, *prāṇa*'s cloth.

Paurṇima, full moon, full moon day.

Phala, fruit, effect.

Pitṛ, ancestors.

Pitṛ aṁśa, ancestral residues that we inherit.

Pitṛ ṛna, debt of gratitude towards ancestors.

Prajāpati, the Creator.

Prāṇa, name of one of Sun's rays, inhalation.

Prāṇa agni hotra, Vedic name for Prāṇāyāma defining the practice of Prāṇāyāma as a daily ritual.

Pravṛtti Mārga, the path that leads the soul to be reborn as a human being as it always leads to rebirth.

Pṛthvī, the 'earth' element, one of the five basic elements that constitutes the created world.

Punar Janma, reborn again, rebirth.

Punar Mṛtyu, dying again.

Puruṣa, Man; the Creator.

Puruṣārtha, the four pillars of man.

Rāma, incarnation de Viṣṇu, principal character in Rāmāyaṇa.

Rāmāyaṇa, one of the two great Indian epics, the Mahā Bhārata being the other.

Ratha, chariot.

Ṛśi aṁśa, residues of Vedic sages that we inherit.

Ṛśi ṛna, debt of gratitude towards the Vedic sages and Masters.

Ṛśi, the seven Vedic sages.

Rohita, the white, the purest. Movement towards the Creator.

Sagarbha Prāṇāyāma, fertile Prāṇāyāma, Prāṇāyāma with invocation of God or with the repetition of a *mantra.*

Samādhi, 'identical to the origin,' identical to the origin of soul in the Creator. Eighth and final stage of Yoga.

Samāna, that which maintains equal distribution in our existence. A function of *prāṇa.*

Saṁsāra, cycle of rebirths.

Saṃdhyā Vandana, ritual carried out at the moment of the three transitions, dawn, mid-day and dusk.

Saṃdhyā, moment of transition. There are three transitions.

Saṃtoṣa, constant happiness.

Saṃnyāsa, complete renunciation.

Sarga, a chapter of a book.

Satya, to do good to all living beings.

Śānti, peace.

Śata Patha Brāhmaṇa, the Brāhmaṇa of hundred and four chapters.

Śauca, physical and mental cleanliness.

Śīrṣa, vital point that is situated just above the fontanel.

Śroṇī, centre of the pelvis.

Śukla Yajur Veda, White Yajur Veda.

Siddhānta Śravaṇa, study that confirms conviction.

Sītā, Rama's wife, incarnation of the Goddess.

Sunanda, Yājñyavalkya's mother.

Sūrya Namaskāra, salutation to Sun.

Sūrya Upasthāna, act of saluting the Sun.

Sūrya, the Sun.

Svātmārāma, author of Haṭha Yoga Pradīpika, a work on Haṭha Yoga.

Tālu Mūla, back of the palate.

Tapas, maintenance of a perfectly clean body, internally as well as externally.

Tāraka, horizon point.

Tejas, 'Fire' element, one of the five elements that constitutes the created world.

Taittirīya, issued from parrots; name of an *Āraṇyaka* and of an *Upaniṣad.*

Tittira, parrot.

Trāṭaka, directing the eyes towards an object with sustained attention.

Trisaṃdhyā, the three moments of transition – dawn, mid-day and dusk.

Ucchiśṭa Prāṇa, principal Prāṇa.

Udaka, water.

Udāna, to go upwards, one of the functions of *prāṇa.*

Ujjāyi, breathing technique specific to Yoga, more particularly, in the practice of Āsanas.

Upaniṣad, philosophical texts which make up part of the Veda and mainly deal with the relation between the soul and the Creator.

Upāsana, meditation.

Vaiśampāyana, Yājñyavalkya's uncle.

Vaiśya, category of men dedicated to business.

Vāk, power of expression.

Valka, bark of a tree used in rites and rituals.

Valkya, clothes made from the leaves and tree bark used in Vedic rituals.

Vālmīki, author of Rāmāyaṇa.

Varuṇa, the Rain God.

Vasiṣṭha, a great sage, Rāma's spiritual master.

Vāyu, God of Wind, 'air' element, one of the five elements that constitutes the created world.

Vedānta, one of the six *Darśanas*, the six philosophical interpretations.

Vimāna, dome of a temple, plane.

Virāj, power of creation.

Viśvāmitra, a Vedic Master.

Viyoga, separation from the stranglehold of matter.

Vrata, strict application of *Dharmas,* which are specific to the individual in searching for the soul.

Vyāna, 'one that goes askew,' meaning that it moves horizontally and vertically.

Yajñya, short Vedic rites.

Yajur Veda, one of the four Vedas, composed of *mantra*-s for rituals.

Yama, *Yama* and *Niyama* are ethical and moral principles with regards to oneself and others.

Yoga Āsana, all of God's posture.

Yoga Āsanagalu, book written by Sri T. Krishnamacharya and published by Mysore University.

Yoga Makaranda, book written by Sri T. Krishnamacharya and published by Mysore University.

Yoga Sādhana, set of practices to regain the power of contemplation.

Index of Sanskrit terms

Annexe

Breath of the Gods

A JOURNEY TO THE ORIGINS OF MODERN YOGA

Shooting impressions

From 2007 to 2011, I produced a feature documentary about Sri T.Krishnamacharya, his school, his teachings and his significance for modern Yoga.

I feel greatly honoured to be granted this opportunity to provide an insight into the process of filming with Sri T. Krishnamacharya's relatives, especially with T. K. Sribhashyam who dedicated a substantial amount of time, work and passion to this project without ever asking for compensation or exerting influence on shape and content of the film.

Thank you, dear Sribhashyam, for your trust.

April 2011, Jan Schmidt-Garre, Germany.

⇧ T. K. Sribhashyam and I at the Parakala Math in Mysore. This monastery was the religious centre for Sri T. Krishnamacharya and his family. Here he first started to lecture on Bhagavad Gita.

⇩ Sribhashyam talking to his aunt Jaya Lakṣmī, the younger sister of Sri T. Krishnamacharya's wife Namagiriammal and of B. K. S. Iyengar. As a young girl she lived with Krishnamacharya and his family.

⇧ At the Lalith Mahāl Palace in Mysore, now turned into a hotel, Krishnamacharya gave Yoga classes to the male members of the Royal family.

⇩ At the vegetable and fruit market in Mysore, Krishnamacharya would buy the ingredients for the ayurvedic medicine he prepared. It was part of his daily routine to visit the market which still looks the same as in Krishnamacharya's days in the 1930s and 40s.

⇳ T. K. Sribhashyam and I at one of the few temples in Chennai dedicated to both Shiva and Viṣṇu. Even though he was staunchly attached to Viṣṇu, Krishnamacharya lectured on Yoga at this temple and gave demonstrations with his children.

⇧ T.K.Sribhashyam at a secondary school in Chennai where he used to perform Yoga demonstrations together with his siblings.

⇩ Sri T.Krishnamacharya's favorite lunch restaurant in downtown Chennai, founded just before he moved here.

⇧ T.K.Sribhashyam was very moved when we visited his father's first own apartment in Chennai on the first floor of this building. The two of them lived here for some time during which Sribhashyam benefited greatly from the closeness to his father and from his tuition.

⇩ T.K.Sribhashyam's elder sisters Alamelu, born 1933, and Pundarikavalli, born 1931.

⇧ Just as Krishnamacharya had taught Yoga to his own children, Sribhashyam teaches this 8-year old boy at the Sanskrit College of Mysore, the beautiful halls of which we were allowed to use for our Yoga demonstrations.

⇩ For our film Sribhashyam's younger sister Sri Shubha, born 1952, did a demonstration of a Yoga sequence she learned from her father. For the opening prayer she asked Sribhashyam to join her.

⇧ The climax of my personal experiences during the shooting of the film: T.K. Sribhashyam teaching me the session that his father called '**Life-saving session**', focusing deeply on concentration (explained in this book in Chapter 8).

Impression :XL Print & Mailing
N° imprimeur : P400301/00
Z.A. de Malacussy – BP 85
F-42010 SAINT-ETIENNE Cedex 2
DEPOT LEGAL : mars 2014
Imprimé en France.